D1414384

Japan and Korea in the 1990s

To Siew Bee, Sarah and Colin

Japan and Korea in the 1990s

From Antagonism to Adjustment

Brian Bridges
Director, Jati International
Associate Fellow, Royal Institute of International Affairs

Edward Elgar

Published by
Edward Elgar Publishing Limited
Gower House
Croft Road
Aldershot
Hants GU11 3HR
England

Edward Elgar Publishing Company
Old Post Road
Brookfield
Vermont 05036
USA

A CIP catalogue record for this book is available from the British Library

ISBN 1 85278 681 7

Printed in Great Britain at the University Press, Cambridge

Contents

Preface

Relations with immediate neighbours often tend to be more troublesome than with those situated further away. This volume derives from my own interest in the relationship between Japan and its two geographically close neighbours on the Korean peninsula. The original impetus for looking at this subject came from my mentor and friend Shibusawa Masahide, who pointed to the difficulties that both Japanese and Koreans have in considering each other and writing about their inter-relationships in an unemotional manner. However, even as a 'third party', it is difficult to avoid making judgements which will annoy either Japanese or Korean friends or, more than likely, both at the same time!

I first started studying this subject while a member of the research staff at the Royal Institute of International Affairs and I have benefited over the years from the helpful inputs and ideas of many colleagues there, including in particular several Japanese and Korean Visiting Fellows, and the then Director of Studies, Dr. William Wallace. I was also fortunate, through RIIA, to spend two months in 1987 as a Visiting Research Fellow at the National Institute of Research Advancement, Tokyo. I am indebted to the Director, Shimokobe Atsushi, and the staff there, who were so helpful in that early period of investigation.

I am particularly grateful to the Leverhulme Trust, which granted me a Research Fellowship in 1990-91 to undertake a research visit to both South Korea and Japan and to prepare this final volume.

Numerous Japanese and Korean academics, officials, journalists, politicians and businessmen have spent time trying to explain particular aspects of this complex subject to me. I cannot list them all, but I do nonetheless wish to express my appreciation of the way in which they have been prepared to share their views with me. I would like, however, to express especial thanks to Choi Jung-il, Lee Jung-hoon, Nagano Shinichiro, Park Jin, and Tanaka Hitoshi. Any mistakes and misrepresentations, however, are my own responsibility.

I would also like to thank Sue Dewar for help with the word-processing and typescript organisation and Edward Elgar for his patience and encouragement.

Last, but not least, I would like to thank Siew Bee, Sarah and Colin, who have seen me too often too preoccupied with this project. Without their support this book would never have been finished.

1 Introduction

The past still casts a long shadow over the present in Japan-Korea relations. During his visit to Seoul in January 1991, Japanese Prime Minister Kaifu Toshiki went to lay a wreath of chrysanthemum flowers at the memorial in Pagoda Park to the Korean independence fighters who had died during the March 1919 revolt against the Japanese colonial authorities. Kaifu was only the second ever Japanese prime minister to officially visit South Korea and he was the first one to visit this particular monument. At the same time, just outside the park, a middle-aged Korean, the grandson of one of those independence heroes, attempted to commit suicide in protest at Kaifu's visit.

Japan and Korea are certainly geographically and culturally close, but the psychological gap seems far from narrow. A long-standing enmity, the origins of which can be traced back to the early phases of the two countries' histories, was exacerbated by the brutal Japanese colonial occupation of Korea from 1910 to 1945. The defeat of Japan did not bring about the united, independent Korean state which the Koreans desired and the establishment of the two Koreas raised a complicated diplomatic dilemma which Japan found difficult to resolve. In fact, not until 1965, 20 years after the end of the Pacific War, were relations between Japan and South Korea normalised and relations between Japan and North Korea have yet to be formalised, although negotiations to achieve that end are now at last in train. Japan's normalisation of relations with North Korea, when achieved, will mark the settling of one of Japan's two final hangovers from the Second World War (the other being the Japan-Russia peace treaty).

Public opinion polls in both Japan and South Korea have, with almost unfailing regularity, depicted the other country unfavourably. Textbook revisions, the finger-printing of Korean residents, intemperate remarks by cabinet ministers and imperial apologies have tended to be rapidly politicised.

Emotions have hampered diplomatic reconciliation. The 1965 agreements were followed by several false starts in political and economic relations and not until the mid-1980s, when a regular exchange of high-level visits began, did the governmental-level relationship improve. Even then popular feelings lagged well behind.

A qualitative change in bilateral relations was achieved with the

1

path-breaking visit to Seoul by Prime Minister Nakasone Yasuhiro in January 1983. Despite the rhetoric accompanying later visits by Kaifu, in January 1991, and Miyazawa Kiichi, in January 1992, they did not mark any significant new phase in the relationship. Rather, the next watershed in Japan-South Korean relations will be marked by the establishment of diplomatic relations between Japan and North Korea, which will rebalance the complex triangular relationship involving Japan and the two Koreas in a new way.

The three states are certainly different polities, with different political and economic systems. Japan is a massive economic presence, with an antiquated but nonetheless pluralistic political system. North Korea is a heavily centralised but stagnating Stalinist-style command economy under the control of a totalitarian leader intent on arranging a dynastic succession. South Korea often seems to be in between: a democratising society throwing off the shackles of authoritarian government and a 'developmental state' economy not as strongly based as the Japanese one. These differences, in turn, impact on how the three states interact.

Japan has become a mature economy, but it is still displaying impressive growth rates by OECD (Organisation of Economic Cooperation and Development) standards, having achieved around 5% growth during the 1987-1990 period. It is a leading trading nation, a massive investor overseas, the world's largest creditor nation, and now the world's largest provider of official development assistance (ODA). Japan, of course, is situated in the world's fastest growing region, the Asia-Pacific, where several countries are growing faster, but it remains a dominating economic force in the region. Its gross national product (GNP) is still more than twice that of the combined total of the other ten major economies in the region. Yet, the nearest - indeed some Japanese would argue the only potential - rival is South Korea. In the second half of the 1980s South Korea accelerated its growth (from 1986-88 it was the world's fastest growing economy), began to register sizeable trade surpluses, and started to export a range of higher technology products. The Japanese came to appreciate that South Korea had become part of their problem of competitive market-sharing; in a number of sectors, South Korea is, or is well on the way to becoming, a serious rival. The Japanese, therefore, are being forced to manage an economic relationship that no longer has the characteristics of traditional developed-developing country interactions. Indeed, even paradigms of the developed-newly industrialising country (NIC) relationships found in other parts of the world are becoming outmoded.

South Korea itself is suffering both the pleasures and the pains of being in a transitional stage in its economic development. Having long since overtaken North Korea, South Korea's drive to 'catch up' now with Japan faces problems of a different order of magnitude. The intense and close inter-linkage between the Japanese and South Korean economies has always been an unbalanced one and tensions over trade deficits and technology transfer, which have long bedevilled the relationship, have only increased in intensity as the South Koreans have striven for a more equitable relationship. South Korea has seen Japan as both model and mentor and has tracked the Japanese development path in a number of ways, but it resents being labelled as a 'second Japan' by other trading partners and fears becoming over-dependent on Japan.

Japan-North Korean economic interaction has been miniscule by comparison with the Japan-South Korean one, even though Japan has been by far the largest non-socialist trading partner of the North (though it is not inconceivable that South Korea might take over that position in the not too distant future). North Korea also faces problems of economic transition, but of a different order - how to resuscitate its economy while resisting those pressures for opening up its society and economy which have had such a dramatic impact on other socialist countries. Nevertheless, the parlous state of its closed economy has forced it to bend its long-held doctrine of self-sufficiency and turn towards Japan as one of the most likely sources of economic assistance and political acceptability.

Japan has been reticent about taking up a political and security profile that could be seen as adequately reflecting its undoubted economic strength. However, the changes in global East-West relations, the slow transfer of the post-Cold War mood to North-east Asia, and the re-emergence of regional disputes are forcing Japan to reconsider its role. Both Japan and South Korea have bilateral security relationships with the United States, but there are no bilateral security ties between themselves. Their security perspectives have differed noticeably in the past, but the regional changes - most notably the North Korean nuclear weapon 'threat' - have caused both countries to look again at their security policies and approaches. How far will this lead to a convergence of interests?

During the 1980s, the Japanese government supported South Korean proposals for the reunification of the peninsula and endeavoured to play a low-key role in promoting an environment for dialogue. The North-South Korean dialogue has been an intermittent and frustrating experience, even though it began to reach a more senior level in late 1990. The degree of competition and the level of distrust between the two remain high, but they both share a suspicion of Japanese motivations and argue that Japan prefers to keep the peninsula divided. Is there scope for German-style '2 + 4' dialogue or broader sub-regional frameworks to moderate the impact of the process of reunification on Japan-Korea inter-relationships?

Ideological divisions between, and within, the two Koreas, and the consequent appeal to different groups within the Japanese political spectrum, have complicated Japanese approaches. Progress in the development of a Japan-North Korean political relationship therefore cannot be isolated from developments in the North-South Korean relationship. The development of Japan's political - and strategic - relations with the Korean peninsula will be a test-case of the Japanese capability and willingness to play a more mature role in ensuring regional stability.

Historical legacies condition many of the psychological attitudes that underpin the relationships between the three countries. Chapter 2, therefore, examines the background of the pre-colonial and colonial period, the different approaches of the early presidents of South Korea, the North Korean aversion to Japan, and the alternating periods of comparative cordiality and severe tension through to the mid-1980s. Chapter 3 broadly surveys popular perceptions and analyses the various inputs into and the contexts of the foreign and economic policy-making processes in Japan, South and North Korea, as far as policies towards either the two Koreas or Japan, respectively, are concerned.

Chapter 4 looks at the politico-strategic issues, focusing on the development of the political, and security, dimensions of the links between Japan and the two Koreas, the development and impact on Japan of moves towards dialogue, political change and reunification on the peninsula, and the enduring territorial and textbook disputes with Japan. Historically, the fate of Korea has always been bound up with the attitudes and policies of its larger neighbours. Chapter 5 examines the external environment - the complex and shifting linkages between the United States, the Soviet Union (and now Russia) and China - and how this impacts on the triangular relationship between Japan and the two Koreas.

Chapter 6 examines the degree of economic interdependence between Japan and the two Koreas, the flows of trade, aid, investment and technology, the economic problems of the North and the hiccups in the South, and the role that these three economies are playing in the embryonic efforts to promote Asian Pacific economic cooperation. The situation of the Korean residents in Japan and the cultural, tourist and educational connections between Japan and the two Koreas, as well as the character of Japanese 'cultural imperialism', are considered in Chapter 7. A separate discussion, in Chapter 8, considers the issues and prospects in the crucial negotiations continuing between Japan and North Korea. The concluding Chapter 9 looks at the issues for the future, including the impact of eventual reunification on the Korean peninsula, and the likely interplay of economic competition versus integration and of convergence versus divergence in politico-strategic outlook.

Throughout this book, Chinese, Japanese and Korean names are shown with the family names first and personal names second. The transliteration of Korean names is complicated by varying personal and official preferences, but the style usually accorded in official publications is taken, even at the apparent cost of consistency. For convenience, South Korea is used for the Republic of Korea and North Korea for the Democratic People's Republic of Korea.

2   The Legacies of History

For both the Japanese and the Koreans, whether living in South or North, the past has a strong influence on how the present is perceived. President Roh Tae-woo's visit to Tokyo in May 1990 was preceded by inordinate consultations on the phraseology to be used by Emperor Akihito in his formal apology for past Japanese actions. A return visit by the Emperor to South Korea has been quietly put on ice to avoid him having to venture into the emotionally-charged atmosphere of South Korea. All formal official visits between Japan and South Korea are now regularly preceded by consultations of this kind, though the results tend to meet diplomatic niceties rather than satisfy emotional needs. Memories of the colonial period and issues that arose as a result of the failure to easily reach a post-war settlement leave issues which can erupt into emotional struggles at short notice.

Japan and the Korean peninsula are close geographically and have a long history of economic and cultural intercourse, but the inter-relationship since the late nineteenth century has been particularly fraught. For a clearer understanding of the present relationships, the differences of perspective between the Japanese and the Koreans on the history of the last century in particular need to be outlined.

The colonial period

Korea became a basically unified country under the Silla kingdom in 668 - and remained that way, apart from occasional and brief periods of political division, until 1945. This has given the Koreans a strong sense of political continuity, unequalled except by the Chinese. Medieval Korea was one of the most centralised and uniformly administered states in pre-colonial Asia, but it never had a fully autocratic system, in the way that the Japanese emperor became divinised or the Chinese emperor was potentially absolute. Under the Yi dynasty, 1392-1910, Chinese cultural influences were strong and Korea became almost a Confucian model of intellectual life and political institution, although some of the traditional social structures survived. However, rivalry between competing cliques of nobles and officials became pronounced and by the eighteenth and nineteenth century Korea was suffering from a lack of strong central leadership and from political stagnation. It had become so inward-looking and weak, politically and economically, that it could offer humiliatingly little resistance to annexation by the Japanese in 1910.

The Japanese and the Koreans have had contacts since ancient times. Japanese travelled to Kyongju and Puyo and on to Luoyang; Koreans went to Asuka, and there were frequent migrations of Koreans to Japan during the fourth to seventh century. The archaeological evidence is by no means undisputed, but some scholars argue that the 'horseriders' of the Koguryo kingdom in fact conquered the Wa people of Kyushu and established the first Japanese state, Yamato, in the fourth century (Lee, C-s. 1985 pp. 151-63). Under the Silla kingdom, Chinese culture and Korean artifacts (and Korean craftsmen) flowed through Korea to Japan. Under the early Yi dynasty relations were cordial, apart from some difficulties with Japanese pirates in the fourteenth century, though not particularly close, until in 1592, as part of the pursuit of his war with the Chinese, Hideyoshi Toyotomi launched an invasion of Korea. In what the Koreans call the 'Imjin war', the Korean army was routed, but the naval commander Yi Sun-sin was able to inflict a naval defeat on the Japanese using his famous 'turtle ships', whose iron-covered decks made them the world's first armoured vessels. The Japanese forces, however, remained on Korean soil for another six years while intermittent peace negotiations occurred and Admiral Yi inflicted further naval defeats (Hoare and Pares 1988 pp. 36-9). In the Korean memory, Hideyoshi's invasion and exploitation of Korea was a precursor of the 1910 action; Admiral Yi is a national hero and has been commemorated on the South Korean 1,000 won note.

Low-level trade continued until the mid-nineteenth century brought the Western challenge to the region. Japan was first jolted out of its seclusion and following the political upheaval of the 1868 Meiji Restoration it, in turn, tried to break down the exclusionism of Korea. In the best tradition of Western gun-boat diplomacy, in 1876, Japan forced Korea to sign the Treaty of Kanghwa, which opened up the country to Japanese diplomatic and commercial operations. Korea became a battleground for contending powers. The threat of the Tonghak reform movement inside Korea led to invited Chinese and uninvited Japanese intervention. The Sino-Japanese War (1894-95) was a surprisingly quick victory for Japan; China was forced to acknowledge formally the ending of Korea's old suzerain-vassal relationship. Yet it was a hollow form of independence for Korea, as Japanese commercial interests grew and strains arose with a new counterforce, the Russians. The struggle for the control of Korea was at the centre of the Russo-Japanese War (1904-5); Japan's victory enabled it to establish a residency-general, held by the veteran politician, Ito Hirobumi. A Korean patriot managed to assassinate him in October 1909, but that only precipitated the final annexation, which was formally dictated in August 1910.[1]

Following on from Taiwan in 1895, Korea was the second acquisition of what was to become Japan's growing formal empire. The beginning of Japan's expansionist phase coincided with the 'high noon' of Western imperialism and, superficially, it seemed simply like an attempt to catch up and imitate Western policies. However, the motivations, at least in the initial stages, were neither as economic nor as idealistic as those of the Europeans. Concerns about national security did rank highly, however. The annexation of Korea was the result of a deliberate governmental decision to secure control of a territory, which, in the old terminology, represented 'a dagger pointing at Japan's heart' (Peattie 1988 pp.229-44). The Japanese were undoubtedly aided by the lack of effective resistance to their moves forward, either from the Koreans or from the neighbouring powers.

From 1910 to 1945 Japanese control was as brutal as it was total. Under Governor General Terauchi Masatake and his successors, a powerful army and bureaucracy forcefully undertook the widespread transformation of Korean society. Korean opinion and political participation was thoroughly suppressed and organised resistance completely broken. The most significant challenge to the Japanese order was the March First independence movement in 1919. Organised initially by a group of religious leaders inspired by Wilsonian ideals of nationalist aspirations, it was the 'first genuine expression of Korean nationalism' (Deuchler 1987 p.18). Although widely supported across the country, it was brutally crushed by the Japanese army within a few weeks. Even within Japan, opinion was horrified by the manner of the suppression and a softer line of 'cultural rule' was instituted.

But the liberalisation soon petered out and in the second half of the 1930s the final phase, the 'Japanisation' of Korea, began. The Japanese tried to totally crush the Korean national identity: use of the Japanese language was made mandatory in schools and public places, Koreans were compelled to adopt Japanese names and to participate in Shinto (the Japanese state religion) rituals. Unwillingly, and at times unconsciously, the Koreans fell under the sway of Japanese habits and patterns that were largely alien to their traditional culture. As the war in China and then the Pacific War intensified, hundreds of thousands of Koreans were conscripted to support the Japanese military machine; at the time of Japan's surrender in 1945, the number of Koreans in Japan alone was over 2 million.

Material improvements did come to Korea, as the Japanese built roads, railways, and ports as well as industrial plant, but they were related to the requirements of the Japanese rather than of the Koreans themselves. Korean agriculture was modernised, but the rice output was increasingly shipped to Japan (per capita consumption levels in Korea actually dropped) as wartime demands from Japan escalated. The Japanese reorganised the primary education system, but Koreans were denied secondary and advanced education or real technical or managerial training. Not only were considerable numbers of Koreans forced abroad, but an estimated 20% lost their homes because of population redeployment policies (Lee, J-h. 1992 p.112).

The balance-sheet of the colonial period is an extremely difficult one to draw up. Historians and economists on both sides draw differing conclusions and attempts by politicians to put their own gloss on events rarely avoid provoking emotional reactions. Korea emerged a more modernised and, through the bitter experience of anti-colonialism, a more nationalistic country, but the benefits of the colonial period pale by comparison with the costs to the Koreans in terms of exploitation and suffering. It is not coincidental that March 1 and August 15 (the date of the Japanese surrender in 1945) are celebrated with particular fervour as national holidays in South Korea. Over the succeeding decades since Japanese defeat, repeated attempts have been made to evaluate and redraw the balance-sheet, particularly by the Japanese. This has complicated and politicised the bilateral relationship on numerous occasions.

Reluctant rapprochement

The Koreans saw the Allied victory over Japan as the chance to regain their lost independence, even though they would not have the satisfaction of winning it with their own hands. However, the Yalta and Potsdam Conferences in 1945 had agreed in principle that there should be Soviet and US occupation zones in Korea for the initial purposes of disarming and evacuating the Japanese. A zonal boundary drawn along the 38th parallel led to the emergence of two separate entities north and south of that line, which, apart from a few minor alterations at the end of the Korean War, has effectively remained the border ever since. To the Koreans, the division of their country is seen as the final and cruellest legacy of the Japanese colonial period.

In the immediate post-war period, US influence was strong in both the southern part of Korea (which formally became the Republic of Korea in August 1948 after UN-sponsored elections) and Japan. But, although the United States had a vested interest in bringing the two sides together in its anti-communist arc as the Cold War atmosphere deepened, it found that that was not at all easy. Only with the restoration of Japanese sovereignty with the signing of the San Francisco peace treaty in September 1951 did formal contacts begin. South Korea had not been invited to the peace conference, because technically Korea had not been at war with Japan. Nevertheless, the first president of South Korea, Syngman Rhee, was determined to extract a formal apology and to secure reparations payments from Japan. Japan, on the other hand, wished to settle the problem of the Koreans in Japan, preferably by repatriating many of them back to Korea (Cheong 1991). The objectives of the two sides did not appear susceptible to easy compromise; to the despair of the Americans the negotiations were to continue, acrimoniously and intermittently, for 14 years.

Rhee, who had been forced into a 33-year exile during the Japanese occupation period, was fervently anti-Japanese; indeed, he even told US Secretary of State John Dulles in 1953 that he feared Japan more than the Soviet Union (Lee and Sato 1982 p.26). Yoshida Shigeru, who was Japanese prime minister in the first half of the 1950s, on the other hand, personally disliked Rhee and even avoided meeting him when the latter visited Japan in January 1953. The differences between the two sides reached their most acrimonious when in an October 1953 negotiation over property claims, the Japanese chief delegate Kubota Kanichiro was so upset by the Koreans' arguments that he defended the Japanese occupation as not an 'unmixed evil' but the provider of considerable economic infrastructure for Korea (Lee, J-h. 1992 pp. 112,123). For over four years the negotiations were suspended.

The downfall of Rhee brought a dramatic change in South Korean-Japanese relations and helped to break the protracted diplomatic deadlock. First the brief but ineffectual democratic government, and then the government headed by General Park Chung Hee, who took power by a military coup in May 1961, demonstrated a desire to improve and settle relations with Japan, not least because Japanese economic aid would solve Korea's own economic problems. Park, in particular, as a graduate of the Japanese Military Academy, spoke Japanese and was an admirer of the Meiji leaders' modernisation model. To Rhee, Japan had appeared as the enemy; to Park, it was a model. Park, therefore, took the decision to push for an agreement with Japan, even at the cost of domestic dissatisfaction; in June 1964 he declared martial law to quell the demonstrations against the proposed treaties. On the Japanese side, the Prime Minister Sato Eisaku and the elder statesmen of the ruling Liberal Democratic Party (LDP), particularly former Prime Minister Kishi Nobusuke, decided to make the most of this opportunity presented by a strong but relatively pro-Japanese Korean leader to reach a settlement. Yet, in Japan too, there were violent protests against the proposed treaties (Baerwald 1968).

The Treaty on Basic Relations and four related agreements, signed on 22 June 1965, and ratified later in the year after violent intra- and extra-parliamentary struggles in both countries, attempted to deal with a number of problems, all of which still remain relevant today. Japan was determined not to foreclose on the possibility of some relations, however tenuous, with North Korea, and tried to avoid agreeing to the South Korean demand for recognition of that government as governing all Korea. The resulting formula, which referred to the 1948 UN resolution on Korea was, and still is, open to differing interpretations by both sides. The Japanese interpret it as referring only to that part of the peninsula under the present jurisdiction of the South Korean government, leaving North Korea separate, while the South Koreans argue that Japan could not establish diplomatic relations with the North without abrogating the treaty itself. Nevertheless, regardless of the legal niceties, it was clear that Japan had through the treaties taken a pronounced step to align itself with one of Korea's two contending governments.

Although the Japanese Foreign Minister, Shiina Etsusaburo, had issued a statement in April 1965 'deeply reflecting on the unfortunate past', the treaties themselves included neither a formal apology nor a reparation clause. Instead, hidden under a cloud of semantics, was an economic cooperation agreement, through which Japan would provide $800 million ($300 million in outright grants and $500 million in loans and credits) over ten years. These amounts were considered essential by the Park government for its economic development plans, but were criticised by opposition groups inside South Korea as being poor compensation for past sufferings. The continued existence of such feelings was to be critical during the 1981-83 aid negotiations.

Fishing disputes were defused by the abolition of the controversial Rhee Line (a South Korean delineation of territorial waters made in 1952), but friction over the activities of the respective countries' fishing boats has never completely disappeared. On the disputed claims to the tiny, normally uninhabited rock islets known as Takeshima in Japanese and Tokdo in Korean, which had erupted in 1952 when the South Koreans followed up their declaration of sovereignty by stationing a small garrison on the islets, the two sides agreed to disagree; the contending claims remain dormant but not dead. Finally, the status of the Koreans living in Japan was only partially solved. Those Koreans who had officially registered as nationals of South Korea could acquire permanent residence, but only about half of the approximately 650,000 ethnic Korean residents in Japan qualified under this criterion; the remainder were left in legal limbo.

Discord and readjustment

The 1965 treaties, however, marked a marriage of convenience rather than a resolution of emotional problems. As a result, the Japan-South Korean relationship since 1965 has been by no means a smooth one, with periods of notable discord, such as in 1972-75 and 1981-83, alternating with periods of readjustment and relative cordiality.

In the immediate post-1965 period, the substantive element of the relationship was economic; a notable rise in trade levels, though with a sustained deficit for South Korea, an influx of Japanese capital into South Korea, and the development of close links between certain political and business sectors in both countries. Bilateral trade (at current prices) rose from a mere $150 million in 1964 to $3 billion in 1973. From 1966 until 1979 Japan was South Korea's largest trading partner, and during most of that period South Korea was Japan's second largest export market. Flows of Japanese foreign direct investment (FDI) into South Korea rose from $4.7 million in the 1962-66 period to $37.4 million in the 1967-71 period. At successive annual meetings of the Korea-Japan Ministerial Conference and the Japan-South Korea Cooperation Committee, a business sector grouping but under strong political influence in both countries, the Korean side sought to draw in further Japanese economic involvement. Japanese business, eager for profits, responded. Although ambitious proposals such as the Yatsugi Plan, unveiled in the spring of 1970 and calling for a cooperative economic zone as a forerunner of an Asian-style EEC to be established (Lee, C-s. 1985 p.77), were clearly ahead of their time, Japanese companies were soon actively involved in the Korean market and export-processing zones.

The period 1972-75 was marked by considerable political strain, as domestic political change and, more significantly, change in the regional environment produced divergent reactions by Japan and South Korea (Hahn 1980 pp.174-95). The government of Tanaka Kakuei abandoned the 'one Korea' policy of his predecessor Sato. Following on the 'Nixon shock' of Sino-US rapprochement, Tanaka first normalised relations with China and, then, tentatively began to explore contacts with North Korea. Park himself began to engage in a dialogue with the North, but its failure was used as a justification for the imposition of a highly authoritarian system under the Yushin (renovation) constitution. Park's increasingly dictatorial style of leadership and desire to perpetuate his power also complicated relations with the Tanaka government. Park's staunchest opponent, Kim Dae-jung, who had come close to defeating him in the 1971 presidential election, was kidnapped in August 1973 from a Tokyo hotel by the Korean Central Intelligence Agency (KCIA). The outrage in Japan over the violation of Japan's sovereignty and Kim's human rights accentuated the Tanaka government's tendency to distance itself from Park (Lee, C-s. 1985 pp.81-4). In August 1974, Mun Se-gwang, a second generation Korean living in Japan, attempted to assassinate Park but succeeded only in killing Park's wife. Anti-Japanese feelings ran high, the Japanese Embassy in Seoul was ransacked, and only US intervention managed to avoid a rupture of relations and secure, eventually, a 'political settlement' (Lee, C-s. 1985 pp.84-5). Commercial relations survived relatively unscathed, as trade increased to $4.7 billion by 1976 and Japanese FDI into South Korea rose to $395.5 million during the 1972-76 period, but the Japanese government felt able to meet few of the Korean requests for economic aid.

A political settlement to the Kim Dae-jung kidnap case secured by the new Japanese prime minister, Miki Takeo, in 1975 ushered in a period of readjustment, though Japan never returned to the one-sided policy characteristic of Sato. Whereas Sato had in his joint communique with US President Richard Nixon in 1969 introduced what came to be known as the 'Korea clause' concept that the security of South Korea was 'essential to Japan's own security', from the time of the Miki government the Japanese identified their security interests with the peace and stability of all Korea, not just South Korea. Miki was more concerned than Sato had been with maintaining a balance of power on the peninsula; the successive governments of Fukuda Takeo and Ohira Masayoshi continued the same basic line. Economic cooperation was resumed and trade and investment links continued to expand. Moreover, a shared concern over President Jimmy Carter's plans for a five-year withdrawal of all US ground forces from South Korea, announced in January 1977, brought the Fukuda and Park governments closer together. The Park government was fearful that the removal of the US deterrent shield would destabilize the peninsula, while the Fukuda government was worried more about the credibility of the US commitment to Japan. Although, therefore, in terms of strategic interests, their starting-points differed, their objective was the same. After repeated representations, assisted by strong political opposition to the US plan both within and without the Carter administration, the two governments succeeded during 1979 in persuading Carter to shelve the planned withdrawal (Nam 1986 pp.139-74). One of the first acts of the incoming president, Ronald Reagan, was to affirm that US troops would not be withdrawn.

The next break in Japan-South Korea relations came with the assassination of President Park in October 1979, the installation of a temporary civilian government and the seizure of effective power in December 1979 by General Chun Doo-hwan, who had himself elected as president in August 1980. Park had been a Japanophile who understood how the political system worked in Japan and wanted to utilise the power and example of the Japanese economy to galvanise his own country's economy. Chun started from a fundamentally different attitude to Japan.

Yet Chun did take over an economy which had benefited from substantial Japanese inputs. After normalisation, the Korean economy recorded average annual GNP growth rates of 9% from 1965 to 1979; total exports grew at a rate of 39% per annum during the same period. South Korea did, of course, benefit from significant US economic inputs during this period as well as from its own indigenous efforts to catch up Japan and other more advanced countries under the 'export or die' mood of the 1970s. Yet, the direct and indirect Japanese inputs were undoubtedly a factor in that successful economic growth record. By 1979, total bilateral trade had reached $10 billion, representing just under 30% of total South Korean trade, though only 9% of total Japanese trade. Japanese FDI into South Korea had reached $610 million on a cumulative basis and Japan had extended over $1.1 billion in government-administered loans and over $2.4 billion in commercial loans.

The Japanese political and business leadership, unhappy though they were with the Kim Dae-jung affair and the increasing repression of Park's later years, nevertheless knew how to operate with Park and appreciated his strong push for economic growth. This understanding, of course, sometimes degenerated into commercial collusion and indirect political influence. Chun came to power determined to break these established 'pipelines' of communication and effect a restructuring of the relationship.

Lurching towards a 'new era'

Chun, like Park, was a professional soldier, but he was a more 'Korean product' than his predecessor. He was not Japanese-trained but a graduate of the first class of the Korean Military Academy to receive US-oriented training; he later commanded a South Korean regiment during the Vietnam War. Chun's ties were, therefore, closer with the United States than with Japan. Moreover, he had been strongly critical at the time of the terms of the 1965 normalisation of relations. When he put forward the massive economic aid request in 1981 he was to talk of offering Japan a second chance to do right by Korea and spoke openly about a 'second diplomatic restoration'.

Almost as soon as Chun became president relations deteriorated, for Kim Dae-jung, arrested on charges of attempted rebellion, was sentenced to death in September 1980. Japan joined with the United States in applying pressure (the government of Suzuki Zenko warned that further economic aid might be halted if the death sentence was carried out). In January 1981 Chun commuted the sentence to life imprisonment and bilateral economic discussions resumed. In the summer of 1981 the Chun government, however, put forward a request for $6 billion of Japanese loans to help finance the Fifth Five Year Socio-economic Plan (1982-86). Chun himself was personally closely involved (indeed, only with difficulty had his advisers persuaded him not to initially request $10 billion), but in so doing left himself little room for manoeuvre. The South Koreans argued that the cumulative trade imbalance since 1965 of over $22 billion deserved more than the roughly $80 million usually received each year from Japan and that the promotion of the economic development of South Korea would help it act as a 'bulwark' against communism and so, in effect, help to defend Japan (Kim, H.N. 1983 pp. 82-7).

Suzuki, in meetings with President Ronald Reagan in May and July 1981, had pledged to increase assistance to South Korea, but his officials were disturbed by the magnitude and the duration of the requested South Korean package and by the linkage with the security of South Korea, since the extension of military aid was precluded under established aid guidelines. Only slowly did signs of flexibility emerge, as the South Koreans dropped the 'bulwark' argument and Japan proposed a $4 billion loan package (Bridges 1984a pp.14-16), but the eruption of a dispute over history textbooks in the summer of 1982 stalled the negotiations completely.

In July 1982 the Japanese and South Korean media began to report that the Japanese Ministry of Education's stricter guidelines for screening history textbooks meant revisions in the descriptions of Japan's pre-war actions in China and Korea. The Koreans were infuriated by reports that the 1919 independence movement would be described as a 'riot' and the Koreans forcibly transported to Japan as 'volunteers'. Although it later became clear that the initial press reports had misrepresented the extent of the revisions (Yayama 1983 pp.301-16), the issue had already become a serious diplomatic problem. In the face of protests from the South Korean - and North Korean and Chinese - governments, the Japanese government was forced to announce changes to the textbook authorisation system and to issue guidelines to teachers about references to Korea and China. The South Korean government reluctantly accepted this statement and the loan negotiations restarted. However, the differences about the package's composition were only resolved by the dramatic visit by the new Japanese prime minister, Nakasone, in January 1983.

Nakasone was critical of the way his predecessor, Suzuki, had allowed relations to deteriorate; he took the initiative to solve the loan question and visit Seoul as his first overseas visit, thereby breaking the accepted rule that a Japanese prime minister's first overseas visit is to Washington. He became the first Japanese prime minister officially to visit South Korea and he went out of his way to please his hosts. He expressed 'deep regret' for the colonial past and high regard for South Korea's defence efforts, agreed to provide a $4 billion loan over seven years, and reconfirmed the 'Korea clause' phraseology, previously confined only to Japan-US communiques. Nakasone also acknowledged Korea's cultural contribution to Japan and even sang a Korean song during one official party. Both countries' media talked of a 'new and vital stage' in Japan-Korea relations (Lee, C-s. 1985 pp. 129-35). While the visit did not quite live up to all that rhetoric, it did, nevertheless, mark a change of atmosphere, at least at the governmental level, and set the tone for the rest of the decade.

President Chun reaped political gains at home by securing, even if in a slightly modified form, the loans to which he had been so personally committed. Even though the finance minister, Kang Kyong-shik, was later to cast doubt on how useful the loan, spread over seven years, would be in solving more immediate economic problems (*Nihon Keizai Shimbun* 17 February 1983), the agreement did much to maintain the credibility of South Korea, which had an external debt of $36 billion at the end of 1982, on the international financial markets. Moreover, Nakasone's expressions of 'high regard' for South Korea's defence efforts in the 'harsh circumstances which currently affect the Korean peninsula' were seen as supportive of Chun's perspectives. The Japanese were less wiling than the Koreans to dwell on the security implications and it was clear from Prime Minister Nakasone's comments in Washington later in January 1983 that he still saw the threat to Japan coming from the Soviet Union not North Korea.

Nevertheless, through his Korean gestures, Nakasone was able to provide early evidence to the Reagan administration of his determination to strike a more positive role for Japan. Domestically, the loan agreement was generally well received, especially by the business community which looked for commercial opportunities arising out of the new Korean projects, but the Japan Socialist Party (JSP), the Japan Communist Party (JCP) and part of the media were critical of both the 'excessive' ODA commitments to an NIC and the security overtones.

The new pattern of high-level exchanges, however, was confirmed by the September 1984 visit to Japan by President Chun, the first ever state visit by a South Korean president. A range of bilateral and multinational issues were discussed, but the success of the visit depended mostly on the phraseology used by Emperor Hirohito in his welcoming speech. By choosing to describe the 'unfortunate past' as 'regrettable', the Emperor pitched his apology at the level of earlier apologies to American and Chinese leaders, but Nakasone amplified this into an expression of 'deep regret' for 'great sufferings' inflicted on the Korean people (Bridges 1984b pp. 406-12). Although accepted by the Koreans, their continued wish for a more explict apology by the Japanese was to haunt the planning of President Roh Tae-woo's 1990 visit to Japan.

Subsequently, Nakasone attended the opening of the Asian Games in Seoul in September 1986, his successor Takeshita Noboru attended the Olympic Games opening ceremony in September 1988 and Kaifu, in January 1991, and Miyazawa Kiichi, in January 1992, have made official visits. South Korean Prime Minister Kang Young-hoon attended the funeral of Emperor Hirohito in February 1989 and President Roh made a state visit to Japan in May 1990.

Foreign ministers visited each others' countries regularly and occasionally met at the United Nations, while the bilateral ministerial meetings reverted to an annual routine until Japanese domestic problems led to a hiatus between early 1989 and late 1990. The greater frequency of high-level meetings since 1983 has not, of course, meant the resolution of all the problems in the Japan-South Korean relationship, but it has encouraged both sides to be more open about discussing them.

The economic links between the two countries grew significantly during the 1980s, as is outlined in more detail in Chapter 6. Bilateral trade rose from $9.4 billion in 1983 to $29.4 billion in 1989. The balance in favour of Japan peaked at $5 billion in 1986, but remained high and even started to rise again at the end of the 1980s. Japanese investment remained the largest source of FDI into South Korea, reaching a cumulative total of $3.9 billion by March 1990. The inter-governmental negotiating emphasis has switched from loans as such to technology transfer and market access as the Koreans push to catch up, and emulate, the Japanese in certain sectors of high technology and manufactured exports.

The rights of the Korean residents in Japan remained a contentious issue, but, under continuous pressure from South Korea, the Japanese government did make a series of minor amendments to finger-printing legislation during the second half of the 1980s, before finally agreeing in early 1991 to abolish the system. Towards the end of the Chun era, the Japanese became more concerned about the human rights issue in South Korea, but the moves after June 1987 towards gradual democratisation defused the potency of that issue. On a number of other issues, slow progress was made, but some minor but often easily politicised issues, such as the territorial dispute over Takeshima/Tokdo, remained dormant rather than dead.

When President Chun installed a new, less ideological generation in power in the early 1980s, the channels of communication - the pipelines - which had existed between Korean and Japanese politicians and officials and, to a lesser extent, businessmen were broken. It took time for the ties to be rebuilt, not least because the new South Korean bureaucrats knew little of Japan and cared more about the global character of Korea's economic and political problems. However, that may well have helped to induce a reappraisal and a new attitude on the Japanese side too, which found its most vivid expression in Nakasone's dramatic visit in 1983.

The North Korean dimension

Throughout the post-Korean War period, Japan has adhered to a policy of non-recognition of North Korea, although on occasions, as shown above, it has tried to edge a little closer. A degree of unofficial contact has been maintained throughout, but the manner of these contacts has often caused tensions in the Japan-South Korean relationship.

The North Koreans have actually maintained an ambiguous attitude towards Japan. The North Korean leadership and media have regularly railed against 'the revival of Japanese militarism', usually in cohorts with US 'imperialism' and the South Korean 'puppet dictatorship'. This theme, of course, derives not only from Kim Il-sung's deep-seated hatred of imperialism but also from his experiences (even allowing for the inflation subsequently by North Korean propaganda of his prowess as an anti-Japanese guerrilla fighter) in exile from Korea prior to 1945. Yet, particularly during the 1980s but also occasionally in earlier decades, the North Koreans have called for the development of cooperative economic relations and Japanese economic inputs. North Korea has also made attempts to distinguish between what it considers the 'reactionary' Japanese government and the 'peace-loving' Japanese people, who might be persuaded to act in a manner more sympathetic to the North.

North Korea has been pursuing three particular objectives in its Japan policy since the early 1950s. The first has been to achieve a diplomatic normalisation with Japan (Shin 1987 pp.281-4). Pre-1965, this was an attempt to beat South Korea, involved in the interminable and fraught negotiations with Japan, to the goal of full relations. The first serious North Korean approach - in the late 1950s - did result in an agreement on the repatriation of Koreans to the North, but brought no further successes. The second North Korean approach - in the early 1970s - was fostered by the North's reluctant acceptance that the Japanese would be unlikely to abrogate the 1965 treaties with the South. The North, therefore, called for equidistant diplomacy by Japan - relations with both Koreas - but the Japanese again saw no real benefits at that time. The North worked hard to cultivate support amongst left-wing Japanese and ethnic Koreans in Japan, but its ideological rigidity and intermittent acts of terrorism (such as the Rangoon bombing in 1983 and the KAL airliner bomb in 1987) hindered the growth of any broader sympathy similar to that which the Chinese were always able to command. Indeed, until 1990 and the emergence of the post-Cold War environment in North-east Asia, the Japanese remained content, while the North continued its stubbornness over a number of bilateral problems, to concentrate on only economic and cultural exchanges.

The second North Korean aim has been to undermine the South Korean links with Japan (Roy 1988 pp. 1280-93). The two Koreas have been engaged in an uncompromising diplomatic, political, economic and military competition for more than four decades. The North tried, therefore, first to prevent a Japan-South Korean rapprochement and then to discourage Japanese business from getting heavily involved only in South Korea. For example, with encouragement from the North, Chinese Premier Zhou Enlai in 1970 enunciated a set of trade principles for those Japanese firms wishing to deal with China (a potentially lucrative market) which included their avoidance of trade or investment deals with South Korea. Despite the intermittent North-South Korean dialogue after 1972, the repeated failure to achieve any real breakthrough ensured that the basic 'zero sum game' mentality persisted, which meant that any small incident involving Japan and one or the other Korea had the potential to be blown up into a serious problem. Typical was the fate of 11 North Korean 'boat people' who sailed their fishing boat down to Japan to seek asylum in January 1987. Hassled by North and South Koreans, who both wanted to 'claim' these people, the Japanese in exasperation finally sent them on to Taiwan.[2]

The third North Korean aim has been to expand commercial interactions (Shin 1987 pp.284-7). In the mid-1950s, the North Koreans opened up trade relations with Japan by concluding private-level trade agreements with Japanese businessmen. These were enhanced, in 1971, by the signing of a memorandum on trade between the Japan Dietmen's League for Friendship with North Korea and the (North) Korean Committee for the Promotion of International Trade. This was seen as a way of spurring trade in the way that earlier Sino-Japanese trade had been formalised. Trade did increase, but mainly through North Korea going on a buying spree for Japanese technology; by the mid-1970s it was finding it difficult to repay the outstanding debts on these purchases. This problem was to bedevil trade relations throughout the 1980s. In addition, as China began to reform its economic system and other openings around the world expanded, Japanese business displayed decreasing interest in the North Korean market. Japan became, and has remained, North Korea's largest non-socialist trading partner, but North Korea found its inputs from Japan to be a mixed blessing.

Based on the assumption that the establishment first of a sound basis to Japan-South Korean relations would remove some of the difficulties that his predecessors faced, Nakasone tentatively explored contacts with the North in the mid-1980s. But North Korean recalcitrance, South Korean and US wariness and internal Japanese political problems prevented any real progress. President Roh's July 1988 policy statement specifically encouraged South Korea's friends to improve relations with the North, but the South Korean government did not cease to watch Japanese-North Korean manoeuvrings with a sceptical eye.

Transition troubles

Towards the end of the 1980s all three countries found themselves coming under new pressures - some domestic, some external - which forced them into a re-examination of their own circumstances and, in turn, impacted on the inter-relationships between them.

In South Korea, when Roh became president in February 1988 there was not such a dramatic impact on the bilateral relationship as when Chun took over. Foreign policy successes and political democratisation encouraged South Korean self-confidence and Roh felt more relaxed about the bilateral relationship than Chun in his early days. Nevertheless, the very fact that South Korea had itself entered into a transition period - taking the first steps in a transition from the authoritarianism of the past to greater pluralism and democracy as well as an attempt to shift from being a newly industrialising country to a high-technology and economically advanced country - inevitably produced tensions which impacted on its relations with Japan.

Japan, despite the occasional political tremor, had seemed stable and controlled under the Liberal Democratic Party (LDP) through most of the 1980s. However, from the autumn of 1988 for a period of 18 months, Japan was hit by a series of domestic political troubles which effectively prevented a concentrated effort to develop foreign policy. At the same time, despite the political paralysis, the economy, having weathered the storms of the 'high yen', began a lengthy boom on the back of a significant restructuring of the economy. But the asset inflation, particularly in land and stock market prices, was to store up problems for the Japanese economy later on. Kaifu's success in restoring some electoral credibility to the LDP in the February 1990 elections opened the way for Japan's foreign policy re-engagement, only for the Gulf crisis to provoke the most serious debate yet within Japan about its role in the region and the world.

North Korea seemed, on the surface, to be far less affected by internal political changes during the late 1980s than either South Korea or Japan, as Kim Il-sung steadily promoted his son Kim Jong-il as his successor. However, the dramatic reversals in the global socialist bloc in 1989-90 and the deteriorating state of its economy left North Korea feeling isolated and vulnerable. The Kims were forced to consider ways in which to amend in practice their much-vaunted juche (self-reliance) philosophy while trying to sustain its ideological purity in theory.

Although all three countries appeared to be embarking on a new transitional phase, the inter-relations between them continued to be influenced by the legacy of the past. As will be seen from the following chapters, few aspects of Japan's relations with either Korea can escape from the emotional scars not just of the past few decades but even going back much further into history.

However, before examining the varied political, economic and cultural dimensions of Japan's contemporary relations with the two Koreas, the following chapter will consider the nature of popular perceptions (and their degree of foundation on the legacies of the past) and the impact of the numerous domestic actors on current policy-making in the three countries.

Notes

1. For further details of Japan's policy towards Korea in the late nineteenth and early twentieth century, see Conroy 1960, Deuchler 1987, and Nish 1985. Press coverage of recently discovered German documents, which cast serious doubt on whether the Korean emperor ever officially signed the 1905 treaty by which Japan initially came to 'protect' Korea, have provided yet another example of the way in which interpretation of the countries' history can become the subject of contemporary controversy. *Korea Newsreview* 20 June 1992.
2. For details of the Japanese dilemma over the 'Zu-Dan' case, see *Asahi Shimbun* 8 February 1987; *Korea Herald* 10,11,12 February 1987. The North Korean government threatened to retaliate against two Japanese fishermen then in its custody, if the escaping family were not returned. The asylum-seeking North Koreans themselves only expressed a desire to go to a 'warm country'. However, as Japanese officials suspected would be the case, the North Korean family were soon allowed entry into South Korea after transiting in Taiwan.

3 Perceptions and Policy-making

The policy-making process in all countries tends to be shrouded to a degree in mystery, which even the opening of official records thirty or more years later does not always clear away. Even in Japan, which is by far the most open of the three countries under consideration here, the actors and processes involved in formulating policy towards the two Koreas are by no means clear. The South Korean political system is becoming more open, under democratisation, but elements of its Japan policy are well hidden. The strict control over information exercised in North Korea makes any analysis of opinion and policy-making extremely difficult; policy towards Japan is no exception to the rule. The following sections examine first the role of popular perceptions in the three countries, particularly as expressed through the medium of public opinion polls, and then the most important domestic actors and elements in the policy-making process of these countries.

Perception gaps

Analysis of perceptions unavoidably draws one into subjective assessments and generalisations, but the clear effect of these perceptions on the bilateral relations between Japan and the two Koreas (or, at least with South Korea) warrants some investigation.

Popular perceptions are not immutable, but since they are the result of accumulated experience, on occasions reinforced by education or government propaganda, they inevitably take time both to form and to change. Policy-makers can be influenced by the prevailing political and cultural climate of popular opinion, often more unconsciously than consciously, into adopting certain negotiating positions or advancing certain analyses of another government's actions. Of course, officials can use public opinion as a justification or excuse for adopting a certain policy stance. Mass popular opinion, however, has only an uncertain and indirect effect on government policy-making, whereas informed opinion - overt expressions of opinion from pressure groups, intellectuals and the mass media - can have more of an impact. On the other hand, governments can take a determined course to influence public opinion in a certain direction.

While Korean perceptions of Japan, or vice versa, may well not be accepted as valid by the nation under consideration, that nation does need to discover how it is perceived by the other in order to understand better which attitudes and policies to adopt.

The impression derived from public opinion polls conducted in Japan and South Korea about how the other country is perceived are invariably dominated not only by negative images on both sides but also by a marked imbalance in the relative lack of knowledge or interest amongst Japanese about Koreans compared with vice versa. Moreover, South Koreans tend to see Japan in hard, concrete terms, focusing on the 36 years of colonial rule or the discrimination against Korean residents in Japan. The Japanese, on the other hand, tend to see Korea in softer, cultural terms, thinking of the Olympic Games or Korean food, such as kimchi.

A joint South Korean-Japanese opinion poll, under the auspices of the *Dong-A Ilbo* and *Asahi Shimbun* newspapers, has been undertaken three times, in 1984, 1988 and 1990 (*Asahi Shimbun* 16 June 1988; *Dong-A Ilbo* September 1990). The questions were slightly different on each occasion and the timing of the polls may have affected some answers - the 1984 poll was taken just after President Chun's visit to Japan when Korean expectations were high, the 1988 poll was taken only three months before the Seoul Olympics opened, and the 1990 poll was taken not long after President Roh's controversial visit to Japan. Nevertheless, it is possible to draw certain broad conclusions from the results. On the basic question of like and dislike, the Japanese responses barely changed between the three polls, with 12% reported as liking and 23% as disliking Korea in the 1990 poll (compared with 11% and 19% respectively in the 1984 poll). However, the Korean responses showed a much wider divergence, with those liking Japan falling from 22% in 1984 to 14% in 1988 and to only 5% in 1990. Those disliking Japan increased from 39% to 51% to 66% over the same period.

Asked in the 1988 and 1990 polls what particularly came to mind when the other country's name was mentioned, for Koreans the past was clearly important; by a wide margin the '36-year colonial rule' was the commonest, followed by 'economic great power'. On the Japanese side, the Olympics and Korean food, such as kimchi, led the list followed by folk dress and dance. However, around a quarter of those interviewed could not think of anything that they particularly associated with South Korea.

When looking at particular aspects of the other's society, positive assessments of the Koreans had grown amongst the Japanese, particularly regarding South Korea's economic development and its vitality; from 37% in 1984 to 48% in 1988. Correspondingly, the negative assessments, such as great disparities of wealth and unstable politics, reduced from 46% to 41%

over the same period. On the Korean side, respect for Japan as a great economic power with a high technological level decreased from 57% in 1984 to 46% in 1988, while the more negative assessments about Japan's economic aggression against neighbours and insufficient technology transfer grew from 38% to 47%.

Public opinion surveys conducted by a team of researchers on behalf of the Japan-Korea 21st Century Committee, a high-level non-governmental body set up in 1988, confirmed several of the perceptions outlined above. The surveys, conducted in late 1989, showed a significant gap amongst the two peoples about the past (Nijuisseiki 1991a pp.3-11). The strength of the suspicion of Japanese as a result of past actions was clear amongst the Koreans. This was to be expected amongst those elderly Koreans, over 60, who had actually experienced the Japanese occupation. However, the surveys suggested that even amongst Korean schoolchildren the negative images of Japan were strong, as a result of parental guidance, the textbooks used in middle-schools, and persistent references in the mass media. Consequently, when asked what Japan should do to improve the Japan-Korea relationship, 48% of those interviewed replied that Japan should recognise and apologise for its past aggression, 24% said that the trade imbalance should be rectified, and 22% said that the conditions of the Korean residents should be improved.

By contrast, the Koreans' knowledge of the present day Japan was comparatively low; only 13% were able to answer three questions about Japanese political parties, population and the second largest city. This probably reflects a feeling amongst older Koreans that because they understand some Japanese language (having been taught it when young) they already know about Japan and have no need to enquire further as well as, for the younger Koreans, being a by-product of the marked discouragement of the study of contemporary Japan in school and college courses.

On the other hand, the Japanese were far less aware of the past than the Koreans. Amongst the Japanese interviewed, a surprising 21% did not even know that Japan had colonised Korea and, of those that did know, 35% had no idea how long that period had been. Echoing the 1988 *Dong-A/Asahi* poll, just over a quarter of those Japanese surveyed could not think of anything in particular to associate with Korea. Around half of the Japanese felt that Japan had already reflected enough on its past, even though, by contrast, 73% of Koreans still felt that Japan had not done enough.

These surveys show a considerable mismatch in perceptions between the South Koreans and the Japanese. Generational differences were not always clear from these surveys, but it is likely that the younger Japanese and Koreans do not hold to their parents' perceptions to the same degree. How far are these perceptions special to the relationship with the other country, or are they typical of popular thinking about a number of other countries?

For the Koreans, until the twentieth century, their world revolved very much around North-east Asia and, in particular, their two large neighbours, China and Japan. The Koreans did not suffer from Western colonialism and, indeed, until 1910 theirs was an independent unified country with a long history, so unlike many other Asians they did not express their yearnings for independence or their nationalism in an anti-Western framework. Instead, Korean nationalism was fermented in an anti-Japanese context. The English word 'nationalism' can be translated in three different ways into Korean, but, arguably, the Koreans are most oriented to 'minjokjui', which could be rendered as nationalism in the sense of 'populism', but which is more appropriately considered as anti-colonialist nationalism.[1]

Since the late 1940s, South Koreans have still confined themselves to thinking in North-east Asian terms, even though during the 1980s South Korea's economic interests became increasingly global. The Koreans have focused on Japan, the United States and, inevitably, North Korea as the countries in which they are most interested. Except amongst the small radical minority, North Korea has been viewed predominantly as a threat to the South Korean polity. In the 1988 *Dong-A/Asahi* poll, a mere 5% of the Koreans held favourable feelings towards North Korea, while 59% positively disliked it. These antagonistic views were softened slightly in the 1990 survey, taken in the build-up to the first ever prime ministerial-level meeting between the two Koreas; those liking North Korea had grown to 12%, while those disliking it had fallen to 46%.

Feelings towards the United States have usually been at the opposite extreme, with appreciation for the US role in the Korean War, post-war reconstruction and continued defence against North Korea clear. Nevertheless, during the second half of the 1980s, the anti-Americanism previously voiced mostly by students drew more sympathetic responses from economic interest groups which felt threatened by US pressure. The three *Dong-A/Asahi* polls recorded a marked fall in those liking the United States from 70% in 1984 to 24% in 1990. In this American context, the falls in the 1988 and 1990 polls in Japan's popularity in South Korea may also be, in part, a reflection of growing South Korean self-confidence vis-à-vis the old traditional partners. Nevertheless, although the South Korean attitude towards the United States is not as clear-cut as it once was, it still has some way to go before it reaches the negative levels accorded to Japan.

If for Koreans Japan has a very clear and separate image, distinct from the rest of Asia, the same does not hold in reverse. For Japanese, the Koreans do not stand out so distinctively from other Asians. Japanese society is not divided into classes in the traditional Western capitalist sense, but there are, nevertheless, very fine gradations in a hierarchical sense which find their expression in inter-personal relations. Tokugawa era Japan was a rigidly regimented 'vertical society' and although the period after the Meiji Restoration, in the second half of the nineteenth century, saw many changes to Japanese society, these ideas maintained their strength. This domestic hierarchical concept was externalised, so that the Japanese looked at surrounding countries and the intruding Western powers in terms of their ranking in power terms on the international ladder (Sato 1974 pp.9-17). Through its economic and military modernisation Japan climbed the ladder, only to fall at the end of the Second World War; but once again, after 1945, it steadily climbed the ladder as its economic power grew.

Although the pre-war Japanese militarists and intellectuals cloaked their expansionist ideas in the rhetoric of pan-Asianism, it was clear that the neighbouring countries were regarded as inferior. The Japanese were aware of their cultural debts to China and Korea, and, in that sense, the Japanese had far greater cultural affinity with their 'colonial' peoples than the Western imperialists ever had with their empires. But the tendency to disparage them for failing to modernise as effectively as themselves was strong. After the Second World War most of the countries of Asia were involved in debilitating independence struggles or internecine wars and Japan, under the US umbrella, made the most of its opportunities to again develop as the most powerful regional economy. Although the desire to avoid a return to the pre-war form of pan-Asianism has been a fundamental belief of post-war Japan, the tendency to view the relationships with Asian countries in an asymmetrical fashion has not disappeared.

The Japanese have talked much about the 'heart-to-heart' relationship with South-east Asians, and the concept even found governmental endorsement after the visit to ASEAN by Prime Minister Fukuda in 1977. Nevertheless, it is difficult to escape the conclusion that when Japanese think of Asians, the Chinese and the Koreans more readily spring to mind. It is tempting to see many similarities in the complex psychological heritages which condition Japanese perceptions of both China and Korea - and those countries' perceptions of Japan. Yet, although Japanese may feel alienated from the post-1949 Chinese experience and the failure, yet again, of the Chinese to get their act together in the way that the Japanese have, they do still hark back to the old cultural linkages. To a surprising degree, despite the intermittent tensions in the relationship, both Chinese and Japanese politicians have a tendency to refer to the 'special relationship' which they see between their two countries (Newby 1988 pp.48-50). These feelings find an echo at the popular level in Japan; the 1988 *Dong-A/Asahi* poll showed a 28% liking for China (higher than for the United States) and a mere 9% saying that they disliked China.

As has been shown above, South Korea has consistently been viewed less favourably than China. North Korea, however, has had an even lower rating;

in the 1988 poll cited above North Korea was liked by a bare 2% and disliked by 51%. The typical Japanese feelings towards Koreans are compounded by a marked lack of sympathy with the North Korean style of dynastic authoritarianism.

Public opinion polls are unknown in North Korea and so it is impossible to judge popular feelings towards Japan. North Koreans certainly share with their southern counterparts a resentment at the past colonial exploitation of their country, and, indeed, Kim Il-sung has played on patriotic sentiments by making a point of mythologising his own role in the anti-Japanese guerrilla resistance movements. North Korean leaders and spokesmen, while critical of past and what is perceived as post-war revived 'Japanese militarism', inextricably linked with American imperialism and South Korean dictatorship, have, nevertheless, taken some pains to differentiate between the Japanese government and the Japanese people (Shin 1987 p.280). The North Korean people, it is argued, join with the Japanese people in wanting relations normalised.

The making of Japan's Korea policy

The literature on the foreign policy decision-making process in Japan has become extensive, but one element common to most analyses is the emphasis on the impact of the 'triad' of the ruling Liberal Democratic Party, the bureaucracy and big business (Scalapino 1977; Drifte 1990). Certainly, by comparison with many Western countries the degree of policy consultation and involvement between these groups is high. However, these three component parts should not be seen as necessarily working in perfect harmony, as the standard bearers of the 'Japan Inc' concept would argue. There are, indeed, significant differences of opinion within each of these three components, for example, between different factions of the LDP or between different ministries, as well as between the three components, such as between LDP politicians and bureaucrats. This inevitably brings tensions and, occasionally, inconsistencies into the policy-making process. These differences appear more clearly on detailed examination of the various actors involved in policy towards a particular country or region. They certainly become more pronounced when policy is concerned with the superpowers, China or the two Koreas than with the relatively 'low key' countries or areas such as ASEAN.

The Foreign Ministry has always considered itself the guiding hand of foreign policy towards South Korea and, despite the absence of diplomatic relations, towards the North too. The Asian Affairs Bureau, through its North-east Asia Division, has always taken the lead, but, as with all aspects of Japanese foreign policy-making, the need to consider the American perspective has also given an important voice to the American Affairs Bureau. While there is a tendency for the 'Asia faction' of diplomats to be rotated within the Asian Affairs Bureau and the Seoul embassy, there have been cases, such as Sunobe Ryozo (1977-81), of 'American faction' diplomats being appointed as ambassador to Seoul. Japanese ambassadors to Seoul have usually been senior career diplomats, often with previous experience either at the embassy in Seoul or in the Asian Affairs Bureau. Their stature has increased during the second half of the 1980s, with Yanai Shinichi actually taking up the ambassadorship after having been deputy vice-minister. Young diplomats are sent on attachment to the embassy in Seoul for language training and a core of 'experts' on Korea has now been effectively built up within the Ministry.

The Foreign Ministry lacks a strong domestic power base by comparison with its fellow ministries and this sometimes weakens its bargaining power in inter-ministerial disputes over policy. Inevitably, with the growing reach of Japanese economic power and the increased complexity of modern international relations, the Foreign Ministry has found that on policy towards Korea, as elsewhere, the number of ministries involved in policy inputs has grown steadily during the 1980s. The Foreign Ministry has worked closely with the Defence Agency on aspects of security and defence policy, particularly where the potential for conflict on the peninsula or merely continued political instability can adversely affect the security of Japan. The Defence Agency contains a number of long-serving analysts who speak Korean and have established good personal contacts with the South's armed forces. The Defence Agency, in its annual white papers, has been careful not to explicitly designate North Korea as a 'threat' to Japan, but there is inevitably a considerable suspicion within the Agency about North Korea's military and, indeed, nuclear capabilities.

The Foreign Ministry's traditional rival in foreign economic policy areas has been the Ministry of International Trade and Industry (MITI). MITI does have a considerable voice in trade and investment problems, anti-dumping disputes and technology transfer squabbles with South Korea. It has not acted as a strong supporter of developing economic contacts with North Korea, unlike its role in the late 1960s-early 1970s in encouraging trade with China prior to the normalisation of relations.

A number of other economic ministries have become more involved. The Ministry of Agriculture and Fisheries has had a long-standing role in fishing disputes with both Koreas. The Finance Ministry was heavily involved in discussions over loans to South Korea (and will be again when the North Korean negotiations lead to an economic cooperation agreement) and over opening up the South Korean market to Japanese financial institutions. The

Justice Ministry has a strong say in resolving the legal issues on the status of Korean residents in Japan. The Construction Ministry has demanded a say on issues of access to the Japanese market for Korean construction companies, the Ministry of Transport is involved in discussions to open up air flights to North Korea, the Ministry of Education becomes involved when textbook contents become controversial and the Ministry of Posts and Telecommunications is interested in satellite broadcasting and other information linkages.

The Foreign Ministry has tried to argue that it should have the supreme coordinating role as 'unifier' (ichigenka) (Drifte 1990 p.22) of policy towards the two Koreas, but, on occasions, when disputes have been hard to settle it has been forced to concede to the Prime Minister's Office, including in some cases the prime minister himself, the final decision. In the Japanese political system, however, the prime minister rarely takes the decisive lead on foreign policy.

In the course of post-war Japanese diplomacy only three prime ministers can be said to have taken a sustained or crucial interest in policy towards the Korean peninsula. Sato, in the early 1960s, took a clear decision to push through the normalisation of relations with South Korea even at the cost of disruption within the national Diet. Miki, in the mid-1970s, tried hard to restore some balance to Japanese relations with the two Koreas after a fraught period in Japan-South Korea relations. Nakasone, in the early 1980s, moved in a dramatic fashion, against the advice of the Foreign Ministry, to make his first overseas visit to Seoul and thereby try again to repair Japan-South Korean relations. Nakasone, in fact, over-rode normal diplomatic channels by first directly telephoning President Chun and then sending a personal emissary, the businessman Sejima Ryozo, to arrange his January 1983 visit.

If Japanese prime ministers have only occasionally been key actors in relations with the two Koreas, this is not the same as saying that the LDP itself has not been deeply involved in Korean policy. There has always been a strong lobby of pro-South Korean politicians within the LDP, particularly in the 1950s and 1960s within the factions of Kishi Nobusuke and of Shiina Etsusaburo, who as foreign minister had negotiated the 1965 Basic Treaty, and later in the 1970s and 1980s in the factions of Nakasone and Fukuda. The faction of Miki (and later as the Komoto Toshio faction) also had good contacts with South Korea, but was less rigidly committed. One element which contributed to the difficulties encountered by the government of Suzuki Zenko in 1981-82 was that the Suzuki faction, like its predecessor the Ohira Masayoshi faction, had poor links with South Korea (Bridges 1984a p.13).

The other important faction of the 1970s and 1980s, that of former Prime Minister Tanaka Kakuei, was, if anything, thought to be more interested in developing greater contacts with North Korea. During the 1981-82 impasse, the South Korean government specifically invited senior Tanaka faction politicians, such as Takeshita Noboru, Gotoda Masaharu and Yamashita Ganri, to Seoul to impress on them an appreciation of the South Korean position.

These committed faction leaders and other senior politicians established informal channels of communication - 'the pipelines' - which enabled Fukuda, for example, to talk out problems with President Park's associates. The main formal line of communication, however, has been the Japan-South Korean Dietmen's League, established in July 1975 (based on an earlier model set up three years before) and which by the late 1980s had a membership of around 300 politicians drawn from LDP and the Democratic Socialist Party (DSP). At its formation, middle-ranking LDP politicians, such as Nakagawa Ichiro and Uno Sosuke, were deliberately given key positions, but the initial chairmanship, after Kishi and Shiina fell out, was given to Funada Naka. During the 1980s the chairmanship was in the hands of Fukuda faction men: from 1981 Yasui Ken, a former Speaker of the Lower House, and later, after his death, Fukuda himself. In March 1990, however, former Prime Minister Takeshita took over the chairmanship. One problem of the League's organisation, apart from the perennial issue of whether the Japan Socialist Party (JSP)[2] would join, has been the increasing age of those LDP politicians most actively interested. There are few signs of a new younger generation of politicians interested enough to take up the mantle.

Contacts by the LDP with North Korea have been far more informal, intermittent and low-key. For decades, few LDP politicians of any standing took an active interest in North Korean affairs, at least until 1990. The LDP's own Afro-Asian Study Group, a small organisation which has always espoused more radical ideas, has followed North Korean affairs occasionally (and even sent groups to North Korea in 1980 and 1982, under Fujii Katsushi of the Miki/Komoto faction). But the main line of communication has been through the Dietmen's League for the Promotion of Japan-North Korean Friendship (Nitcho yuko sokushin giin renmei). This League, established in November 1971 by LDP and JSP politicians, is smaller and more vulnerable than its Japan-South Korean counterpart. When its chairman, Kuno Chuji (a member of the Tanaka faction), lost his seat in the 1983 Lower House election, the work of the League practically ground to a halt through lack of someone to take over his role; in the end a Nakasone faction member, Tani Yoichi, temporarily took over until Kuno was returned to the Diet in 1986.

Not until 1990 did senior LDP politicians begin to take a serious interest in developing relations with North Korea. When they did the impact was significant. First Ishii Hajime, a Takeshita faction member, and then Kanemaru Shin, a former deputy prime minister and the acting leader of the Takeshita faction (and, ironically, one of the few senior members of the preceding Tanaka faction that had been obviously in the pro-South Korean lobby), began to take the initiative. As is discussed further in Chapter 8 both visited North Korea in September 1990 and, in a joint delegation with the JSP, opened the way for governmental-level negotiations. In February 1991 Ishii was elected chairman of the revamped Dietmen's League.

The opposition parties play a lesser role than the LDP in the development of relations with the two Koreas, although the JSP has been an important channel of communication with North Korea. The largest opposition party, the JSP, long maintained a severely critical attitude towards South Korea. Incensed at the 1965 Japan-South Korea Basic Treaty, the JSP announced that it would even refuse to 'recognise' the existence of South Korea as a state; a bizarre stance that it held to stubbornly until 1989. Then, the democratic election of President Roh and the JSP's own electoral needs within Japan, when it began to seriously visualise a coalition with other opposition parties, led the party into much agonising over policy towards South Korea. In February 1988 the long-standing ban on party members visiting South Korea was lifted and contacts with South Korean opposition parties were formalised. First former party chairman Ishibashi Masashi and then, in December 1989, JSP Secretary-General Yamaguchi Tsuruo visited Seoul at the invitation of Kim Young-sam's Reunification Democratic Party. After Kim Young-sam joined the Democratic Liberal Party (DLP) in February 1990, the JSP decided to develop contacts with the new government party. These contacts may well be up-graded if Kim Young-sam, chosen as the DLP's candidate for the presidential elections due in December 1992, wins that election. Nevertheless, the process of developing contacts with the South will continue to be subject to powerful restraints from the pro-North Korean factions within the JSP, not least because the current chairman, Tanabe Makoto, who replaced Doi Takako in June 1991, is so personally associated with the push for normalising relations with the North.

Having effectively cut itself out of policy-making towards South Korea, the JSP has concentrated on trying to promote trading, cultural and, ultimately, diplomatic contacts with North Korea. Successive party leaders have visited Pyongyang; Asukata Ichio in 1978 and 1981, Ishibashi in 1984, Doi in 1987 and 1990, and Tanabe in 1992. While the Foreign Ministry has rarely approved of the statements that emanated from visits by these leaders and other JSP senior politicians, it has recognised the utility of maintaining contacts with the North through the JSP. Moreover, since the first 'private-level' agreement in 1972, the JSP has negotiated a series of fishing agreements and even a form of 'memorandum trade' (on the lines of earlier Japan-China unofficial trade agreements) with North Korea. The JSP has, therefore, acted as a constant lobbying group for better relations with North Korea, but, ironically, has found itself being used not just by the North

Koreans but even by the Japanese government.

The other opposition parties have not been so actively involved. The Democratic Socialist Party (DSP) has been generally pro-South Korean, and it was the only party to vote with the LDP in 1965 in favour of the normalisation of Japan-South Korean relations. Within the DSP, the most pro-South Korean faction was led by Kasuga Ikko, who for many years in the 1970s was the number two in the Japan-South Korean Dietmen's League. The Japan Communist Party, on the other hand, has been strongly critical of the South (unlike the JSP it refused to attend President Roh's speech to the Diet in May 1990) and supportive of better relations with the North, although since the early 1970s it has been unhappy about the personality cult of the Kim family. The Komeito has tended to see itself as playing a mediating role, if in a minor key, and party chairman Takeiri Yoshikatsu visited both Koreas (the North for the first time in 1972 and the South in 1981).

The Japanese business community can be considered a heterogeneous player; the interests of the leaders of the major economic organisations, the industry sectoral groups and the individual corporations are different and competing. Nevertheless, in general, Japanese business has been keenly interested in the prospects for trade and investment with South Korea, but has shown little sustained interest in the North's market.

The 1965 normalisation of Japan-South Korean relations had been supported by business groups in Japan and there was a rapid expansion of commercial contacts afterwards. In 1969 the Japan-Korea Cooperation Committee was formed by senior businessmen and politicians (and headed for the first decade by former prime minister Kishi). The importance of this committee, although it has continued to hold joint meetings with its Korean counterpart, began to be down-graded under the Chun administration and is now no longer so influential. Another organisation which has regular contacts with its South Korean counterpart but which is basically a business grouping is the Japan-South Korea Economic Committee, which has been headed for many years by Sugiura Binsuke, President of the Long-Term Credit Bank. The Keidanren (the Federation of Economic Organisations) has been an active supporter of this organisation and Keidanren leaders have often led business delegations put together by this committee to South Korea.

The business community has basically encouraged and supported the Japanese government's efforts to expand economic contacts with South Korea after the 1965 normalisation, through, for example, urging greater liberalisation of the Korean market and improved investment incentives. These considerations, however, became less paramount in the second half of the 1980s as the South Korean market became noticeably more open, though the Japanese banks and securities houses still continued to urge the Japanese government to press the South Korean government to carry out the planned, but often postponed, liberalisation of its financial markets. By contrast, some sectors of Japanese industry became increasingly concerned about the competitive success of South Korean industry. This had been a problem for the Japanese ship-building industry since the late 1970s, but in the 1980s the textiles and consumer electronics sectors came under pressure from cheaper imports from South Korea. This culminated in pressure on MITI from textile companies to institute anti-dumping actions against South Korean producers; in 1988, therefore, the South Koreans were forced into agreeing to an export restraint agreement on knitwear exports to Japan. Lobbying on the Japanese government by other sectors worried about Korean competition is likely to increase.

Apart from a brief flurry of interest in the early 1970s, when the North Korean government embarked on a short-lived campaign to import machinery and plant, the Japanese business community has shown little enthusiasm for the North Korean market. Indeed, the main concern of both MITI and the business circles concerned has been to secure repayment from North Korea of the debts incurred at that time. In the period immediately before the normalisation of relations with China, in 1971-72, Japanese business leaders accelerated the change of political climate amongst both the major factions of the LDP and the general public and helped realise the formation of a new cabinet committed to a new policy towards China (Ogata 1977 pp.175-203). Although some companies are interested in the long-term prospects for the North Korean market, there is nothing comparable to the China case in terms of pressure from business leaders for normalising relations with the North.

There is a wide range of private groups and individuals (from academics to activists) who are interested in aspects of relations with both South and North Korea, but their influence on Japanese policy-making is marginal. The Korean residents in Japan are the major group outside the 'triad' of influentials, but the splits within the community have tended to turn the residents' organisations into irritants rather than positive factors in Japanese government policy-making. The situation of the Korean residents will be examined in more detail in Chapter 7, but it should be noted here that the two main organisations, Mindan, which represents the pro-South residents, and Chongnyon, which represents the pro-North residents, seem to act more as subsidiary agents for their respective governments than as overseas Korean welfare organisations (Lee and De Vos 1981, pp. 127-9). So, although Mindan does lobby, in conjunction with South Korean governmental activities, for the abolition of finger-printing for example, and Chongnyon tries to join with the JSP and the JCP in political campaigns, the majority of Korean residents have become disillusioned with them (Colbert 1986 pp. 285-6). Their direct impact on Japanese government policy seems be limited.

South Korea's policy-making process

The Confucian Korean political culture is oriented towards the acceptance of elite leadership and hierarchical bureaucracy. Apart from a very brief period in 1960-61, the South Korean political system has been presidential in both style and substance. Even under the post-1987 democratisation, this has constrained the input and influence of the prime minister and cabinet ministers in particular, and, to a lesser degree, the bureaucracy and big business. The inputs of the president and his aides which form the presidential secretariat are, therefore, still crucial though inevitably elusive in detail. Presidential pre-eminence applies as much to foreign policy-making as to domestic policies (Koh 1984 pp.114-21).

The personality and perceptions of the successive presidents have had a marked effect on South Korea's policies towards Japan. In both a personal and an institutional sense, Syngman Rhee and Park Chung-hee dominated foreign policy decision-making, though they adopted very different policies towards Japan. Rhee was dedicated to driving Japanese influence out of Korea, whereas Park took a more pragmatic view of Japanese economic achievements. He not only pushed through the 1965 Basic Treaty against considerable domestic opposition, but also promoted what was seen as a favourable reception for Japanese trade and investment. Park had many Japanese friends and knew how to operate in the Japanese system; he preferred to use personal ties and informal contacts. Given his strong central control, he was able to switch means for pursuing his policy with Japan at will. During the negotiations with the Japanese in 1961-65, for example, he used the director of the Korean Central Intelligence Agency (KCIA) Kim Jong-pil (an ex-military colleague of his), the technocrat-politician and Deputy Prime Minister Kim Yu-taek, or the young politician Lee Dong-won (appointing him foreign minister), depending on whom he thought might be the most effective.

Chun Doo-hwan, while also operating a strong central control, did allow a slightly wider sharing of power amongst the various government organs than Rhee or Park. Although Chun's early moves to reorganise the presidential secretariat were intended to reduce the distance between him and his cabinet ministers, the prime ministers under Chun, who were usually chosen from 'civilian' backgrounds, were even less influential than under Park, who at least installed some of his inner group of former military colleagues (such as Kim Jong-pil in 1971-75) in that post. Chun came to power with no knowledge of foreign affairs in general or of Japan in particular. The same could be said about the inner circle of military men, retired or still on active service, who came to power with him (future President Roh Tae-woo was in this category).

Significantly, therefore, Chun had to bring expertise on foreign policy into his secretariat. His first three chiefs of the secretariat all had foreign policy backgrounds; one of them, Lee Bum-suk, a fluent Japanese speaker, was moved to be foreign minister in June 1982 at a crucial stage in the Japan-South Korean loan negotiations.

Chun insisted on dealing with Japan in a very different way from his predecessor. He purged most of the senior politicians and even bureaucrats who had built up long-standing contacts with Japanese opposite numbers. Determined to extract a better deal from Japan, he was personally closely involved in the proposal to Japan for a $6 billion loan. However, after the settlement of the loan issue and, subsequently, his own visit to Japan in 1984, he seems to have taken a less direct interest in policy towards Japan, leaving more responsibility to his aides and to the Foreign Ministry.

His successor, Roh, had gained some experience of international affairs through his work preparing for the 1988 Seoul Olympics and he did visit Japan, when Democratic Justice Party (DJP) presidential candidate, in September 1987. Roh has retained most of the decision-making power of his predecessor, but has opened up the flow of information more; the presidential secretariat assistants act more as 'liaisons' between the cabinet and the president (Kim, Hakjoon 1989 pp.32-6). His foreign policy aides within the secretariat tend to be drawn from academic rather than party political or career diplomatic backgrounds. Roh's reputation is one of being a 'good listener' rather than a decisive advocate himself. He certainly does not have the strong views on Japan that Chun brought with him and there has been far more continuity in Japan policy than either Park or Chun allowed when they became president.

The Foreign Ministry is involved in handling the day-to-day administration of relations with Japan. The Ministry has an Asian Affairs Bureau, with a North-east Asia Division which deals directly with Japan. In the 1960s and 1970s ambassadors to Japan tended to be political appointees, but in the 1980s more career diplomats began to be appointed. Roh's first ambassador, Lee Won-kyung, was a former foreign minister who had studied in Japan in his youth, and the current ambassador, Oh Jay-hee, although from the same high school as Roh, is nonetheless a senior career diplomat. Similarly, the foreign ministers themselves have ceased during the 1980s to be politicians or presidential comrades and, starting with Lee Won-kyung in 1985, there has been a succesion of senior career diplomats as minister. This has certainly provided ministers with diplomatic expertise, but it has not necessarily given them political clout. Of the foreign ministers since 1980, moreover, only Lee Bum-suk (1982-83) and Lee Won-kyung (1985-88) had a deep knowledge of Japan. One of the weaknesses of the Foreign Ministry has been in long-term research and analysis; in 1988 the attached Institute for Foreign Afairs and

National Security was reorganised and in 1991 a Policy Research and Analysis Division was created within the Ministry to try to meet these needs.

As in the case of Japan, the increasing complexity of issues on the international agenda has given a growing range of ministries a say in foreign policy-making. On foreign economic policy, the Economic Planning Board (EPB), under the control of the deputy prime minister, has acted as a very powerful voice, especially through using its coordinating functions over inputs from other economic ministries such as the Ministry of Trade and Industry, the Ministry of Agriculture, Forestry and Fisheries, and the Ministry of Science and Technology. However, the Ministry of Finance has always tried to operate in a more independent fashion and, recently, under democratisation, the other less powerful economic ministries have differed more openly with the EPB over aspects of economic policy towards Japan.

Defence and security aspects involving Japan, the United States and the North-east Asian strategic environment require the heavy involvement of the Ministry of National Defence and the Agency for National Security Planning (as the Korean CIA was renamed in 1981). The National Unification Board is closely concerned with watching North Korean policies, and, therefore, of course, North Korean policy towards Japan. However, its political standing has tended to be rather lightweight; despite the switch of the then Foreign Minister Choi Ho-joong to that agency and his promotion to become, at the same time, the second deputy prime minister, in March 1990, the Board still tends to act as a research and analysis rather than a decision-making organ.

As mentioned above, the prime ministers do not have as much impact on foreign policy as their title might suggest. Much will depend on their expertise and their rapport with the president; Roh's first four prime ministers all came from academic backgrounds and only one, Roh Jai-bong, who was in the post for less than six months, had any real political standing. None of the prime ministers of the 1980s and early 1990s can be said to have had strong inputs on policy towards Japan, with the exception of Lho Shin-yong, who was prime minister in 1985-87 after having served earlier as foreign minister during the early tense stages of the loan negotiations.

Political parties in South Korea are far more unstable and short-lived than the semi-permanent Japanese parties; they form, merge and break up with great rapidity. Presidents often create their own parties on coming to power; Park formed the Democratic Republican Party, Chun the Democratic Justice Party (DJP), and Roh, after continuing with the DJP for two years, the Democratic Liberal Party (DLP). Except for the period 1986-88 and for a few days after the March 1992 elections before some independents were wooed into the DLP, the president's ruling party has always had a majority in the National Assembly. Party politicians do not have such a strong say in foreign policy towards Japan, although several have played an important role in acting as 'pipelines' to Japanese politicians. The main official organisation is the Korea-Japan Parliamentarians' League, which was created at the same time as its Japanese counterpart in 1975. Kim Jong-pil, the prime minister 1971-75, was one of the instigators and became its first formal chairman the following year. Active in this Korean initiative was Lee Pyong-hee, minister without portfolio in the Kim cabinets, who developed good contacts with Japanese politicians. However, both Kim and Lee were purged when Chun took power and not until 1981 was a new Korean chairman appointed, Lee Chae-hyong, who was chairman of the DJP. Subsequently, the chairman of the South Korean side has always been a senior ruling party politician, which suggests a higher political profile than on the Japanese side, at least until the late 1980s, when the Japanese began to follow the same practice.

The formation of the DLP in February 1990 brought into the new ruling party two opposition politicians who had good contacts with Japan. Kim Young-sam, leader of the RDP, had visited Japan and held talks with the JSP. More important, however, was Kim Jong-pil, leader of the New Democratic Republican Party, who has sustained his contacts from decades earlier. The other important DLP politician with good Japanese connections is Park Tae-joon, the co-chairman and a leading steel industrialist. Kim Dae-jung, the leading opposition politician and leader of the Party for Democracy and Peace (PDP), has his own contacts with Japanese opposition politicians and he was actually in exile in Japan in 1973 when he was kidnapped back to Korea by the KCIA (Nakagawa 1981 pp. 136-50).

As in Japan there is a close partnership between government and business, especially the huge conglomerates, the chaebol, whose birth the Park government deliberately encouraged in the 1960s through the provision of cheap credit and preferential treatment. As the Park and Chun governments were less dependent on business for political support than their Japanese equivalents, the system appeared to become much more officially directed 'from the top down'. Nevertheless, the relationship has been, at times, an uneasy one. Even under Park and Chun the government did not always get its own way; under Roh the government has found it even harder to curb the power of the chaebol. There has been a proliferation of quasi-governmental organisations, such as the Korea Trade Promotion Corporation (KOTRA), and business associations (often formed on government initiatives), such as the Federation of Korean Industries (FKI). Although all the leading industrialists join the FKI, its main role is reactive, responding to government proposals rather than initiating policies (Park, M.K. 1987 pp. 904-8). Instead, in their lobbying for and against policies the business leaders use more informal methods deriving from family, alumni and other personal relationships which are the key to Korean society.

The chaebol are, of course, modelled on the Japanese pre-war zaibatsu; the

Korean general trading companies set up after 1975 to focus the exporting activities of each chaebol also owe much in inspiration to the Japanese sogoshosha. Many senior Korean executives are fluent Japanese speakers or are familiar with Japanese business practices. However, in the bilateral trade between the two countries, the Japanese companies are much stronger than their Korean counterparts, who, therefore, try hard to persuade the Korean government to support their needs. This can result in the Korean conglomerates pushing for government support to open up the Japanese market or to resist anti-dumping actions or to exclude certain Japanese goods from South Korea. In 1984, Korean industrialists hastily compiled a list of 23 technologies they wanted to obtain from Japan and presented it to President Chun just before his state visit to Japan; the list even included the names of Japanese corporations from which they wanted specific technologies. However, the intention to seek greater technology transfer from Japan was already an integral part of Korean government policy; the details of which exact technologies to ask for was where corporate opinion counted.

As in Japan there is a range of pressure groups and individuals who, particularly since the advent of the Roh administration, can play a role in influencing specific aspects of policy towards Japan, for example over the treatment of Koreans in Japan. Academics tend to be involved in the policy-making process to a greater degree than in Japan. For example, the text of Roh's July 1988 declaration, which encouraged countries friendly to South Korea, including Japan, to develop contacts with North Korea, was discussed in depth with a group of university academics prior to its finalising. Few amongst this elite group of academic experts, however, are specialists in Japan alone.

North Korea's policy-making

The last four decades have seen several transfers of power in South Korea and each president has operated in a different manner. For North Korea, however, there has been no such transfer of power, although Kim Il-sung, now the world's longest-serving ruler, is faced with a crucial problem of succession. Kim may not be a particularly charismatic figure, but he has shown himself to be a survivor and master of political intrigue. He came to power in North Korea with the blessings and help of the Soviet army (after being in exile from the Japanese in Manchuria in 1937-41, he fled to the Soviet Maritime Provinces). After 1948, he fought off internal challenges from other factions and became chairman of the unified Korean Workers Party (KWP) and concurrently prime minister (Suh 1983 pp. 43-64).

Under the 1972 constitution, however, Kim was elected president and his own political thought, juche (self-reliance), became the official ideology of the state. Despite the continued constitutional pre-eminence of the KWP, Kim actually began to shift some of the power to the state, although the considerable overlap of personnel in the top echelons of party and government blurs the distinction between the two (Chung, C-w. 1983 pp. 19-42). In practice, the office of president and a new administrative organ, a kind of 'super-cabinet' known as the Central People's Committee, have taken over some of the KWP Politburo's decision-making functions.

Views vary over the role of Kim's son, Jong-il, in the decision-making process. After having toyed with the idea of using his own younger brother as his successor, Kim Il-sung turned in the mid-1970s to his own son, who was promoted into the KWP Politburo in 1980. He is now number two in the KWP hierarchy and, in December 1991, he was promoted to Supreme Commander of the Armed Forces, the first time he has held a military post. Significantly, however, he has not yet held a government post. The elder Kim has invested considerable effort into creating such a suffocating cult of personality around him and his son that it is difficult to separate out fact from reality (Cotton 1987 pp. 745-68). Kim Jong-il is reportedly exercising day-to-day control over the party and chairing Politburo meetings, but on major decisions his father's is still the crucial voice. According to a defecting North Korean diplomat, Kim Jong-il began to take control of the Foreign Ministry in 1984, but he has rarely come up with any ideas about what direction to take in foreign policy (FBIS-EAS-91-091, 2 October 1991).

On policy towards Japan, particularly where the crucial linkage with the nuclear inspection issue is involved, the elder Kim can certainly be considered as supreme. Kim Jong-il does not seem to have been involved to the same extent as he has been, for example, in policy towards China. The important LDP-JSP Japanese mission in September 1990 did not meet him once despite staying five days in Pyongyang. Indeed, not until a similar LDP-JSP mission visited Pyongyang for the April 1992 celebration of Kim Il-sung's eightieth birthday, did Kim Jong-il meet any senior Japanese politician or negotiator. Even then, there was no conversation beyond an exchange of simple greetings. At the same time, the North Korean media began to talk of Kim Jong-il's important input into the negotiations with Japan. But this may well be designed more to enhance the son's political importance by giving him credit for progress in the Japan negotiations than a reflection of the reality of the negotiating process.

The Foreign Ministry, which operates as part of the State Administrative Council, is responsible for the implementation of policy. Its role in policy formulation is more problematic. According to a defecting North Korean diplomat, since the mid-1980s, the KWP's International Department has lost ground to the Foreign Ministry in the decision-making process. Certainly, the

Ministry has usually been headed by political heavyweights, such as Ho Dam (1970-83) and Kim Yong-nam (since 1983), who have also been members of the KWP Politburo. In October 1990, after the LDP-JSP delegation visit to Pyongyang heralded the development of relations with Japan, the Ministry's North-east Asia Department, which had handled contacts with Japan through a small-scale office, was reorganised. A new Japan Bureau was created and the number of officials increased from 2 to 15. In the preliminary negotiations in November-December 1990, the North Korean delegation was led by the bureau head, Chu Chin-kuk.

The KWP also acts as a crucial channel of communication with Japan in the absence of formal diplomatic routes. In particular, the International Department of the KWP Central Committee, which Kim Yong-nam headed before becoming foreign minister, has been heavily involved in arranging contacts with Japanese politicians. Kim Yong-sun, the party secretary in charge of international affairs, has been particularly active in cultivating party-to-party contacts with Japan since 1990; he visited Tokyo in February 1991 at a crucial early stage of the normalisation negotiations. However, according to a defecting North Korean diplomat, Kim's role is more that of putting a human face on North Korean policy and helping from the sidelines than of actually initiating policy (FBIS-EAS-91-191, 2 October 1991).

The KWP's Committee for Cultural Relations with Foreign Countries also plays a general role in conducting people-to-people diplomacy and cultural exchange, but the main formal organ for contact with all groups in Japan throughout most of the 1970s and 1980s was the Korea-Japan Friendship Promotion Association (KJFPA). Despite the longevity of Kim Il-sung and the fixed position of his son as number two in the hierarchy, the North Korean political system is characterised by a relatively high turnover in middle-level party and government posts. Such has been the case also with the KJPFA leadership, so that there has been a fairly regular change in the chairmanship throughout the 1980s. The successive chairmen have often had past contact with Japan; Kim Dak-jon, for example, had been a Foreign Ministry official specialising in Asian affairs and as a KWP official had visited Japan four times prior to becoming chairman in 1984. But, unlike the case of Liao Chengzhi, who became a long-standing activist for closer Sino-Japanese relations (Radtke 1990), the North Koreans have not allowed anyone to achieve the special role that Liao created for himself in China.

The KWP also maintains close contacts with the pro-North resident Koreans in Japan. The pro-North organisation, Chongnyon, founded in 1955, is technically organised as an affiliate of the KWP; the chairman and several Chongnyon Central Committee members are also invariably elected to the North Korean Supreme People's Assembly (SPA).

In a formal and functional sense, other ministries, such as the Ministry of

External Economic Relations and the Ministry of the People's Armed Forces, provide an input. So too does the Korean Committee for the Promotion of International Trade, which was responsible for negotiating the 1971 memorandum governing trade relations, and has continued to act as the main body for trade and fishery negotiations with the Japanese. There will also be inputs into the policy process from KWP- and government-affiliated research organisations, such as the Academy of Social Sciences and the Research Institute for Peace and Disarmament.

Nevertheless, the notable lack of concrete data on North Korea means that the answer to the question of how these various structures and personalities actually interact to make foreign policy in general, and policy towards Japan in particular, remains, in the words of Koh Byung Chul, 'elusive' (Koh 1987 p. 54). The necessity to follow the personality cult of Kim Il-sung and adhere to his personal philosophy of juche must impose constraints on the debates within the policy-making process and on the nature of the proposals put before Kim. As a result, the conflictual tendencies between 'red' (ideological consciousness) and 'expert' (technocratic expertise), which have been often noted in other communist societies, may be more suppressed in North Korea than, for example, in China. In North Korea, the juche ideology is supposed to imbue even technocrats and bureaucrats with the revolutionary spirit. Nevertheless, there are a number of issues, including the relationship with Japan (in the past a powerful ideological enemy), on which the leadership is being presented with important decisions as to the weight to be given to pragmatic as against ideological considerations. As will be shown in Chapter 8, Kim Il-sung has had to make significant compromises with the spirit of self-reliance in order to develop the much needed practical contacts with Japan.

The expression 'flexible rigidities', first used to describe the adaptive qualities of the Japanese economy (Dore 1986 pp. 6-7), can be aptly used to describe the decision-making processes in the three countries under consideration. Of course, in the North Korean case, rigidity is more common than flexibility, but, as the subsequent chapters will show, even in the North policy change in response to differing internal and external influences is not impossible. The following chapters examine in detail aspects of the politico-strategic, economic and cultural interconnections between Japan and the two Koreas and highlight how the various actors, and their perceptions, outlined in this chapter impact on these relationships.

Notes

1. 'Nationalism' can be translated by three words in Korean. Gukminjui which means the form of

nationalism displayed, for example, by the citizenry during the French Revolution. Gukkajui which is taken as 'statism' of expansionist nationalism, such as Germany under Nazism. Minjokjui which is more a kind of 'populism', but which is taken by Koreans to mean anti-colonial nationalism. (Choi 1978 pp.172-4)

2. The Japan Socialist Party (JSP) formally changed its English name to the Social Democratic Party of Japan in January 1991, but kept its original name in Japanese, Nihon shakaito. For convenience, JSP will be used throughout this book.

4 The Political and Security Triangle

A Korean proverb warns that the prawn (Korea) will have its back broken by the convulsions of the whales (the neighbouring great powers). Since 1945 there have been two prawns (or perhaps, more accurately, one prawn broken into two) and four whales: China, the Soviet Union, the United States and Japan. The Korean peninsula is regarded by all these four major powers as being of political and strategic importance; it lies at the heart of the East Asian theatre.

Because of its geographical position, Korea has served both as a buffer and as an invasion route for its more powerful neighbours. The Koreans have been invaded by the Chinese (in the seventh century), the Manchus (in the thirteenth century), and the Japanese (in the sixteenth and twentieth centuries). In the last century alone, three wars have been fought on Korean territory for control and influence over the peninsula - the Sino-Japanese War in 1894-95, the Russo-Japanese War in 1904-5 and, of course, the Korean War, in 1950-53.

Inevitably, therefore, any discussion of the political and security aspects of the relationships between the two Koreas and Japan will involve some consideration of the role of the other three major powers interested in the peninsula, the subject of the following chapter. However, much of the complexity of the Japan-Korea relationship has to do with the nature of the relationship between the two Koreas themselves, so that situation will be examined first.

North-South competition

North and South Korea have been waging a competitive struggle for prestige and legitimacy for more than four decades. This has been based on economic, military and diplomatic power. In recent years, the balance has been shifting increasingly in favour of the South, but that has not meant any lessening in the manoeuvring for advantage.

A precarious truce has survived on the border for nearly 40 years, since the end of the fratricidal Korean War. To borrow the phrase used in a different context by Leon Trotsky as long ago as 1918, it is 'neither war nor peace'. Bitter memories of the Korean War still play a dominating role in military strategy on the peninsula. The North Koreans cannot forget the US blanket-bombing which reduced their major centres to rubble; Pyongyang is only 90 miles from the border. In the South, the industrial and political nerve-centre of Seoul is only 30 miles away from the border, well within range of North Korean artillery and, drawing on the 1991 Gulf War example, Scud missiles as well. The South Koreans, therefore, remain obsessed by the fear of a surprise attack across the border in the manner of the invasion of 1950, probably in combination with guerrilla infiltration (in 1990 a fourth North Korean infiltration tunnel, dug under the demilitarized zone (DMZ), was uncovered).

Excluding the US forces from the comparison, the military balance in quantitative terms favours the North. According to statistics from the International Institute of Strategic Studies' *Military Balance* (1991), in 1991 North Korean armed forces totalled 1,111,000 men while the South Korean armed forces totalled 750,000. In weaponry, the North has 4,100 tanks, 5,800 artillery pieces, 732 combat aircraft, and 438 naval vessels (including 22 submarines) compared with the South's 1,550 tanks, 4,100 artillery pieces, 457 combat aircraft, and 145 naval vessels (including 4 submarines). The North Korean numerical advantage, however, does not mean a qualitative advantage. Although the North does have a few MiG-29s and Su-25s, most of its aircraft are outmoded and inferior to the South's fighters. Over three-quarters of the North's naval vessels are in fact fast-attack or landing craft and, in terms of total tonnage, the South Korean navy is superior.Both sides are continuing to upgrade their capabilities, but mounting costs have produced a drain on both economies.

The military implications of the rapid defeat of the Iraqi forces must have been disturbing for the North Koreans. They will have noted the relative ease with which the high-technology US-led forces defeated the Soviet-armed Iraqis. North Korea, like Iraq, has relied on mass conscript armed forces and has been exposed to Soviet strategic thinking and training (although Kim Il-sung, since his adoption of his own 'Four Great Military Doctrines' in the early 1960s, has utilised a modification of Soviet thinking). Of course, the battlefields of Iraq/Kuwait and the Korean peninsula are very different, and the North Korean forces, given their much longer period of preparation, are far better entrenched in underground bunkers than the Iraqis. Nevertheless, the North's need to modernise its military equipment and rethink its military strategy was obvious. However, North Korea found it increasingly difficult to obtain the desired advanced Soviet/Russian military technology as relations with the disintegrating Soviet Union worsened. The successor state of Russia has signed a new military agreement with North Korea, but claims not to have supplied any new military hardware to the North. The North has turned to the Chinese, who, under strong pressure from Kim Il-sung when he visited China in October 1991, did agree to increase their military equipment sales to the North (FBIS-EAS-91-200,16 October 1991). It is still unclear, however, how far this would include missiles and other advanced weaponry.

South Korea has been having second thoughts about its next-generation fighter programme and is likely to go for the cheaper F-16s rather than F-18s; some of them will be built under licence from the United States. The United States has also agreed, in late 1991, to the South Korean request to be supplied with Patriot missiles in order to cope with any Scud attack launched from the North.

In per capita terms and in proportion to GNP, defence expenditure is significantly lower in the South than the North, although the absolute value for defence expenditure in the South is much higher. South Korean military authorities claim that the South should be able to reach military parity with the North in the mid-1990s if current trends are continued, but, in reality, South Korea is already more than capable of resisting a North Korean frontal attack. Confidence in South Korean abilities is implicit in the US decision, made public in the spring of 1990, to reduce the number of US Army and Air Force troops stationed in South Korea by 7,000 over the period 1990-92 (DOD 1990). This was followed during 1990-91 with further agreements to give the South Koreans a greater role in the command of the joint US-South Korean force structure. Nevertheless, the South Koreans continue to be extremely watchful of the North Korean military build-up and, since 1990, emerging evidence of the potential for nuclear weapon development. In November 1991 the United States and South Korea decided to postpone the second phase of US troop withdrawals, which probably would have involved 5-7,000 troops in the 1993-95 period, until the uncertainties of the North Korean nuclear programme were addressed (*Korea Times* 22 November 1991).

When Korea was divided in 1945, most of the industrial raw materials, the heavy industry developed by the Japanese and the coal and hydro-electric sources passed to the North, whereas the South inherited most of the strategic harbours, the best agricultural land, considerable light industry and around two-thirds of the population. Both states have managed to transform backward 'part-economies' ravaged by war into predominantly industrial economies, but, although both share a commitment to planning for economic development, their economies have increasingly diverged. South Korea has become one of the leaders of the NICs, and is on the verge of membership of the rich countries' club, the OECD. It is now on the edge of the world's top ten of trading nations; for three years (1986-88) it was the world's fastest growing economy, its per capita GNP is now greater than at least one EC country (Portugal) and it has risen significantly up the technological ladder. This does not mean that South Korea is not without its difficulties, for in 1990, for the first time for five years, the country again slipped into trade and current account deficits, and these deficits worsened in 1991. It is, indeed, as is shown in more detail in Chapter 6, an economy which is in transition, but which nonetheless is a powerful one.

The lack of real data from the North is a handicap in making effective comparisons, but probably until the early 1970s the tight Stalinist-style centrally-controlled northern economy was performing better than the South. However, this command style of economy, while well-suited to the early stages of industrialisation, has proved to be poor at adapting to the demands of managing a more complex and modern economy. In contrast to a number of other socialist countries, including China, which during the 1980s undertook reform to some degree by incorporating some market elements, North Korea has remained wedded to its rigid centralisation under Kim Il-sung's goal of 'self-sufficiency'. The economy is now faced with poor productivity, persistent external debt, sluggish foreign trade, and declining economic aid from its heretofore main supporters, the Soviet Union/Russia and China. The GNP growth rate and foreign trade growth rate are even believed to have been negative in both 1990 and 1991. Even normally tight-lipped North Korean officials have talked about 'difficulties' with energy and food supplies. In almost all economic indicators South Korea appears well ahead of the North.

The record of the 1980s suggests that the South has been winning the economic competition; the same could be said for the diplomatic one (Clough 1987a pp.274-304). The South has hosted the 1988 Olympics as well as receiving a wide range of international leaders including the Pope. It is recognised by more countries than is the North and, most significantly, it has made serious diplomatic inroads into the group of socialist and former socialist countries closest to North Korea. After a series of East European countries, headed by Hungary in early 1989, recognised South Korea, the key prize of diplomatic recognition by the Soviet Union was achieved in September 1990. Finally, China moved first to exchange quasi-diplomatic trade offices in early 1991 and then to full diplomatic relations in August 1992.

Moreover, after continually expressing its opposition to both Koreas entering the United Nations, North Korea was forced in May 1991 to alter its policy. Having realised that the diplomatic balance had shifted sufficiently to allow the South's intended application for membership to succeed, the North too decided to apply. Both Koreas were, therefore, admitted simultaneously but separately in September 1991 (Kim, H.N. 1991 pp. 397-409). As North Korea has found itself increasingly diplomatically isolated since 1989, it has been forced into a reactive mode by the South's diplomatic successes. Its attempts to foster relations with Japan, and even the United States, have yet to produce enough fruits to go even part-way to equalising the balance. Hosting international events too has proved a mixed blessing: the July 1989 World Youth Festival almost certainly produced a massive drain on the government budget and the May 1991 Inter-Parliamentary Union's annual conference was marked by strong criticisms on the North's human rights record from some of the European delegates.

Relations between the two Koreas themselves have been hesitant and insubstantial. In fact, they have worked hard to keep themselves and their people well apart. Even now there are no direct exchanges of postal or telephonic communications (except for an official hotline between the two governments) and no crossings of the border by individuals, except for a limited number of officials involved in talks and one limited 'separated family visit' in September 1985. Official dialogues have been spasmodic and insubstantial, characterised by the 'one step forward and two backwards' kind of syndrome. There have been brief dialogues in 1972-73, 1979-80, 1984-86 and, intermittently, since 1990 (Kim, Hakjoon 1978; Lee, J.S. 1992).

National unification has loomed large in the policy pronouncements of both sides, but the flow of proposals and counter-proposals has long been characterised by an exchange of unacceptable plans and mutual recriminations. The North Korean position has become concentrated on the Democratic Confederal Republic of Koryo (DCRK) concept, which was first espoused in its existing form by Kim Il-sung in October 1980. Foreshadowing what later became popularised in China as 'one country, two systems', two separate social and governmental systems would coexist, for the foreseeable future, under the rubric of the DCRK and its 'supreme national confederal assembly'; but there would be only one 'national army' and unified foreign and defence policies (Kihl 1984 pp.213-6).

The South Koreans have tended to be more reactive to North Korean proposals and, indeed, until the late 1980s were clearly losing the propaganda initiative to the North. The step-by-step ideas advanced by South Korea during the 1970s and 1980s, while more practical than the North's more dramatic proposals for a sudden breakthrough, lacked broader appeal. Currently, the South's position has found expression in the Korean Commonwealth concept, first enunciated by President Roh in September 1989. It stresses 'one people, two governments', thereby building not 'one house' but a 'condominium' for the coexistence of two political systems, as an interim stage to final unification. The Korean Commonwealth would include joint councils of the presidents, ministers and parliamentary representatives (Lee, H. 1990 pp. 601-9).

Despite the differences in the concepts, during 1990 the two sides began to show some flexibility and edge warily towards each other. A series of unprecedented prime-ministerial meetings took place in September, October and December 1990; although progress was limited the very fact that they occurred was significant. The North postponed the fourth prime-ministerial meeting planned for February 1991 because of the joint US-South Korean Team Spirit exercises, but some lower level contacts continued. Some indirect trade developed and, in July 1991, the first authorised direct barter trade took place. A joint table-tennis team participated in the world championships in Japan (actually winning the women's doubles) in June 1991 and further joint sporting teams came up for discussion.

North Korea's partially changed approach reflected its disquiet at its political isolation and economic difficulties. It had been shocked first by the events in China leading up to the Tiananmen Square massacre and by the disintegration of its socialist allies in Eastern Europe in the second half of 1989. Just when it seemed to be recovering from those set-backs, it was hit by the South Korean-Soviet rapprochement in mid-1990. South Korea, on the other hand, felt more self-confident and able to consider a slightly more flexible approach.

In the autumn of 1991, North Korea agreed to restart the prime-minsterial meetings. Then discussions moved much faster than expected. The October meeting in Pyongyang produced a draft, which was fleshed out into an Agreement on Reconciliation and Non-aggression, signed on 13 December 1991 in Seoul (*Korea Times* 14 December 1991). In this most significant breakthrough in North-South relations since the July 1972 North-South Declaration, the two Koreas guaranteed non-interference and non-aggression and proposed military confidence-building measures. They also agreed to stimulate economic exchanges - trade, investment and transport links - and facilitate the flow of mail and people. Both sides had made concessions, but both could draw satisfaction from the terms. The South had accepted the North's non-aggresssion concept, but could expect that in the medium term the North's society would be opened up to the kinds of influences that would slowly undermine the power of the Kim dynasty. The North was, of course, wary about these broader humanitarian contacts (and balked at the South's suggestion of unrestricted exchanges of newspapers and television programmes), but it had gained a way out of its international isolation and a more immediate infusion of economic inputs than was likely to come from either Japan or the United States and the West.

The contentious nuclear issue had not been covered, but, on 31 December, the two sides agreed to a joint Declaration on a Non-nuclear Korean Peninsula (*Korea Times* 1 January 1992), in which both sides pledged the peaceful use of nuclear energy, no nuclear weapons and no nuclear reprocessing and uranium enrichment facilities.

During the first part of 1992 a series of working-level meetings was held to set up the mechanisms for implementing these two agreements. In May, at the seventh prime-ministerial meeting, protocols establishing three joint commissions to promote exchanges and two liaison offices at the joint security area at Panmunjom were signed. It was also agreed that the two sides would exchange visits of 100 long-separated elderly family members just after the 15 August anniversary of liberation from Japan (*Korea Times* 7, 8 May 1992), though this exchange ultimately did not materialise . In July 1992, North Korean Deputy Prime Minister Kim Dal-hyon, charged with responsibility for external economic affairs, visited the South. He spent four days touring South Korean industrial plants and he succeeded, without making any concessions on the nuclear issue, in getting the Roh administration to unfreeze its temporary ban on South Korean businessmen visiting the North. In September the prime ministers signed accords establishing a joint commission on reconciliation, but failed to set up an exchange of visits programme. Moreover, continuing differences over the sites to be inspected (the North insisted on access to all US military bases in the South) and the timing and frequency of the inspections continued to make progress on the implementation of the de-nuclearisation agreement painstakingly slow.

Both sides continue to be extremely suspicious of each other; the process of building up mutual trust is likely to be slow. Tensions are not far below the surface, as was graphically demonstrated by the exchange of fire across the DMZ in May 1992, which left three North Korean soldiers dead, the worst inter-Korean incident for more than a decade. Significant progress - and the possibility of an unprecedented summit meeting between the two presidents - depends on clear and acceptable assurances that the North has given up its ambitions to become a nuclear power. As will be seen from the coming chapters the varied relationships of the two Koreas with Japan and the other major powers feed on or stimulate these tensions as much as they ameliorate them.

Japan and North-east Asia

Ever since it was opened up to the West in the mid-nineteenth century, Japan has grappled with the dichotomy of its positions in Asia and in the West. While it is geographically and culturally part of Asia, its post-war history has pushed it economically and politically into the 'West'. However, unlike West Germany, which was gradually brought back into the evolving post-war regional order in Western Europe through membership of NATO and the EC, Japan found itself isolated in North-east Asia, surrounded by either communist or authoritarian neighbours and dependent ultimately on the United States alone.

For more than four decades, therefore, Japanese foreign policy has been heavily coloured by the one crucial relationship with the United States. No alliance relationship is ever built on perfectly symmetrical and identical economic, political and security outlooks. Despite the gradual shift in consciousness from US patronage to greater equality, or burden-sharing, the terms of the Japan-US security arangements remain lop-sided. The United States has an obligation to defend Japan which is not reciprocated in reverse; indeed, many Japanese claim that its Peace Constitution specifically prohibits Japanese participation in collective security.

Successive leaders of the LDP and its precursors endorsed the line of Prime Minister Yoshida, who had been inclined to rely extensively on US military protection under the 1951 Security Treaty (its modified 1960 successor remains in force today), undertaking little more than the barest minimum rearmament while concentrating on economic activities. In the 1970s, changing international circumstances and the relative economic and military decline of the United States forced the Japanese to think more actively about their political and security role. The nebulous concept of 'comprehensive security', articulated in the early 1980s, became the rationale for measures to strengthen the capability of the Self-Defence Forces (SDF), to facilitate the smooth operation of US forces in Japan and to step up diplomatic and economic activities supportive of common security interests (Chapman, Drifte and Gow 1983). Well aware of the significant Soviet military build-up in the Far East and the heightened pressure from President Reagan's administration for burden-sharing, Nakasone, in the mid-1980s, made a number of moves to enhance Japan's security role: he pushed defence expenditure over the psychological barrier of 1% of GNP (a cabinet directive in force from 1976 until breached in 1986), agreed to export certain defence-related technologies to the United States and to cooperate in the Strategic Defence Initiative programme, and improved the SDF's naval and air surveillance capabilities (Maswood 1990 pp.45-77).

The nature of the security challenge in North-east Asia is vastly different from the clear-cut confrontation that existed in Europe until 1989. There has always been a far less clear configuration of forces and the competition for power and influence has been acted out amongst a more diversified cast of actors (Segal 1990a pp. 184-279). Moreover, the growing complexity of the region's security environment during the 1980s has been a cause of concern for the Japanese. In general terms, however, the Japanese think of threats as being indirect rather than direct, economic rather than military (Akao 1983 pp. 6-7), and more likely to come from Third World conflict arenas than direct superpower confrontation in Europe or North-east Asia.

With the ending of detente and the worsening of global East-West relations at the beginning of the 1980s, Japan did go as far as to designate one 'potential threat' - the Soviet Union - which was so described in successive Defence White Papers from 1980. Not until the 1990 edition was the phrase deleted, after Prime Minister Kaifu's direct intervention. North Korea was not described as a threat to Japan; nor was China seen in such terms. The very real Soviet military build-up from the late 1970s was used as the rationale for Japan's own military build-up, but, even so, few Japanese defence planners seriously expected the Soviet Union to invade, however far relations deteriorated, as long as the Japan-US security relationship remained stable. But the Japanese concerns about the Soviet military posture were symbolically expressed through the long-standing quest to secure the return of the four 'northern territories' which had been occupied by the Soviets at the end of the Second World War (Mendl 1990 pp. 174-87; Segal 1991 pp. 8-14).

Given that the United States was, and still is, a major actor in any consideration of security in the region, the internal Japanese debate over security policy has usually been cast in terms of ameliorating the tension between domestic political and budgetary constraints and US admonitions for greater 'burden-sharing'. This in turn affected, as will be seen below, how the Japanese interpreted their security role vis-à-vis the Korean peninsula.

After mid-1989, the spillover effect from heightened Japan-US trade friction, the electoral advances of the leading pacifist-inclined opposition party (the JSP) and the changes in global East-West relations made the Japanese government more concerned about the relevance of its military build-up and even the Japan-US Security Treaty. The Japanese government at first argued that the size and posture of Soviet nuclear and conventional forces in North-east Asia remained threatening, that the 'end of the Cold War' was slower in coming to the region than in Europe, and that a strong alliance with the United States was indispensable for Japan in promoting an active dialogue with the Soviet Union.

However, during 1990, developments on the Korean peninsula and within the Soviet Union itself suggested that the Soviet Union might be becoming less of an external threat and the Americans suggested reducing troop deployments and concentrating on maintaining a steady balance of power for regional economic prosperity to flourish. So, the Japanese government began to reconsider its defence planning and threat perceptions. However, there had not been sufficient time for the old security philosophy to be changed before the cabinet, in mid-December 1990, had to endorse the new defence expenditure programme for 1991-95. For the moment, the lack of a framework for regional stability and the danger of a 'vacuum of power' justified a continued defence build-up and reliance on the security relationship with the United States (*Nihon Keizai Shimbun* 18, 20, 21 December 1990).

The 1991 Defence White Paper stressed that the 1991-95 Defence Programme had been predicated on the continued qualitative extension of Soviet military capabilities in the Far East. However, just as the programme began, the Soviet Union disintegrated. Caught between demands from the Americans for greater burden-sharing, both financially and operationally, and efforts by the Finance Ministry, who anticipated a large revenue short-fall, to slash the defence budget (an endeavour suported by the JSP, which called for zero growth), the Defence Agency and the Foreign Ministry were forced onto the defensive. Miyazawa himself, on taking office in November 1991, also made it clear that he preferred to emphasise social welfare expenditure and an enhanced 'lifestyle' rather than a sustained military build-up.

The 1992-3 defence budget, therefore, showed only a 3.8% increase, the lowest for 32 years, and accounted for only 0.94% of estimated GNP, the lowest ratio in nine years. Faced with a popular desire for a 'peace dividend', the Defence Agency will have to work hard to mend political fences if it is to avoid deeper cuts in future years. Miyazawa has already instructed the relevant agencies and ministries to begin a review of the five-year defence procurement programme, well ahead of the intended 1993 date. This review will stimulate further consideration of the rationale of the crucial Japan-US relationship and Japan's role in North-east Asian security.

Although the Japanese have been deepening their economic involvement in the East Asian region through massive trade, aid and investment flows and have been participating in the embryonic discussions about creating regional economic organisations, they have not been impressed by the various ideas that have been floated since the mid-1980s for regional security frameworks. Proposals put forward by Mikhail Gorbachev in his Vladivostock and Krasnoyarsk speeches for an Asian security conference and his later proposal in Tokyo in April 1991 for a five-power consultative body, as well as Canadian and Australian ideas about an Asian equivalent of the Conference for Security and Cooperation in Europe (CSCE), were greeted with a caution verging on scepticism (Araki 1991 pp. 16, 24-30).

Instead, the Japanese tended to treat North-east Asia and South-east Asia separately; as Foreign Minister Nakayama Taro emphasised in January 1991, priority should be given to solving bilateral conflicts such as the Korean peninsula confrontation or the 'northern territories' as a means of strengthening 'dialogue and cooperative relations on sub-regional bases' (Araki 1991 pp. 25-6).

However, in the summer of 1991 the Japanese began to change tack. Nakayama, speaking at the post-ministerial ASEAN dialogue meeting in July, proposed that security issues should be taken up on a regular basis. The initial reaction was cautious, but the January 1992 ASEAN Summit did, in effect, endorse these Japanese ideas, with a reference in the Singapore declaration to the intensification of political and security dialogues with external partners (*Far Eastern Economic Review* 6 February 1992). By the summer of 1992, the Japanese appeared to be moving even further forward. Some officials began to mull over ideas of a security 'multiplex', which would add multilateral efforts to the already existing bilateral arrangements in the Asia Pacific region. Prime Minister Miyazawa, in some of his speeches, also began to talk vaguely about the need for regional security structures. This, however, was still some way from a definite initiative to establish a regional or even sub-regional security organisation. Japan, well aware of regional sensitivities, is certainly not yet going to make the leap to proposing a security organisation for either North-east or South-east Asia.

Japan-South Korean connections

The Japanese have traditionally thought of Korea as the dagger pointing at their heart. This has meant a continuing interest in the power situation on the peninsula; on at least one occasion, in 1904-5, Japan directly intervened to prevent a hostile power extending its influence there. This concern about Korean political stability and security did not disappear with the end of the Japanese colonial occupation and the division of Korea, even though the Americans took over the direct burden of security.

As discussed in Chapter 2, it took 20 years for diplomatic relations to be established between Japan and South Korea and there have been numerous ups and downs in political relations since 1965. Of course, both Japan and South Korea have long-standing bilateral security alliances with the United States, but there are no direct security ties between themselves. Indeed, the Japanese have gone out of their way to play down the strategic linkages with South Korea.

Of course, Japanese policy-makers do realise, as one Foreign Ministry official admitted, that 'any large-scale military conflict in the peninsula would involve Japan, at least indirectly' (Satoh 1982 p.12). In the event of North-South armed conflict, the United States, in support of South Korea, would depend on the use of its bases in Japan. Although the Japanese argue that the use by US forces of facilities and areas in Japan as bases for military combat operations is subject to prior consultation with Japan, in practice the Japanese government would find it very difficult to refuse US requests. Moreover, prolonged conflict could well result in refugees and 'boat people' leaving Korea; geographical closeness and family ties with the Koreans already resident in Japan would make Japan the probable destination. Japan also, of course, has considerable economic interests at stake, almost exclusively in the South. Japan would, therefore, find it impossible to remain detached from any such conflict.

The Japanese, however, have been reticent about publicly conceding this in terms of a concern with the security of South Korea. Not until November 1969, for the first time in a US-Japanese communique, did Prime Minister Sato, together with President Nixon, state that 'the security of the Republic of Korea was essential to Japan's own security'; this became known as the 'Korea clause'. Although the Korea clause reappeared in subsequent US-Japanese summit communiques during the 1970s, the phraseology was altered subtly. The Tanaka administration tried to introduce a more equidistant relationship with the two Koreas and Foreign Minister Kimura Toshio, in 1974, re-formulated the Korea clause into peace and security on the 'entire peninsula' being essential to Japan. However, the changed regional situation after the fall of Indochina prompted the 1975 Miki-Gerald Ford and the 1977 Fukuda-Carter communiques to refer to the importance of the maintenance of peace and stability on the Korean peninsula for the security of Japan and East Asia as a whole; the 1981 Suzuki-Reagan communique also used similar phraseology (Lee, C-s. 1985 pp. 68-96).

Although the Japanese had made such statements to the United States, they avoided making such commitments explicit to the South Koreans. President Park, in 1975, called for a special security relationship, but with no Japanese response, and his successor Chun actually set Japan-South Korean relations on a deteriorating course in 1981 by requesting a $6 billion loan from Japan which would promote the economic development of South Korea and help it act as a 'bulwark' against communism, contribute to stability on the Korean peninsula and, in effect, help to defend Japan. The Japanese baulked at this explicit security linkage; the Koreans eventually dropped the formal linkage, but not until Nakasone became prime minister was the loan deal concluded. On his January 1983 visit Nakasone agreed, for the first time, for a Japan-South Korean communique to include the Korea clause phraseology; he also publicly expressed his 'high regard' for South Korea's defence efforts (Kim, H.N. 1983 pp. 95-7).

The Americans and the South Koreans were pleased by Nakasone's action, though the North Koreans interpreted it as the 'rounding off' of a 'tripartite military alliance'. Yet the reality was far from this. Nakasone made it clear, even before he left Seoul, that Japan could not engage in military cooperation with other countries because collective defence was prohibited under the constitution. Article 9 of the 1947 Constitution prohibited Japan from maintaining land, sea and air forces; but, after 1954 when the SDF was created, the government argued that this did not preclude the legitimate right of the nation to 'self-defence' (Araki 1991 pp. 3-7). The phrase 'collective defence' does not actually appear in the Constitution, but the reference in Article 9 to the renunciation of 'the threat or use of force as a means of settling international disputes' is taken to imply it.

The degree of security cooperation between Japan and South Korea, therefore, has been extremely limited. There have been some 'goodwill visits' from officers in the South Korean armed forces and the SDF to their opposite numbers, especially between the naval and air force services (the ground forces revive too many memories of the Japanese army's role in the occupation of Korea from 1910-45). The number of exchanges was slowly built up during the 1980s. In 1991, for example, one South Korean navy officer and one air force officer joined the Japanese staff college for training. Information exchange meetings began on a twice-yearly basis in 1977 and have become more frequent and informal since. In 1990, both countries did participate together, for the first time, in the bi-annual multinational RIMPAC exercises, although the Americans were careful to ensure that they participated in different teams in those exercises. In late 1990 it was agreed to increase consultation over an 'Air Defence Intercept Zone', which, for example, would avoid either country's air force scrambling to intercept Soviet intruders without being aware that the other country's air force was also responding.

Yet the caution on both sides is clear. In 1979 Yamashita Ganri became the first Defence Agency director-general to visit South Korea, but not until November 1990, when Ishikawa Yozo went, did any of his successors visit South Korea. No South Korean defence minister has ever visited Japan, although the chairmen of the Joint Chiefs of Staff did accompany Presidents Chun and Roh on their visits to Tokyo in, respectively, 1984 and 1990. In the months immediately preceding the October 1988 Seoul Olympics a joint Japanese-South Korean-American security and intelligence group met to combat possible North Korean and Japanese Red Army terrorist action against the Olympics, but that was treated as a one-off organisation and subsequently disbanded.

Moreover, it is inconceivable that emotional legacies, apart from constitutional niceties in Japan, would permit Japanese soldiers to join with South Koreans in joint action on Korean soil. In fact, despite the degree of reconciliation achieved by Nakasone and Chun, two problems hampered security cooperation throughout the 1980s: differences in perception between the two countries on external security threats and South Korean suspicions of the continued Japanese build-up of the SDF and its external role.

Despite Nakasone's implicit recognition that economic assistance to the South played a strategic as well as purely economic role, there were clearly still differences of perception between the Japanese and the South Koreans about threats. The South Koreans, of course, saw North Korea as the main threat, while the Japanese saw the Soviet Union as the main disruptive factor in North-east Asia. This, indeed, was confirmed by Nakasone's comments in Washington the week after his Seoul visit, when he called Japan a 'large aircraft carrier' acting as a 'bulwark of defence' against Soviet bombers.[1] The South Koreans believed that the Japanese, to use Chun's own words, saw the threat from North Korea as merely 'a fire across an ocean'. Certainly, the Japanese did not designate North Korea as a threat; successive Defence White Papers during the 1980s referred only to the continuing 'military tension' on the peninsula and the efforts by South Korea, as a result of its perception of a 'serious threat' from the North, to build up its armed forces. When a Foreign Ministry official on attachment to the Defence Agency, in 1980, did describe North Korea as a 'potential threat' to Japan, his comment was quickly disowned (Olsen 1985 p. 57). The Japanese have not felt themselves threatened by North Korean conventional weapons, but, particularly since 1990, they have been concerned about reports that North Korea was becoming capable of developing nuclear weapons. Reports in 1991 that North Korea had developed new long-range missiles capable of reaching all of Japan also added to their worries. In July 1992 the director-general of the Defence Agency publicly expressed his concern for the first time that these missiles were an 'element of instability' in the region, a sentiment that was repeated in the 1992 Defence White Paper issued the following month. Nevertheless, the predominant Japanese concern about North Korea is similar to their feeling about China: instability rather than a direct threat.

As a result of Nakasone's attempts to revamp the relationship with the United States, Japan and the United States did begin joint studies in the mid-1980s on how to respond to a number of emergencies, one of which was an outbreak of fighting on the Korean peninsula. The results have not been made public, but it is certain that Japan's contribution would be, as it has been so far, confined to the provision of bases to allow the US forces to carry out their commitments to defend South Korea.

The South Koreans have, in fact, remained ambivalent about the Japanese military build-up during the 1980s. The South Koreans welcomed Japanese commitments to do more for regional defence, not least because they felt, rather like many Americans, that Japan had been 'free-riding' at their expense. Nevertheless, they did not want this to be an excuse for the remilitarisation of Japan. Chun set the tone with his comments that Japan's increased defence efforts were 'justifiable' but that they should be 'limited to complementing US defence capabilities'. This was maintained as the official line throughout the 1980s, even though some politicians and sections of the media became vocal in warning about the Japanese abandonment of the '1% of GNP' barrier in 1986.

Psychologically more difficult to accept, however, were signs that the Japanese might actually use this newly-acquired military capability overseas. This did not become a real possibility, however, until the 1990-91 Gulf crisis, when, under pressure from the United States and other allies, Japan went through an agonising internal debate about how to respond to calls to join the multinational forces opposed to Saddam Hussein's occupation of Kuwait. The Japanese government's plans, first, to send SDF members under a UN Peace Cooperation Bill, and then, when that legislation was defeated, to send SDF aircraft to transport refugees (also ultimately aborted) aroused considerable suspicion in South Korea. Of course, South Korea was itself under pressure from the Americans to contribute to the multinational effort - it did actually send military medical teams in January 1991 - and was concerned that a significant Japanese commitment would increase the pressure on itself to commit more (Bridges 1992 p. 147).

But the main fear was, to use the words of Foreign Minister Choi Ho-joong in October 1990, that sending SDF troops overseas would be 'the starting point of the remilitarisation of Japan' (FBIS-EAS-90-210, 30 October 1990). When eventually , in April 1991, Japan did send SDF mine-sweepers to the Gulf, after the fighting had finished, South Korea remained one of the few Asian countries which openly expressed some reservations about the precedent being set (FBIS-EAS-91-081, 26 April 1991).

South Korean officials continued to express their concern during the autumn of 1991 as the Japanese government pushed through the lower house of the Diet a new bill which would allow the SDF to participate in UN peace-keeping operations. The Japanese Foreign Ministry was even moved to protest after the annual South Korean Defence White Paper, issued in October 1991, characterised the SDF as being 'transformed into offensive forces for the purpose of forward defence' by the on-going defence programmes (FBIS-EAS-91-232, 3 December 1991). Clearly some within the Defence Ministry and the armed forces in South Korea have been trying to justify increased defence expenditure - at a time when the South's economic problems and a slight lowering of tension with the North might be expected to increase calls for a 'peace dividend' - by warning about the growing military power of Japan. But there has been a rare degree of coincidence of interest even with the political opposition. Kim Dae-jung, leader of the Democratic Party, also warned against Japanese 'rearmament' and argued for American troops staying in South Korea not just to counter the North Korean threat but also to prevent a power vacuum which Japan might fill with the SDF (*Korea Times* 7 December 1991). While these arguments are not shared by the majority of the civilian members of the South Korean government, there is no doubt that the debates within Japan since the Gulf crisis have been watched with heightened concern.

The final passage of the peace-keeping operation legislation through the Japanese Upper House in June 1992 was greeted with considerable media criticism in South Korea, but with a comparatively restrained reaction from the government itself. When the Japanese ambassador in Seoul, Yanai, visited him to explain the final version passed into law, Foreign Minister Lee Sang-ock asked that Japan be prudent in dispatching its troops overseas (*Korea Times* 20 June 1992). The restrictions on the circumstances under which the Japanese SDF could actually take part in UN operations (it would not, for example, be able to take part in any multilateral force such as that put together against Iraq in the Gulf War nor in the current Yugoslav crisis, where fighting is still occurring) may well have assuaged some of the South Korean government's doubts. Nevertheless, neither public opinion nor the media will allow the government to forget that the sensitivities about Japan's military reappearance overseas are still very strong.

Japan and North Korea

When it accorded recognition to South Korea in 1965, Japan was determined not to foreclose on the possibility of some form of relations, however tenuous, with North Korea. Differing interpretations of the recognition formula, based on the 1948 UN resolution, remained. For many years the South Korean government's view was that Japan could not establish diplomatic relations with the North while the 1965 Japan-South Korean Basic Treaty remained in force. However, the practicalities of this legal argument were altered by President Roh's 7 July 1988 speech, when he expressed his country's willingness 'to cooperate with North Korea in its efforts to improve relations with countries friendly to us including the United States and Japan' (*Korea Newsreview* 9 July 1988). The South Korean government now accepts that even if Japan-North Korean relations are established, there is no need to abrogate the Japan-South Korean treaty. Moreover, when both Koreas joined the United Nations in September 1991, article 3 of the Japan-South Korean treaty effectively lost its validity.

In public, the Japanese government has supported the South Korean proposals for the reunification of the Korean peninsula, but it has long believed that a truly neutral, unified Korea is a distant goal. Some Japanese do fear the potential economic power and latent anti-Japanism of a unified Korea (of whatever political hue) and, therefore, prefer to maintain the status quo of a divided peninsula. Koreans, too, often characterise Japanese attitudes as being of this view.

The Japanese government, however, has been more concerned about the process than the end result, even though it would clearly be worried about an aggressive communist unified state emerging. The avoidance of the destabilising effects of violent reunification has been paramount. During the 1980s, therefore, the Japanese government operated on the principle that the promotion of 'peaceful co-existence' or a modus vivendi between the two Koreas by encouraging them to expand the scope of their contacts would assist the way forward to eventual peaceful reunification.

Japanese government officials and LDP and opposition politicians also tried to play a low-key role in 'creating an environment for dialogue' by talking to the Russians and the Chinese about the Korean situation. Yet the role of mediator between the two Koreas or between South Korea and the socialist allies of the North was neither clearly articulated nor openly welcomed. For example, in May 1983, when a Chinese airliner was hijacked to South Korea, it was at China's request not South Korea's that Japan became involved as the means of transmitting the initial messages from and to the Chinese side for the return of the aircraft, crew and passengers. Later, in August that year, when the Soviet air force shot down the KAL airliner off Sakhalin, the South Koreans turned to the Americans rather than the Japanese to request an explanation and compensation from the Soviets. Later in the decade, as South Korea's own diplomatic and semi-diplomatic contacts with China and the Soviet Union developed, there was even less scope for a Japanese intermediary role, but Japanese politicians and officials have, nevertheless, continued to raise the Korean problem during bilateral discussions with Chinese and Soviet counterparts.

The final strand of Japanese policies towards North Korea during the 1980s has been to keep open a window of communication with the North. Not surprisingly, however, Japan's own contacts with North Korea have been watched with a great deal of caution by the South Koreans. Historically, as shown in Chapter 2, there have been two upsurges in attempts to further Japan-North Korean political relations, in the second half of the 1950s and the early part of the 1970s. Both occurred at times of relative East-West detente, both were initiated by North Korea, and both coincided with sour Japan-South Korean relations (Okonogi 1989 pp. 331-46). The results, therefore, were meagre, as the greater importance to Japan of the relationship with South Korea adversely affected the moves by the North to cultivate the Japanese.

Working from the assumption that the establishment first of a sound basis to Japan-South Korea relations would remove some of the difficulties that his predecessors had faced, Nakasone began to tentatively explore contacts with North Korea in the mid-1980s. However, North Korean intransigence effectively destroyed Japanese interest. The North Koreans refused to maintain the rescheduled arrangements for repayment of debts run up during the early 1970s. In November 1983, North Korea imprisoned two Japanese seamen, on grounds of espionage but really for assisting a North Korean, Min Hong-gu, to escape to Japan (the Fujisan-maru incident), and refused all Japanese requests for their release. The North Koreans also reacted fiercely to the Japanese decision to allow 11 North Korean 'boat people', who sailed into Tsuruga port in January 1987, to leave for Taiwan, from where they flew to South Korea. Finally, and most seriously, North Korean terrorist activity against South Korea left Japan little alternative but to impose diplomatic sanctions. After the Burmese revelations of North Korean complicity in the 1983 Rangoon bombing, which missed President Chun but did kill several cabinet ministers, and again, after the arrest of North Korean agent Kim Hyon-hui for the destruction of the KAL airliner off the coast of Burma in November 1987, the Japanese government sharply reduced contacts.[2]

Nevertheless, after the safe conclusion of the 1988 Seoul Olympics, the Japanese government returned to the possibility of developing relations with North Korea. As shown by Roh's July 1988 pronouncement and his comments to visiting Japanese Prime Minister Takeshita, during the Olympic Games, the more self-confident South Korea was prepared to allow Japan more diplomatic lee-way. The Japanese government, which had maintained some indirect and low-level contact with the North through visits by JSP politicians to Pyongyang, remained sceptical about a real change in North Korean policies just because the Olympics had not been disrupted, but felt that it was important to keep an open mind and test the waters. In March 1989, Takeshita expressed for the first time officially Japan's 'deep regret and reflection' for the past unhappy history of relations with the North (Tanaka 1989 pp. 22-9). This comment was received with a notable lack of criticism by North Korea, but the subsequent confusion in Japanese policy-making, as the Recruit share scandal and other scandals began to take their toll of the Japanese leadership, prevented any follow-up. North Korea too became preoccupied with the need to maintain its ideological purity and internal discipline as the shock waves of the events in China in April-June 1989 and, later, in Eastern Europe reverberated across the Korean peninsula.

So, the third serious attempt to promote relations did not begin until the autumn of 1990. North Korea took advantage of a visit to Pyongyang by a joint LDP-JSP delegation, headed by the senior LDP politician Kanemaru, in September 1990 to secure commitments to normalise relations and pay 'compensation'. The Japanese Foreign Ministry was not enthusiastic about all these commitments, but preliminary negotiations did begin, leading in January 1991 to the full negotiations which are still continuing. The motivations, course and implications of these negotiations are discussed below, in Chapter 8, but it should be noted here that, while it is the North Korean side which again took the initiative, on this occasion the foundation of Japan-South Korean relations was much securer than in the earlier periods of attempted rapprochement.

Textbooks and territory

Although relations with North Korea have been the most significant political problem between Japan and South Korea, a number of other political issues - or issues which have become easily politicised - have clouded the relationship during the 1980s. Of these, emotionally the most difficult to solve has been the Japanese attitude to past activities in Korea as expressed through intemperate remarks by senior politicians and by reported attempts to sanitise history textbooks. This has helped to make the phraseology used by Emperors Hirohito and Akihito when receiving South Korean Presidents Chun and Roh, respectively, of great political sensitivity.

Although there had been occasions since the late 1970s when South Korean officials had picked up and criticised descriptions in Japanese history textbooks of the colonial period, not until 1982 did this issue become a major diplomatic incident. In June 1982 the Japanese media began reporting that the Ministry of Education's Textbook Authorisation Committee had forced changes in the wording of certain new high school history textbooks, such as altering the references to the Japanese invasion of North China to 'advance' and the 1919 Korean independence movement to a 'riot'. Both the Chinese and South Korean governments officially protested. During the summer, the South Korean media ran extensive articles and numerous demonstrations and public meetings were held about the Japanese distortions. In late August, after an intense internal debate pitching the Ministry of Education against the Foreign Ministry, the Japanese government agreed to review the authorisation system and to issue guidelines to teachers reminding them of the spirit of the 1965 Japan-South Korean treaty (Lee, C-s. 1985 pp. 141-53; Yayama 1983 pp. 301-16).

The most remarkable aspect of this dispute was that, as the Japanese media grudgingly came to admit during September, the initial furore had actually been based on mis-reporting, for the most commonly cited 'revisions' had not actually taken place. This incident, in fact, grew out of the long-standing domestic struggle between the conservative bureaucrats in the Ministry of Education and the radical Japan Teachers' Union. The textbook authorisation system was the main bone of contention and clearly needed some improvement. One of the ironies of the dispute was that those LDP members - the bunkyozoku - who favoured more 'patriotic' textbooks included many who were normally in the pro-South Korea lobby and, therefore, were in rather a dilemma about how to respond to 'foreign interference' (*Japan Times*

2 September 1982).

Though the initial reporting was clearly erroneous, the reaction of both sides to this controversy, which came at a time when relations were already tense because of disagreements over the South Korean loan request, demonstrated much about the deeper emotions of politicians and the public in both countries. South Koreans right across the political spectrum reacted with fierce denunciations of Japanese attitudes to the colonial period in general (and the government was criticised for not being stronger in its protests). But in Japan there was a polarisation between those who saw the incident as yet another example of the shift to the right in the political climate in Japan and those who argued that there were just as many inaccuracies in foreign textbooks (including Korean ones) and that the government should not brook foreign interference.

The textbook issue remains a latent one with the potential for bursting into life again easily. In 1986, the Education Ministry authorised a textbook compiled by the right-wing National Council for the Protection of Japan, but, after protests from China and South Korea about its 'militaristic' tone, it was partially revised. The outspoken Education Minister, Fujio Masayuki, was angry with these protests and told reporters that countries that complained should also look at their own history to see whether they had not committed similar actions themselves (*Far Eastern Economic Review* 21 August 1986). He followed this up by giving an interview, published in September in a respected monthly journal, *Bungei Shunju*, in which he argued that Korea too should take responsibility for agreeing to the annexation by Japan in 1910. He was supported by a small group of young right-wing LDP politicians, who actually visited the Korean ambassador in Tokyo, and told him that the raising of the textbook issue was causing unnecessary stress in the bilateral relationship. Embarassed by the controversy provoked by Fujio's remarks, Prime Minister Nakasone was forced to sack him and apologise to the South Koreans (Fujio 1986 pp. 122-33; Kuroda 1986 pp. 14-15).

Japan has moved towards greater coverage of the past in its textbooks, but the progress has been slow. In May 1990, the then education minister directed teachers to teach schoolchildren the 'full historical facts' about the colonisation of Korea, including the use of forced labour (BBC-SWB FE0777, 30 May 1990). But this did not prevent another clash of views when the controversy over the 'comfort women' - the forced prostitution of Korean women by the Japanese army - surfaced in early 1992. The Korean education minister, Yoon Hyung-sop, called on the Japanese government to correct distortions in Japanese textbooks, while Kato Koichi, the Japanese chief cabinet secretary, said that South Korea should stop education which 'calls for continued hatred towards the Japanese'. Yoon retorted that Korean textbooks had actually been restrained in their criticism of past Japanese actions, but that, in future, they would contain more detailed descriptions of Japanese wartime atrocities (*Korea Newsreview* 25 January 1992). It was perhaps in response to this heated exchange that the Japanese Ministry of Education, in approving new textbooks for use from April 1993, was more open than usual in allowing in critical references to Japan's past military actions; six history textbooks even positively described the Korean patriot who assassinated Ito Hirobumi.

Nevertheless, the coverage accorded to the past in current textbooks in both countries is likely to remain an issue with the potential for erupting into a political problem. Indeed, the issue of Japan's acknowledgement of its past has continued, and will continue, to act as an irritant. As indicated by the heated feelings engendered in late 1991-early 1992 during the run-up to the fiftieth anniversaries of Pearl Harbour and the fall of Singapore, other countries too are watching closely how the Japanese come to terms with their past.

In the Korean case, however, particular symbolism has been attached to the phraseology used by Emperor Hirohito when receiving President Chun in 1984 and by Emperor Akihito when receiving President Roh in 1990. On both occasions, there was considerable diplomatic and media discussion beforehand about the wording to be used, although, of course, it was the Japanese side, by consultation between the Imperial Household Agency and the Foreign Ministry, that made the final decision.

For the Japanese, the problem was to find a phraseology which would appease Korean sentiment but would not provoke discontent within Japan itself. Hirohito, in fact, pitched his remarks at the level of earlier apologies to Chinese and American leaders. He referred to the 'unfortunate past' which was 'regrettable' and then added some complimentary remarks on Japan's cultural borrowings from Korea in the sixth and seventh centuries. The Japanese felt that the use of the word ikan (regrettable) was a sophisticated and delicate way of apologising. However, the North Koreans denounced this as 'not an apology but a crafty trick ....to cover up the criminal colonial rule' and, although the Chun administration declared itself satisfied, many within South Korea shared the North's feelings that Hirohito had avoided a direct apology by using 'so refined' language (*Nihon Keizai Shimbun* 7 September 1984; BBC-SWB FE7744, 10 September 1984).

For South Koreans, Hirohito personally symbolised the harsh colonial rule. Even more than Chun's visit, the illness and subsequent death of Emperor Hirohito in January 1989 reawakened Korean memories. There was considerable media and public discussion of Hirohito's role in Japan's expansionist policies and opinion was divided over who should represent the country at his state funeral in February. After briefly toying with the idea of sending the president, who had had to postpone a planned visit to Tokyo the previous year because of the Emperor's illness, it was decided to send Prime Minister Kang Young-hoon (*Korea Newsreview* 14 January 1989).

When the Japanese domestic political situation did finally allow Roh to make his visit, in May 1990, again the words to be used by the new Emperor Akihito at the official banquet became the subject of controversy. In the run-up to the visit a succession of South Korean politicians and officials called for a more forthright expression from Akihito than his father had given; President Roh himself commented that Hirohito's 1984 speech had fallen short of an apology. Several senior LDP politicians opposed an imperial apology - one was quoted as saying that 'there is no need to throw ourselves down on our knees and bow our heads'. LDP Secretary-General Ozawa Ichiro deployed the argument that, as the Emperor was not allowed to comment on behalf of the government but only acted as a 'symbol' of the nation, it would be 'unconstitutional' for him to give an apology (a line of reasoning that was supported by opposition parties such as the JSP). The intensity of the media coverage of this issue, which Roh had of course helped to encourage, did shock him and at one stage he apparently contemplated calling off his visit. In the end, Akihito went further than his father by expressing his 'deepest regret' for the suffering inflicted on the Korean people but it was left to Prime Minister Kaifu to express 'sincere remorse and honest apologies' (*Nihon Keizai Shimbun* 15, 25 May 1990; FBIS-EAS-90-094, 15 May 1990).

Roh said, on his return to Seoul, that it was his intention to lay this 'thorny question' to rest. This may be easier said than done, for he had officially invited Akihito to visit South Korea. While Akihito had still been Crown Prince, in 1986, there had been plans mooted to invite him to Seoul but they had been postponed, officially because of the Crown Princess's ill-health but in reality because of fears for his safety. Although there had been an implicit understanding between the two foreign ministries that Emperor Akihito's first overseas trip, once the period of official mourning for his father had ended, should be to South Korea, that did not happen, for both personal security and political reasons. Instead, in October 1991, Akihito visited South-east Asia, the first visit by a Japanese emperor to the region, and he was scheduled to visit China in October 1992.

Emperor Akihito now has a number of outstanding invitations. The visit to South Korea is now dropping down the order of priorities. Enthusiasm on the South Korean side has cooled, and the political schedule there would not allow an imperial visit before mid-1993 at the earliest. Whenever Emperor Akihito does make the first ever imperial visit to South Korea undoubtedly the question of what he will say during his visit will be raised. The degree of diplomatic friction caused by this issue will depend very much on how far the then South Korean government (presumably the successor to the Roh administration) is prepared to head off the inevitable domestic pressures by emphasising the satisfactory nature of the 1990 apology from the Japanese leaders.

Japan's territorial disputes with the Soviet Union over the 'northern territories' and with China over the Senkaku islands are well known, but Japan does have an equally long-standing dispute with South Korea over two tiny rock islands known as Takeshima to the Japanese and Tokdo to the Koreans. While a territorial dispute is a fundamental problem involving national sovereignty, the methods and timing by which it is brought to the diplomatic table are political questions. Certainly this dispute has some political potency and, indeed, in 1965 even threatened to wreck the normalisation negotiations at the final stage. These tiny barren islands lie about 38 miles south-east of the Korean island of Ullungdo and, historically, were used as a haven for Japanese and Korean fishermen. No specific mention was made of the status of the islands in the San Francisco Peace Treaty, but in 1952 President Syngman Rhee, in asserting South Korea's sovereignty over the continental shelf, included the islands within what became known as the 'Rhee Line'; the following year, in response to a Japanese diplomatic protest, he sent a small garrison unit to occupy the islands.

Despite the normalisation of relations in 1965, when both sides finally agreed to disagree and all direct mention of the islands was omitted from the agreements signed, and the more recent governmental-level reconciliation, the situation has changed little in practice since 1953 (Bridges 1986 pp. 55-60). Both sides continue to parade various historical and legal justifications for their respective claims, the South Koreans maintain their maritime guard unit there, and the Japanese government makes a ritualistic protest every year to which the South Koreans respond in kind. For Japan, the islands lack the strategic value and emotional appeal of the northern territories and the potential economic (in terms of natural resources) value of the Senkaku islands. For South Korea, the claim has more emotional content, not least because it cannot afford to be seen as giving way on a territorial issue which might compromise its claims to sovereignty over the whole peninsula. The occasions when the dispute has risen to prominence have usually been when tension has already entered the relationship for some other reason, such as in 1982 and in 1986; it can be used to raise the tension a notch further.

With the gradual extension of national jurisdiction over maritime resources, Japan and the two Koreas have been drawn into other overlapping claims. However, after extensive negotiation, a Japan-South Korean agreement was reached in 1974 to set up a Joint Development Zone (JDZ) in the Yellow Sea for the cooperative exploration and exploitation of off-shore oil and natural gas resources. China registered strong objections to the JDZ not only because of its own claims to the area but also because it wished to act as a proxy for North Korea. After a protracted internal struggle within Japan between the pro-China and pro-South Korea, as well as the energy and fisheries, lobbies, the agreement was ratified in 1978 and drilling begun (Harrison 1977 pp.136-45). Although commercially-realisable deposits were not found during the initial eight-year co-development programme, a second eight-year exploration programme began in September 1991. This is, therefore, a case where the desire for exploitation of significant natural resources has overcome the issues of sovereignty, which have been left, without prejudice, for later decision, in this case fifty years. The bait of such potential resources does not seem to exist around Takeshima/Tokdo.

The political and security framework of this complex triangular relationship can be seen on two levels: one, the relations between the two Koreas themselves and with Japan, and the other, the inter-relationships of these three with the other three interested major powers - China, the Soviet Union (now Russia) and the United States. In turn, the changing inter-relationships between these three external powers also affects the central triangular relationship. The following chapter addresses the multilateral context of the Japan-Korea relationship.

Notes

1. A translation error led to the reports that Nakasone had said 'unsinkable aircraft carrier', an expression which carries odious wartime connotations for the Japanese. *International Herald Tribune* 21 March 1992.
2. For further details of the Japanese reaction to these various incidents see Kantaiheiyo Mondai Kenkyujo, *Kankoku kitachosen soran*, Vol. II (Tokyo 1988), pp. 101-2, and JETRO, *Kitachosen no keizai to boeki no tenbo* (1988), pp. 74-5.

5 The Major Powers and the Korean Conundrum

Japan's relationship with the two Koreas does not exist in a vacuum. The changing nature of that relationship is influenced by, and does itself influence, the complex interactions between both South and North Korea and the other major powers, China, the Soviet Union/Russia and the United States, as well as Japan's own relationships with those three powers. In the international context, particularly, the sense of increasing flux is pronounced.

South Korea's 'nordpolitik'

For decades, the two Koreas competed in a 'zero sum game' over relations with the four major powers, Japan, China, the Soviet Union and the United States, but gradually since 1988, and particularly since 1990, the nature of the game has altered as South Korea has forged ahead of its northern rival in the diplomatic competition.

For two decades after the end of the Korean War, South Korea followed a version of the earlier German Hallstein doctrine, that is not recognising any country which recognised North Korea. However, in 1973 South Korea made a switch in policy, when President Park announced that he was prepared to establish contacts with 'non-hostile' communist states. Neither China nor the Soviet Union responded publicly, but very slowly some informal contacts were established. China took the hardest line in the 1970s, for a South Korean citizen attended an international conference in Moscow in 1973, something that did not happen in China until 1981. However, in the first half of the 1980s, China began to prove more responsive than the Soviet Union to South Korean advances. The hijacking of a civilian Chinese airliner to South Korea in May 1983 and the entry of a Chinese torpedo boat into South Korean waters, after a mutiny on board, in February 1985, provided fortuitous opportunities for representatives of both sides to meet. In June 1983, capitalising on the earlier incident, South Korean Foreign Minister Lee Bum Suk announced a nordpolitik (northward policy) to 'normalise relations with the Soviet Union and mainland China' (Kim, D. 1989 pp. 322-9; Kurata 1989 pp. 80-95).

A limited number of contacts, mostly sporting, with China followed and unofficial trade, primarily through Hong Kong, rose from $285 million in 1983 to $1.5 billion by 1987. A number of senior South Korean industrialists began visiting China, but Chinese sensitivity over the North Korean reaction to South Korean investment meant that the first joint venture, with Daewoo to produce refrigerators, had a rocky start in 1986. The Soviets were far more reticent than the Chinese in widening contacts, which were anyway broken for a year after the destruction of the KAL airliner by a Soviet fighter in August 1983, and by 1987 trade had only reached $154 million.

Although the Chinese did send a large delegation to attend the September 1986 Asian Games, held in Seoul, in the late 1980s it was the Soviet Union which suddenly switched to being the more positive about relations with South Korea. The bait of participation in the October 1988 Seoul Olympics (after the Soviet Union had boycotted the 1984 Los Angeles Games) was important, but so too was President Gorbachev's growing interest in tapping into South Korean economic prowess. Gorbachev's response to President Roh's July 1988 speech, when he outlined in more detail his hopes of developing contacts with North Korea and other socialist states, came in his speech in Krasnoyarsk in September 1988. He spoke publicly for the first time about 'forming economic relations' with South Korea (*Soviet News* 21 September 1988). After Soviet participation in the Olympics, trade, sports and cultural exchanges increased greatly.

As the disintegration of the communist bloc in Eastern Europe led to a series of first trade and then diplomatic representative breakthroughs for South Korea, the Soviet Union followed only slightly behind its former allies. In December 1989, the Soviet Union agreed to consular relations. In June 1990, Roh himself met Gorbachev in an unprecedented meeting in San Francisco. Official relations were established in September 1990, after which Roh visited Moscow in December 1990, when he agreed a $3 billion aid package to the Soviet Union. Gorbachev, in turn, became the first Soviet president to visit either part of Korea by visiting the South (though only Cheju island) in April 1991 (*The Times* 28 June 1991).

South Korea, however, did find itself in a quandary over the disintegration of the Soviet Union in late 1991. It suspended the outstanding half of its aid programme in December 1991 and its worst fears seemed to be confirmed when the successor Russian government, in May 1992, defaulted on an interest repayment (*Far Eastern Economic Review* 11 June 1992). But negotiations are now underway for a new debt-repayment pact, an agreement on energy resource exploitation (a key target of the South Korean companies) has been signed and Russian President Boris Yeltsin is planning to sign a friendship treaty with South Korea when he visits in November 1992. The South Koreans have also been developing contacts with the Central Asian members of the Commonwealth of Independent States (CIS), particularly Kazakhstan and Uzbekistan, where there are sizeable ethnic Korean minorities, a legacy of Josef Stalin's forced migration of ethnic Koreans from the Soviet Far Eastern territories in the 1930s.

China, on the other hand, became far more cautious than the Soviet Union, putting most emphasis on the burgeoning economic ties with South Korea. Despite the Chinese austerity programmes, bilateral trade reached over $3 billion in both 1989 and 1990, though in both years the South Koreans were in deficit. Deng Xiaoping's youngest son paid a private visit to Seoul in the spring of 1990 and South Korean conglomerates donated millions of dollars to help China host the Asian Games in Beijing in October. Immediately thereafter, the South Koreans were rewarded with an agreement to set up trade offices, which would also be empowered to handle consular affairs; these offices began operations in the spring of 1991. A trade agreement was signed later in 1991 and an investment guarantee pact initialled in April 1992; these certainly helped to stimulate economic contacts. Bilateral trade reached nearly $6 billion in 1991 and it is estimated that in 1992 it will reach $10 billion and South Korea will become China's fourth largest trading partner.

At the first ever official meeting between South Korean and Chinese foreign ministers, which took place at the United Nations in New York in early October 1991, after South and North Korea had been admitted to that body, Foreign Minister Lee Sang-ock asked Chinese Foreign Minister Qian Qichen to establish diplomatic relations. Lee repeated this request, in the form of a personal message from President Roh, when he became the first South Korean cabinet minister ever to visit China in April 1992 (*Korea Newsreview* 18 April 1992).

The Chinese government, mindful of its close ideological relationship with North Korea, had been reluctant to take that final step. Reportedly, Kim Il-sung has secured a commitment from Chinese leaders, probably during his 'secret' October 1990 visit to Shenyang, that China would not recognise South Korea until North Korean-Japanese relations were normalised.[1] Nevertheless, the Chinese seem to have become increasingly unhappy with the pace of the Japan-North Korea normalisation negotiations, which, since the third round, in May 1991, they have actually been hosting in Beijing. Their policy, therefore, was to try to encourage both North Korea and Japan to be more flexible in their negotiating stances, while, at the same time, to develop substantial relations with South Korea 'quietly and gradually', to use the words of Foreign Minister Qian (*Korea Times* 4 October 1991).

Finally, strong pressure from the South Koreans (President Roh clearly wanted a diplomatic success to divert domestic criticism of him as a 'lame-duck' president in his final months), coupled with frustration with the North Koreans, and gradually mounting concern at Taiwanese diplomatic successes, pushed the Chinese into full diplomatic relations, which were established in August 1992. At the end of the following month, Roh actually visited China and signed further trade and technological cooperation agreements.

The successes of South Korea's nordpolitik, of course, have impacted on North Korea's own relations with its two major supporters but also on those two countries' relationships with Japan. This has much to do with the differing motivations behind South Korean, Soviet and Chinese policies.

For the South Korean government, the rationale behind Roh's policy was primarily political. By developing political and economic contacts with the socialist allies of North Korea, the North could be pushed into a more positive mode. When North Korea failed to respond, for even the prime ministerial-level meetings in late 1990 produced no real breakthrough in North-South relations, good relations with the Soviet Union and China became important in their own right. They certainly helped to ensure that the two powers, members of the UN Security Council, did not vote against the South Korean application for membership in 1991. Thus, South Korea was able to ensure itself a 'very inexpensive security' (Sanford 1990 p.69).

The nordpolitik has also helped to boost Roh's image domestically, particularly in the face of considerable popular disillusionment over political in-fighting and economic difficulties. It is these economic problems which are making the economic element, initially less significant, increasingly important. When South Korea opened its quasi-diplomatic trade office in Beijing in February 1991, its new head argued that the past 'ocean-bound' trade patterns were changing to 'continent-bound' ones (*Korea Times* 5 February 1991). This is an over-simplification, but it is true that South Korea, faced with what it sees as growing protectionism in Europe and North America and still heavily dependent on imported natural resources, has looked to both China and the Soviet Union/CIS as potential markets for its consumer goods and intermediate technology and as sources of raw materials. Here, the South Korean chaebol found themselves searching for commercial opportunities in which the Japanese were the main rivals. The chaebol leaders felt that the absence of diplomatic relations left them exposed; they lacked the leverage of Japanese companies in negotiating deals and securing the removal of discriminatory duties on Korean products.

The establishment of diplomatic relations first with the Soviet Union and now with China has helped, but South Korean businessmen and officials are still concerned at signs that the Soviets and the Chinese use the 'Japan card' in negotiations with them. Both states naturally try to play off Japanese companies against South Korean companies to get the best deal. But, in addition the South Koreans felt that, for example, Gorbachev was using the potentiality of massive Japanese aid (though it did not actually materialise) in the run-up to his April 1991 visit to both Japan and South Korea to keep the South Koreans on track with their own commitments to aid the Soviets. On the other hand, the South Koreans are aware that, particularly where large-scale resource projects in Siberia are concerned, they do not on their own have sufficient capital and technological expertise. They do need to work together with Japanese (or American) companies and Japanese official and private financial organisations, if their ambitious plans are to be realised. As such, both the competitive and cooperative elements of Japan-South Korean relations co-exist in the Soviet/Russian market to an extent that they do not in the Chinese market, where the competitive element is overwhelmingly dominant.

From the Soviet point of view, the economic motivation for relations with South Korea was more important than the political. Of course, by establishing relations with the South, Gorbachev would help to stabilise the peninsula, encourage US troop and weaponry withdrawals, and increase its own leverage (as the only major power to recognise both Koreas) in the North-east Asian region. However, the Soviet Union's 'intrinsic interest' in the Korean peninsula lay in economic contacts with the South (Segal 1990b p.59). As the Soviet Union's economic problems mounted, Gorbachev's interest switched from acting as a provider of aid to ailing North Korea to being a recipient of aid, trade and investment from the South.

Gorbachev, of course, tried not only to use the 'Japan card' against the South Koreans but also to use the 'Korean card' against the Japanese. His successor, Yeltsin, has also tried to follow the same tactics. First Soviet and now Russian officials have tried to suggest that the Japanese might lose significant economic opportunities to the South Koreans, if they do not adopt a more positive attitude, especially over economic assistance. The Japanese government, however, has not been impressed by such arguments, since it sees resolution of the disputed 'northern territories' issue as a precondition for substantial aid; neither have Japanese businessmen been very tempted by the Soviet/Russian market (Bridges 1991 pp. 56-62). Indeed, during 1990-91, the attitude amongst Japanese businessmen towards the South Korean endeavours to get into the Soviet market was 'good luck to them'.

Even though, under the reforming Russia/CIS, Japanese businessmen have been busy in sending inspection and survey teams, they have been cautious about getting definitely committed to the major projects that the Russians are offering. The Japanese government did decide to give some limited humanitarian assistance to Russia/CIS, but it continued to argue against its G-7 partners' efforts to put together an economic aid package for Russia without a settlement of the territorial dispute. Yeltsin's decision to call off, at short notice, his planned September 1992 visit to Japan and South Korea (primarily because of domestic contraints that would not allow him to cede territory to Japan) but re-schedule only the South Korean trip (for November) suggests that he may have, at least temporarily, given up on the Japanese and decided to concentrate on the South Koreans. The continued evidence of Russian economic chaos, however, makes South Korean businessmen concerned almost as much as their Japanese counterparts, so Yeltsin's leverage to play off the two countries is weakening.

For China, too, the economic motivation is paramount. Whereas Soviet disillusionment with the North Koreans grew rapidly during 1990-91 and contributed to the decision for political recognition of South Korea, the Chinese, especially under the post-Tiananmen Square massacre leadership, have been reluctant to further upset their ideological soul-mate Kim Il-sung. They have, however, talked quietly to the North Koreans about the way things are moving. President Yang Shangkun, on his visit to Pyongyang in April 1992, in fact warned the North Koreans that China would be moving soon to establish diplomatic relations with the South.

The Chinese were happy to concentrate first on economic contacts with the South. Despite China's long-standing economic relations with the North, the stagnation of the North Korean economy meant that from the mid-1980s South Korea overtook the North in the value of its trade with China. The Chinese began to look on South Korea as an important source of the intermediate goods and technology necessary for modernisation, but at prices which were competitive with the Japanese. As Chinese resentment against the burgeoning trade deficit with Japan mounted, South Korea seemed the perfect foil. Even though the Sino-Japanese trade situation has turned around since 1989, the Chinese, like the Russians, can see advantages to playing off South Korean and Japanese businessmen. With more success too, since the prospects for commercial activity in China are much greater than in Russia/CIS. Also important for China was that it was able to insist that as part of the agreement on full diplomatic recognition South Korea would de-recognise Taiwan (whereas China was required to take no such equivalent step with the North). In fact, Taiwan, having got wind of the impending China-South Korean rapprochement, pre-empted it by severing relations with South Korea first.

North Korea: losing its balance

Because it shared borders with both China and the Soviet Union, North Korea developed special ties with them both. Notwithstanding Kim Il-sung's juche philosophy of self-reliance, they were North Korea's principal sources of economic, technical and military aid. The Russians, in particular, in recent years have made a point of emphasising the crucial role that they played in developing the economic infrastructure of North Korea. However, over four decades, Kim has managed to maintain a posture of independence by balancing his much larger allies: siding with one or the other on particular issues but aligning with neither. While the two giant communist powers were at odds, Kim was able to play off one against the other, but in the second half of the 1980s the gradual move towards Sino-Soviet rapprochement, which reached its peak with Gorbachev's visit to Beijing in May 1989, drastically reduced Kim's leverage.

After mid-1989, however, the responses of China and the Soviet Union to the challenges of economic and political reform became increasingly divergent: the Tiananmen Square massacre and clampdown in China contrasting with the disintegration of socialism in Eastern Europe and, ultimately, the Soviet Union (Lin 1991). Ironically, however, this has not revived North Korean leverage, for Kim has found himself increasingly out of sorts with the direction of Soviet - and subsequently Russian - policies and has been forced to rely to an ever greater degree on China.

The Soviet Union had long thought North Korea an awkward ally, but, from 1988 onwards, relations gradually deteriorated as Gorbachev began to see the economic advantages of coming closer to the South. The North Koreans felt betrayed by this movement and tried to prevent it; they even threatened to switch to supporting the Japanese claim to the disputed 'northern territories' against the Soviet Union. However, when they failed and the Soviet Union recognised South Korea in September 1990 their reaction was limited to a brief fit of pique, for the North Koreans still wished to hold on to Soviet economic and military assistance. Here again, they were disappointed, as the deteriorating Soviet economic situation led to a Soviet decision to switch to 'hard currency' transactions with North Korea from the beginning of 1991, and the Soviets suspended technical assistance for the North Korean nuclear development programme as a way of increasing pressure on the North Koreans to open up their nuclear facilities to outside inspection. Gorbachev's April 1991 visit to the South, rather than to the North, was a humiliating demonstration of the way the wind was blowing. The North Koreans' support for the August 1991 hard-line coup against Gorbachev and their subsequent embarassment and frustration at its failure only served to further chill the relationship.

During 1991 imports from the Soviet Union virtually disappeared to around 2% of the previous year's total; exports held up slightly better, but still fell to around one-third of the 1990 level. Yeltsin's Russia has been prepared to maintain the diplomatic relationship with the North, but both sides appear to be doing little more than going through the motions. The ideological bonds have been completely broken. Further economic and military assistance from Russia or the other CIS states is unlikely. Indeed, Yeltsin specifically told visiting South Korean Foreign Minister Lee Sang-ock in June 1992 that Russia no longer provided 'financial, military or any other form of assistance' to North Korea (*Korea Times* 1 July 1992). Kim Il-sung has attempted to buy Russian expertise and materials for the one project that is strategically important to him, the development of his nuclear programme. In April 1992, a Russian newspaper reported that North Korea had, indeed, succeeded in getting hold of 56 kilos of plutonium from a smuggling ring in the CIS (*Korea Times* 25 April 1992).

Depressed by the turn of events in the former Soviet Union, Kim turned to China, which was prepared to recognise his ideological inclinations, even though it took a more pragmatic line about economic reform and developing economic contacts with the capitalist world, including South Korea. Since late 1989 there have been regular exchanges of visits by Chinese and North Korean leaders, culminating in Kim's own visit to China in October 1991. However, Kim has found it difficult to obtain from China, beset by its own economic problems and going through a period of austerity, anything like the economic inputs that would replace the loss of Soviet aid. The Chinese offered some small-scale help with food supplies, but during 1991 they stopped using 'friendship prices' for oil (one of the North's major imports) and began charging close to world prices. Instead, the Chinese tried to persuade Kim and other North Korean leaders of the advantages of opening up to the outside world along the Chinese path. On his October 1991 visit, Kim was specifically taken by the Chinese to one of their special economic zones as a way of showing him how some 'capitalist' inputs might save his economy.

He does not seem to have been converted to the faith, although the North has become involved in discussions sponsored by the UN Development Programme about developing an ambitious economic zone straddling the borders of North Korea, China and the Soviet Union/Russia in the inhospitable Tumen river basin. These plans are discussed further in Chapter 6, but suffice it to say here that the countries involved have different motivations and that there are significant infrastructural, labour and capital problems to be solved.

The net result of Kim's ideological rupture with the former Soviet Union and the failure to receive real economic compensation from China was to push him into looking to Japan as the only viable source of assistance to his struggling economy. With the West Europeans preoccupied with the 1992 single market process and the resuscitation of Eastern Europe and the Americans not yet interested in developing serious contacts, Kim calculated that only Japan would have both the will and the means to meet his needs. As is discussed further in Chapter 8, this accounts for the North Korean decision in the autumn of 1990 to push for the normalisation of relations with Japan.

Kim's position, however, became increasingly isolated as even the Chinese edged towards the South Koreans. Kim had long tried to dissuade the Chinese from developing their contacts with the South and was upset by the establishment of Sino-South Korean relations in August 1992. However, unlike the 1990 Soviet-South Korean rapprochement, when North Korean officials and media reacted vehemently and threatened reprisals, the reaction to the Sino-South Korean rapprochement was more muted. This undoubtedly reflected the fact that Kim could not afford to cut contacts with his last mentor. The Chinese tried to mollify him by explaining that the new relationship with the South did not prevent the continuation of the close relations with the North, but it was clear that the Chinese, like the Russians two years earlier, had moved to accept the reality of the 'two Koreas'.

The role of the United States

Historically, the world for Koreans revolved around their two immediate neighbours, China and Japan. However, since the Second World War, for South Korea at least it is the United States, one of the newer forces in the region, that has now become its most important partner. For three decades after the Korean War, the relationship was a deeply asymmetrical one, but in recent years South Korea has exhibited the desire and the ability to act more independently. South Korea, however, has always been aware of the close Japan-US relationship, both economically and politico-strategically, which has always acted as a factor complicating the simple bilateral US-South Korean relationship.

Throughout the twentieth century, US foreign policy in the Asian Pacific region has been driven by the belief that no one power should become dominant in the whole region. This concept led the United States not only to take on the Japanese expansionism of the 1930s but also to become embroiled in the Korean and Vietnam Wars. But, additionally, US involvement in the Korean War was crucially affected by the Japan factor. Indeed, despite all the high-sounding rhetoric about combating communism, the US decision to fight for the survival of South Korea only made sense as a means of defending the newly-reconstructed Japan (Gordon 1990 pp. 9-11).

However, US hopes for a harmonious trilateral relationship among itself, Japan and South Korea were frustrated by President Rhee's intransigent anti-Japanism. For more than a decade, repeated US attempts to coax and sponsor its two 'clients' to normalise relations ended in failure. Even after 1965, as shown in Chapter 2, Japan-South Korean relations remained tense and the United States was forced to rely on two sets of bilateral, patron-client relationships (Lee and Sato 1982 p.27 ff.).

Moreover, until the early 1980s at least, US policy-makers tended to continue the Korean War tradition of seeing South Korea through the 'prism' of Japan, initially in security terms, but later in economic terms too. This meant that the US preoccupation was with Soviet (and, to a lesser extent, Chinese) activity in the region and, only secondarily, with the North Korean threat to the South. The Reagan administration, however, put a strong emphasis on a continued commitment to South Korea's defence. It buried President Carter's abortive plans to withdraw US forces from there, which both the South Koreans and the Japanese strongly argued against. At the same time it began pushing Japan to take on more of a regional defence role.

Just as for the Japanese in the 1970s, so for the Koreans in the 1980s their economic success and growing self-confidence altered the balance in the relationship with the United States. The US-South Korean relationship became less asymmetrical but not less complex. This was, partly, because the United States began to see South Korea as a growing economic threat, and, partly, because South Koreans thought that they could afford to display more anti-Americanism.

Trilateral interdependence is more pronounced in the economic than the security field. For South Korea, Japan still remains its primary source of imports (particularly intermediate parts and technology), while the United States is its primary market. The US experience with Japan's exporting techniques and its 'closed' domestic market conditioned much of the response to South Korea's economic development too. The United States reacted to Japanese exports of successive products, through textiles, televisions, and cars, to video-cassette recorders (VCRs) etc., by negotiating 'voluntary export restraints' and other arrangements. The Koreans initially exploited this Japanese restraint, until they, in turn, found themselves being pressurised by the Americans. In responding to US complaints, South Korea has argued that its heavy trade deficit with Japan, which fluctuated during the 1980s but remained sizeable, requires it to continue exporting to the United States and that opening up its own market too rapidly only benefits the Japanese not the Americans. The South Koreans, therefore, have followed the Japanese in exporting an increasingly sophisticated range of consumer goods to the United States and, subsequently, in investing in manufacturing plants inside the United States.

Whereas in the US-Japan relationship it has been the US side which has tried to link defence and economic issues, in the US-South Korean relationship it has been the South Korean side which has tried to link the two by arguing that its economic practices should be given special consideration because of the costs of defending its people against the communist North.

Problems with the burgeoning budget deficit and the changing nature of the global and regional competition with the Soviet Union, however, forced the Bush administration to reassess its policies towards Japan and South Korea. This has meant little change in the basic economic relationship, where intermittent disputes and frictions continue much as before. The Bush administration placed considerable weight on the Structural Impediments Initiative (SII) talks in 1989-90 and various follow-up activities in its efforts to rebalance the economic relationship with Japan, and on the threatening use of the 'super-301' trade legislation to encourage the Koreans to open their markets more. But, by 1991, the Japanese surplus with the United States had begun to increase again and, although the South Koreans actually slipped into a slim deficit with the United States, there seemed to be only grudging progress on the market-opening issues by South Korea. Trade issues are set to remain high on the agenda.

The more crucial changes were in the defence and security relationship. An April 1990 Department of Defense plan called for a continued and substantial US air and naval presence in North-east Asia, but measured reductions of ground and some air forces in Japan and South Korea (DOD 1990). In a phased programme, US forces would be reduced over a three-year period to the end of 1992 by 7,000 men in South Korea and 5-6,000 men in Japan; further reductions could follow in two subsequent phases. In addition, both the allies were expected to contribute more financially to the upkeep of those US forces still remaining on their soil, and, more so in the case of Japan than South Korea, to themselves play a greater role in regional defence operations. As in the case of President Carter's 1977 troop withdrawal plans, the South Koreans and the Japanese found themselves at one in their reservations about US policy, though once again from different starting-points. Both felt that the North-east Asian situation had not changed as dramatically as in Europe - the South Koreans citing their northern neighbours, the Japanese the continued Soviet refusal to return the 'northern territories'.

However, there were no second thoughts within the Bush administration as there had been under Carter and both the Japanese and South Koreans were this time more easily convinced of the logic behind the US moves. Grudgingly, after hard bargaining, they both agreed to greater financial contributions to the upkeep of the US troops on their territories. They then found themselves again in a similar position when asked by the Americans, and other members of the multinational forces, to contribute to the resolution of the 1990-91 Gulf crisis. Both agonised over how to respond. In the end, the Japanese contributed large financial assistance ($11 billion), but eventually sent only minesweepers, in April 1992, after the fighting had finished (Maswood 1992 p.154). The South Koreans gave a much smaller amount of money but did send a military medical team to the front. For the Japanese, the marker against which to judge their response was (West) Germany, which had similar constitutional and psychological sensitivities about sending troops overseas; they were far less concerned about South Korean policy. For the South Koreans, however, much depended on the Japanese attitude, not just because of their long-standing suspicion, even fear, of seeing Japanese troops going overseas, but because a significant Japanese response would have increased the onus on them to follow the Japanese precedent (Bridges 1992 p. 147).

President Bush's September 1991 initiative to withdraw ground-based tactical nuclear weapons from around the world, implicitly including South Korea, discussed in the next section, was a further example of US policy towards one ally indirectly affecting the other. Despite a certain initial nervousness in some defence circles in South Korea, both South Korea and Japan welcomed this initiative. For both, it represented a chance to break the log-jam in relations with North Korea, if the latter were prepared to respond by allowing IAEA inspection.

The Bush administration, however, has ruled out direct negotiations between itself and North Korea over nuclear issues, which it says are primarily for the two Koreas to settle and, to a lesser extent, for North Korea and Japan to discuss. The United States, in fact, remains very suspicious of North Korea; it not only holds the North responsible for the outbreak of the Korean War and perpetrating a series of incidents against the South but it also points to a long list of incidents, from the capture of the US spy ship Pueblo in 1968 onwards, against American interests. Since 1985, North Korea has been specifically mentioned on the US government's list of 'terrorist' regimes around the world.

In North Korean eyes, the US domination of South Korea is indisputable and the presence of US troops in the South represents the greatest single obstacle to reunification. Although the North Koreans undoubtedly do wish to remove the US forces as a way of weakening the South, these forces do also, in themselves, appear as a threat to the North. For the North Koreans cannot forget the US blanket-bombing during the Korean War, which reduced their major centres to rubble. Nevertheless, as in their relationship with Japan, the North Koreans have practised a certain duality in their attitude to the Americans. While vilifying the Americans as 'war-thirsty imperialists' propping up successive South Korean 'fascist' regimes, North Korea has on a number of occasions sought to obtain some recognition from the United States and to develop some cultural and economic links. Since 1974, in fact, the North has frequently proposed direct negotiations between the two countries (Clough 1987b pp.255-73).

The United States has consistently rejected the idea of high-level bilateral talks, but, since 1988, it has been carrying on a low-level intermittent dialogue through diplomats based in Beijing. By September 1992 20 meetings had been held, without any substantial progress. The North Koreans have occasionally pressed for the level of representation to be raised, even to ambassadorial level, but the United States has seen no incentive to do so. Occasional conciliatory gestures, such as the returning of the bodies of a few missing-in-action US soldiers in May 1990, June 1991 and May 1992, have been reciprocated by allowing North Koreans to attend academic meetings in the United States and some former US government officials and congressmen to visit the North. In January 1992, Kim Yong-sun, the KWP secretary for international affairs, was allowed to visit Washington and meet Under-Secretary of State Arnold Kanter, the most senior US diplomat to meet a North Korean official so far, but the United States made it clear that this was a one-off meeting to discuss the nuclear inspection problem (*Korea Times* 24 January 1992).

In April 1992, in a rare interview with a US newspaper, Kim Il-sung called for the normalisation of relations with the United States, but US State Department officials made it clear that for there to be an improvement in relations, North Korea would have to address a number of US concerns, which included constructive North-South talks, the return of MIAs (missing-in-action soldiers), nuclear inspection, an end to missile exports and improved human rights (*Korea Times* 17 April 1992). As President Bush emphasised during his January 1992 visit to Seoul, the United States was not going to go round the back of the South to establish relations with the North (*Korea Newsreview* 11 January 1992). Close consultation between the US and South Korean administrations remains the order of the day and the United States is still waiting for more substantial evidence that the North is seriously changing its approach.

The nuclear dimension

The United States has long been concerned about the heavy North Korean military presence close to the DMZ, but since 1989 it has also become worried about signs of possible nuclear weapon development in the North, an eventuality which it regards as 'extremely destabilising'. This has accounted for its strong insistence on North Korea adhering to the IAEA nuclear-safeguards agreement and for its pressure on Japan to maintain that issue as a precondition for its establishment of diplomatic relations with the North.

The issue of North Korean nuclear weapons development and the opening up of its nuclear facilities to inspection by the IAEA has now become a key area in which the complex interactions between China, the Soviet Union/CIS and the United States have impacted on Japan's relations with the two Koreas. North Korea, at Soviet behest, signed the Nuclear Non-Proliferation Treaty (NPT) in 1985, but it did not sign the associated mandatory safeguards accord with the IAEA. A small research reactor was built in the 1960s with Soviet assistance, but in 1980 work had began on a large-scale (20-30 megawatt) nuclear research reactor at Yongbyon, 60 miles north of Pyongyang; this reactor came into operation in 1987. By 1991 US and South Korean intelligence authorities had begun to suspect that a nuclear-fuel reprocessing plant and another reactor were under construction at Yongbyon.

After a visit to Yongbyon in May 1992, Hans Blix, the IAEA director general, reported that the main reactor was outdated and primitive, but that a large building, which could certainly be a reprocessing plant, was about 80% complete. He also confirmed an earlier statement by the North's chief negotiator in the Japan-North Korean negotiations that the North had extracted 'a tiny quantity of plutonium' during a test in 1990 (*Korea Times* 16, 17 May, 12 June 1992). A North Korean defector also claimed that underground nuclear test facilities existed at Pakchon. North Korea does have some uranium deposits, close to the border with the South, but their extent is unknown. Its nuclear scientists and technicians have been trained in the Soviet Union and Eastern Europe. Together, it is believed, these would give North Korea the capability to produce a nuclear bomb within the next few years, at the latest by 1995.

Speaking to the National Assembly in September 1991, Defence Minister Lee Jong-koo warned that the North could be capable of producing 50 kilograms of plutonium a year by 1993, enough for six or seven bombs of the power of those dropped at Hiroshima. During 1991, therefore, as UN and world interest focused on the nuclear weapon-making potential of Iraq, an increasing number of, often contradictory, reports about the state of North Korea's nuclear programme also appeared. These ranged from denials by the North Koreans that they had any capability or intention of making nuclear weapons to assessments that the North was only a few months away from completing a bomb.[2]

Under the requirements of the NPT, acceding powers are expected to sign the nuclear safeguards agreement within 18 months. This North Korea failed to do, arguing that the United States must first remove its tactical nuclear weapons from South Korean soil. Only in June 1991 did the North Korean government announce its intention of signing this agreement, but, within a few days, its spokesmen had started to attach conditions for its implementation, once again implying that the US nuclear threat was a 'major obstacle'. Negotiations over a draft agreement continued with the IAEA, but in September on the eve of signing this agreement the North Koreans drew back again (*International Herald Tribune* 14 August 1991).

The major powers share a desire to prevent the proliferation of nuclear weapons on the Korean peninsula. The United States has always maintained a 'neither confirm nor deny' policy regarding its own nuclear weapons in South Korea; the South Korean government too has been reticent about admitting to the US nuclear presence. According to the Greenpeace organisation, the number of US nuclear weapons in South Korea has declined from about 680 in the 1970s, to about 150 by the early 1980s, and to around 100 - 40 army artillery projectiles and 60 air-delivered bombs - stored at the Kunsan air base south of Seoul by early 1991 (*Far Eastern Economic Review* 10 October 1991). President Bush's initiative in September 1991 to reduce US ground-based nuclear weapon stockpiles overseas covered the ground-based artillery weapons in South Korea, but the fate of the air-delivered nuclear bombs was less immediately clear. However, when the US government began quietly removing its nuclear weapons from South Korea both categories were included.

The Bush initiative was, of course, primarily a part of the ongoing US-Soviet discussions about reducing nuclear and conventional weapons. Nevertheless, it was greeted favourably in North-east Asia, as being bound to have an impact on the nuclear balance in and around the Korean peninsula. In fact, the United States had been talking not just to South Korea but also to the other three major powers about North Korean nuclear ambitions for some time. Although the Soviets supplied the initial expertise to the North Korean nuclear programme in the 1960s, they did become increasingly concerned to keep the North Koreans under control. They not only encouraged the North to join the NPT, but when it refused to accede to the safeguards agreement, they held up the implementation of a 1985 contract to supply four modern reactors to the North (a decision which has been reaffirmed by the successor Russian government).

There was a series of consultations between senior Soviet and US officials about the North Korean nuclear programme from the autumn of 1989, including at the February 1990 Bush-Gorbachev Summit. In the autumn of 1990, as Soviet-North Korean relations deteriorated, the North Koreans told the Soviets that their opening of relations with South Korea relieved the North of its obligation not to make nuclear weapons. In return, the Soviets warned that they would withhold vital nuclear fuel and technology, if North Korea did not allow IAEA inspection of its facilities (*Korea Times* 16 April 1991; *Newsweek* 29 April 1991). When Gorbachev visited Japan in April 1991, he and Kaifu issued a joint statement which included an expression of hope that the North would agree to IAEA inspection. The successor Russian government has made it clear that it shares Western concerns about the North Korean nuclear programme.

US defence and intelligence experts visited Japan in October 1990, and again in the autumn of 1991, to specifically brief Japanese officials about the North Korean nuclear programme. As is discussed further in Chapter 8, the IAEA inspection issue has become one of the two key sticking-points in the Japan-North Korean normalisation process. Apart from their own sensitivities, having been the first and only nation to suffer an atomic bomb attack, the Japanese are certainly well aware of the American concerns.

China claims that it has not provided nuclear weapons' development assistance to the North, and has frequently expressed its belief in the desirability of a nuclear-free Korean peninsula. Chinese leaders reiterated that point to President Roh on his visit to China in September 1992. In refusing to openly side with the diplomatic offensive put together by the United States and its Asian allies, China is not saying that it is less concerned than the other major powers about the North Korean nuclear programme. Rather, it feels that the best way to encourage the North to conform to international inspection procedures is through subtle persuasion rather than more blatant pressure which might be counter-productive.

However, all the other interested powers have tried to encourage China to use its influence over the North to allow IAEA inspection. China has not been very responsive to US and Soviet/Russian persuasion on this point, not least because its bilateral relations with both of these countries have been cooled by other factors. However, China did take the opportunity of Kaifu's August 1991 visit to Beijing to announce that it itself would sign the main NPT in the near future (*Far Eastern Economic Review* 22 August 1991). This change of policy, by switching from past denunciations of the NPT as an imperialist tool to accepting international mechanisms, was taken as a sign to North Korea that it too should fully adhere to international agreements. In his October 1991 meeting with his South Korean counterpart, Chinese Foreign Minister Qian avoided a direct commitment to exert pressure on the North but did say that China hoped that nuclear weapons would not exist on the Korean peninsula. Moreover, the public pronouncements which accompanied Kim Il-sung's October 1991 visit to China studiously avoided mentioning the nuclear issue, which may be a sign that the two sides did not completely see eye-to-eye on this point.

The nuclear inspection issue has become tightly wound up not just with the Japan-North Korean normalisation negotiations but also with the prospects of any real breakthrough in the North's relations with the South and with the United States. In fact, as the North Koreans showed alternating signs of concession and foot-dragging on the IAEA inspection during late 1991-early 1992, both the United States and South Korea began to emphasise the importance of South-North inspections as well. This, in turn, impacted on the Japanese negotiating stance; by the spring of 1992 Japan too was calling for not just IAEA inspections but for South Korean inspections too.

The South-North inspections are provided for in the December 1991 agreement on de-nuclearisation of the Korean peninsula, the culmination of a series of shifts in policy stances by both Koreas during the autumn of 1991. Following on from the Bush initiative to remove its nuclear weapons from South Korea, President Roh anounced on 8 November that South Korea would 'not manufacture, possess, store, deploy or use nuclear weapons' (*Korea Times* 9 November 1991). This brought South Korea almost exactly into line with stated Japanese practice. On 18 December, Roh was able to declare that there were no longer any nuclear weapons on South Korean territory and he suggested the simultaneous inspection of all facilities in the two Koreas, including US military bases in South Korea (*Korea Times* 19 December 1991). The South Koreans and the United States used the stick as well as the carrot. In late November 1991 Defense Secretary Dick Cheney and Defence Minister Lee agreed to postpone the second phase of US troop withdrawals, scheduled to begin in early 1993, until North Korea complied with international inspection procedures. A decision on whether to scale down the annual 'Team Spirit' exercises was also said to depend on North Korean actions (the 1992 exercises were subsequently cancelled after the December North-South agreement).

Following on from their prime-ministerial level agreement on general relations in mid-December, the North and South issued a joint declaration on 31 December. Both sides pledged the peaceful use of nuclear energy and agreed to possess neither nuclear weapons nor nuclear reprocessing and uranium enrichment facilities (Lehmann 1992 pp.13-22). A Joint Nuclear Control Commission (JNCC) began discussions in March 1992, with a timetable of two months for working out the sites to be inspected and the mechanisms for implementing the inspections. However, the JNCC's meetings have been marked by wrangling over details, particularly over the South's insistence on 'challenge inspections' of North Korean sites and the North's demand for access to all US bases in the South, and the initial deadlines have been passed. The North made some slow moves forward in its discussions with IAEA, however. It signed the IAEA safeguards agreement at the end of March, ratified it in April, provided a list of its nuclear facilities in May and allowed an initial IAEA inspection of the Yongbyon facilities in early June. The results of that and a subsequent inspection were inconclusive, mainly because the North Koreans would not allow the IAEA to take samples from the reactor core.

The problem lies not just with the foot-dragging of the North Koreans, but in the inadequacy of the IAEA inspection procedures (something which the

IAEA themselves admit). The Iraqi case has demonstrated that even though a country has signed the NPT and the safeguards agreement it is no absolute guarantee that the country concerned is not covertly producing weapons-grade fissile material or manufacturing nuclear weapons. For, in North Korea, as in Iraq prior to the Gulf War, IAEA inspectors can only visit those sites designated by the North Korean government. Although discussions are going on within the IAEA to strengthen inspection procedures, enhanced powers have not yet been agreed. Hence the view of the United States (and now Japan) that South Korean inspections are important to complement and strengthen the IAEA's coverage.

While the technical capability of the North Koreans to develop an effective bomb at an early date must be doubtful, the balance of evidence and the constant prevarication over IAEA inspection and South Korean inspection does suggest that the North has, indeed, been trying to perfect a bomb, but that it has not yet succeeded.

The key question is whether Kim Il-sung sees it as a cheap 'strategic equaliser' with the South, enabling him to reduce expenditure on conventional weaponry (and so help to save his economy), or whether he is just developing it as a bargaining card, first to irritate and off-balance his 'capitalist opponents' and then to be used - even negotiated away - for a better deal in recognition and economic assistance. It may even be that Kim has failed and has given up trying to develop a bomb, but wishes to still use its potential as a card to be played. Kim has certainly used the nuclear card to achieve at least one of his long-standing objectives - the removal of US nuclear weapons from South Korea. But he has not yet achieved the diplomatic recognition and economic assistance that he craves. Both Japan and the United States have made it clear that IAEA inspections of June 1992 would not suffice; inter-Korean inspections must also take place.

With the North's two old allies, the former Soviet Union quite openly and China more covertly, pushing for North Korean acquiescence to full inspections, the international pressure on the North is mounting steadily. What options are open to the major powers to induce North Korea to give up its nuclear weapon programme?

One option which has been ruled out is that of a pre-emptive military strike against the North Korean facilities, rather on the lines of Israel's June 1981 attack on Iraq's Osirak reactor. In April 1991 South Korean Defence Minister Lee suggested that a commando team should be sent to destroy the Yongbyon facilities, but he was quickly forced to retract (*Economist* 20 April 1991).

Another option would be to bring a special resolution before the UN Security Council which would involve UN-mandated economic and other sanctions against North Korea. China, however, would probably veto any move to introduce economic sanctions and the North's acceptance of partial IAEA inspections in June 1992 would delay the creation of a consensus for UN action. The fall-back alternative might be to arrange for G-7 (plus Russian) economic sanctions against North Korea, but doubts remain as to whether Japan would be able to place a complete embargo on links between the ethnic Koreans in Japan and the North (Niksch 1992 pp.77-8).

For the moment the best option may be to continue to make it clear that the international community is solidly behind South Korean policies. South Korea has argued that full-scale economic cooperation with the North is dependent on inter-Korean nuclear inspections; in July 1992, the South Koreans did begin again to dangle a carrot by allowing the chaebol to investigate joint venture prospects in Nanpo, but they have emphasised that no pilot projects can occur without North Korean movement on nuclear inspection. Japan, the United States and the EC countries have also clearly linked recognition and aid to the same criteria. At the same time, it is important to consider possible further inducements to the North. In early June, ideas began to be floated that North Korea might be prepared to abandon plans to reprocess plutonium in exchange for US, Japanese and even South Korean technological assistance on developing alternative light-water reactors (*Korea Times* 12 June 1992). This may provide a way out of the diplomatic stalemate.

Realising cross-recognition

Roh's July 1988 speech opened up the possibilities of improving ties between the South's friends and allies and the North. The South, however, has kept a very cautious eye on the Japanese dialogue with the North; it has been less suspicious of the US dialogue, which is, anyway, far less advanced than the Japanese one. Indeed, the South has looked to the United States to act as restraining factor on Japan, to prevent premature recognition. The very fact that the South and the United States are deeply concerned about the North's nuclear weapon programme has helped to stimulate and reinforce the Japanese concern about this issue.

The more fluid situation on the Korean peninsula and the frequency with which leaders of the four major powers met with each other and the leaders of their respective Korean allies from the early 1980s gave rise to reconsideration of the concept of cross-recognition. This idea, briefly given some prominence by US Secretary of State Henry Kissinger in 1975, but revived after Nakasone's visits to Seoul and Washington in 1983, depicted the United States and Japan recognising North Korea and China and the Soviet Union recognising South Korea, after which both Koreas could join the

United Nations. The North opposed the idea, which it saw as meaning the consolidation of the existing division of the peninsula.

However, in practice, moves have been made in reverse order with UN membership coming after only one strand of the cross-recognition plan (the Soviet Union recognising South Korea) has come into place. Now China has recognised the South, making the recognition pattern extremely one-sided. Japan and, finally, the United States will no doubt in due course recognise the North and complete the cross-recognition scenario, but by then the North will have been left well behind in the diplomatic struggle.

Notes

1. According to a report by Ko Young-hwan, a senior North Korean diplomat who defected to the South in May 1991, Deng Xiaoping personally made this promise to Kim (*Korea Times* 14 September 1991).
2. On the changes in estimates of the capability and pace of the North Korean nuclear weapon programme see Mack 1991 pp. 87-104; Song 1991 pp. 473-8; *Newsweek* 29 April 1991; *Jane's Defence Weekly* 14 September 1991; *Christian Science Monitor* 4 October 1991.

6 Economic Interdependence

In the 1980s, East Asia was the fastest growing region in the world and the World Bank expects it to repeat that record during the 1990s. Japan became a mature and slower growing economy, but, nevertheless, ended the 1980s with its longest-ever post-war period of continuous economic growth. South Korea recovered from a hiccup in 1980 to become the fastest growing economy in the world for three years in succession, with over 12% GNP growth in 1986-88. North Korea, however, in common with almost all the socialist economies of the region apart from China, struggled to maintain growth and its Stalinist-style command economy seemed increasingly out of tune with the dynamism elsewhere in the region.

This chapter looks at Japan's economic linkages with the two Koreas, of which that with the South is by far the most important. It examines the flows of trade, aid, FDI and technology, which are binding them closer and yet at the same time forcing them to turn outwards as well. It looks also at this particular manifestation in East Asia of the developed country-NIC relationship found elsewhere in the world, and, finally, sets these relationships in the context of the aspirations for regional economic cooperation and even a regional economic 'bloc'.

Japan as 'master' and 'model'

Japanese economists like to refer to the phenomenon of the 'flying geese' pattern of economic development in East Asia. Japan is depicted as being at the head, followed by the NICs and then the ASEAN countries, in a regular formation, with shifting comparative advantage as the countries advance in technological sophistication. Part of the interest of East Asia's flying-geese pattern is that these geese are not of the same size or breed, nor are they flying at the same speed (Shibusawa, Ahmad and Bridges 1991 pp.4-8; Awanohara 1989 pp.198-208). Thus the resource-rich ASEAN countries contrast with the resource-poor NICs and Japan; per capita income levels and export dependency ratios vary considerably. Growth rates, too, have differed widely. Over the years 1980-90, in fact, China and South Korea performed the best, both of them at just under 10% average annual GNP growth. Several ASEAN countries were hit by the oil and commodity price falls in 1983-85; neither have the NICs been totally immune to fluctuations (both South Korea and Singapore did experience negative growth, in 1980 and 1985 respectively). In the late 1980s, it was the NICs which recorded the fastest rates, but as the 1990s opened some of the ASEAN countries, notably Malaysia and Thailand, took the lead. With the exception of China, the socialist economies in the region have languished; North Korea looks like one of the geese that has not yet taken off.

Japan's growth during 1980-90 averaged 4%, low by earlier standards but higher than the OECD average. By regional standards, however, Japan has matured into an affluent but less dynamic economy. Nevertheless, it continues to dominate - by virtue of its sheer size. The combined GNP of the NICs and ASEAN is still less than one-third that of Japan. Even if China's GNP of around $370 billion were added, the total would be less than half of Japan's GNP. This means that Japan is still a massive economic presence by comparison with its two Korean neighbours. Accurate data on the North Korean economy are extremely difficult to obtain (even the World Bank has stopped providing estimates since the early 1980s), but, even so, Table 6.1 does give some measure of the differences between the three countries.

Table 6.1   Japan's economy compared with that of North and South Korea

	Population 1990 mill.	GDP 1990 $ bn.	GDP per capita 1990	GDP growth rate 1980-90 av.anl	Export growth rate 1980-90 av.anl
Japan	124	2943	25430	4.1	4.2
South Korea	43	236	5400	9.7	12.8
North Korea	23	21	1144	2.0	0.5

Sources: World Bank (1992); author's own calculations from data in Foster-Carter (1992) and in South Korean National Unification Board materials.

The spectacular economic growth of Japan since the early 1960s has obscured the strong element of continuity in Japanese economic growth throughout this century, interrupted only by the war years and the oil shocks of the 1970s. There is now an active debate amongst observers as to how far Japan has merely benefited from being a 'late developer', following the path of other industrialised countries, or whether it has developed in a totally 'unique' and different way which puts it at odds with the other 'Western' capitalist countries (Johnson 1982; Wolferen 1989; Komiya *et al.* 1988).

Undoubtedly, the Japanese post-war 'economic miracle' owed something to the land, labour and corporate structure reforms introduced during the Allied Occupation period. But much also depended on certain socio-political features which survived from the pre-war period and earlier. Primary amongst these was a tolerance of the government's flexible involvement in promoting economic growth - the history of Japanese economic development since the Meiji period, indeed, is one of a continually shifting balance between reliance on market forces and resort to government intervention.

The 1960s marked a spectacular burst in Japan's economic growth, making it the second largest economy in the 'free world'. The 1970s started with a series of shocks, first through US policies on textiles and the dollar and then by the Arab oil embargo. Yet these actually acted as blessings in disguise for Japan. Huge efforts were made to conserve energy and raw materials, and the shift away from heavy and capital goods industries and towards high-technology and high value-added industries was accelerated. The achievement of a shift in comparative advantage laid the foundation for the remarkable expansion of its exports in the early 1980s. This led to large trade surpluses, reaching a peak of $87 billion in 1987, which generated considerable criticism from abroad.

In order to defuse trade friction and further promote structural change, the 1986 Maekawa Report, commissioned from an *ad hoc* committee of experts by Prime Minister Nakasone, recommended that Japan should transform its economy by reducing its export orientation and stimulating imports and domestic demand. Although the report was meant as a vision for the 1990s rather than for the 1980s, some of its ideas have already been implemented as the 'high yen' of 1987-89 dictated the pace. FDI grew massively in the late 1980s, domestic demand took over the driving seat of the economy and manufactured imports topped the 50% mark of total imports in 1989. Japan experienced the longest boom period in its post-war history; the 'Heisei boom', like earlier booms in 1958-61 and 1965-70, came, therefore, at a period of significant restructuring. But it also covered a period of tremendous asset inflation, particularly in share and land prices. In the second half of 1991 these 'bubbles' began to deflate rapidly. Stock prices fell the sharpest, so that by July 1992 the stock exchange was 60% below its October 1989 zenith. Land prices also began to decline. Domestic demand stagnated, thereby cutting back on import growth, and exports again took over, raising the trade surplus to a record $103 billion in 1991. Overseas investment peaked and growth declined to 4% in 1991 and was set to worsen to almost half that level in 1992. This does not signal the end of Japanese economic strength, for the fundamentals remained strong, but does imply a subdued period of regathering.

For South Korea, this huge and dynamic economic entity, Japan, has been impossible to ignore. Japan has played three roles in South Korean economic development: as master through the legacies of social and economic ideas and patterns imposed during its colonial occupation of Korea, as model through the example of how to penetrate Western markets with manufactured goods and, later, FDI, and as mentor by its provision of aid and technology. North Korea, however, has tried to turn against the legacies of Japan as its master, has never acknowledged Japan as any kind of model for its own particular form of economic development, and, only recently, when confronted with dire economic straits, has it seriously begun to consider Japan as a possible mentor.

As shown in Chapter 2, it was the Japanese colonial period which saw the establishment of the basic infrastructure of a modern economy in Korea - railways, roads, mines, factories and scientific agriculture - even though these were for Japan's benefit and they were severely disrupted by the Korean War destruction. More subtly, however, the Japanese supervision of the Korean education system brought about a new post-independence and post-Korean War elite in South Korea who turned first to Japanese publications and information to learn of Western scientific and economic knowledge.

Thus, in the 1960s, it was President Park and his advisers who drew inspiration from the post-war economic development of Japan and the even earlier foundations during the Meiji period. Although a strong nationalist by nature, Park admired the Japanese success in emerging as a modern economic power. However, he modified the characteristics of this model, not just to suit the different character of the Korean people, but also to justify his own particular military-inspired governmental system.

He inaugurated a series of five-year plans, which were far more comprehensive than the Japanese more sectorally-based rationalisation plans of the 1950s, and created the Economic Plannning Board (EPB) to act as an economic overlord (to a degree that its Japanese equivalent, the Economic Planning Agency, has never achieved). He fostered close government-business links, as in Japan, with government officials working closely with businesss leaders in giving strategic guidance for industrial development. Park also encouraged the growth of the chaebol, the large company groups which, through their family ownership and control, resembled strongly the pre-war Japanese zaibatsu. These have spread their interests across a large number of industries, not always wisely, preferring to take over older companies or found new ones rather than go in for sub-contracting chains on the Japanese scale. But they have followed the Japanese, again in the mid-1970s, in setting up associated general trading companies, which bore a close resemblance to the Japanese sogoshosha.

Like the Japanese, the Koreans have always respected education. Faced in 1945 with an adult population of whom over three-quarters were illiterate (a result of the limited spread of education in the Japanese colonial period), the South Korean government put a strong emphasis on improving educational standards. Illiteracy has been virtually eliminated, secondary school education expanded and, now, a greater percentage of young Koreans go on to university than in Britain. However, the quality has not always kept up with the quantity. The rote-learning type of education that Korean children receive is conducive to producing an efficient and well-qualified labour force, but it is probably less suited to producing managers with initiative and, as in Japan, there is a growing concern about whether it is producing sufficient scientists able to push the country up the technological ladder.

To outside observers, however, the basis for judging the degree to which South Korea has taken Japan as a model has less to do with conscious or unconscious borrowings from Japanese corporate or educational systems, but rather with the way that South Korea has tracked the Japanese export strategy. This has inevitably led to widespread perceptions of South Korea as a 'second Japan'. In the second half of the 1980s, indeed, the South Koreans became so concerned about this image, which they felt led to them being unfairly subject to 'protectionist' actions in their major markets, that the government inaugurated an 'unofficial' campaign to promote the idea that South Korea was 'not a second Japan'. This was actually counter-productive in two respects: it raised some suspicions in the West that, maybe after all, South Korea was just operating like Japan (the psychology of 'me thinks he doth protest too much') and it provoked protests from Japanese officials and businessmen that by implication Japan was being type-cast as an unfair trader.

In the early 1960s, less than a decade after Japan, South Korea switched from an import substitution policy to an export-oriented strategy. But how far were, and are, the Japanese and the South Koreans operating on the same paths? Both countries have a serious lack of natural resources, which makes a course of self-sufficiency impossible. Japan, however, has a much larger population, so that its post-war domestic industrial build-up fuelled rapid growth rates in exports as it turned towards the international market-place. At the risk of over-simplification, Japan has gradually shifted from heavy industry into lighter, more capital-intensive assembly-type operations; its exported products have become steadily more technologically advanced. Textiles, ships, and iron and steel products, which together represented 29% of Japanese exports in 1977, accounted for only 10% a decade later. Televisions and radios declined from around 6% of exports to under 2% over the same period. Automobiles rose steadily through the 1980s until their share of exports peaked in 1986; the new growth areas in the mid-1980s were video cassette recorders (VCRs) and scientific and optical equipment.

Lacking the large domestic market that Japan possesses, South Korea followed a slightly different route, emphasising light, labour-intensive industries first, followed by a move into certain heavy industries, with mixed results. Nevertheless, in 1982 the value of heavy and chemical exports surpassed that of light manufactured exports and this sector has gradually grown to account for 55% of exports by 1989. South Korea, too, has been technologically up-grading its exports, and now exports VCRs as well as a wide range of consumer and office electrical goods. The pace of this development of electronics exports has been rapid: Korean manufacturers did not start exporting microwave ovens until 1980, yet by 1987 they were the largest exporters, with 30% of the world market by comparison with Japan's 25%. However, the range of South Korean manufactured exports is still much more limited than in Japan. As late as 1985, textiles still represented the largest export item, and, even now, the top ten export items account for around three-quarters of all exports.

Although the range, depth and sophistication of Korean exports is less than the Japanese, the manner in which they tend to grow rapidly and to be concentrated in certain export markets is similar. As far as the trading partners of both South Korea and Japan are concerned, the obverse of the sectorally-concentrated exporting pattern is a home market which is difficult to penetrate. Both did begin their exporting from behind heavily-protected markets, but since the late 1970s in the case of Japan and the mid-1980s in the case of South Korea they have made considerable efforts to reduce restrictions on market access. Japan now has all but eliminated tariff barriers - certainly it has one of the lowest levels of any OECD country - while in South Korea the liberalisation ratio has reached 96%. Although agriculture - and rice in particular - remain highly protected in both countries, the emphasis of foreign pressure has now shifted to non-tariff barriers, including the distribution systems in both countries. As in its export policies, so in its import (and financial market) liberalisation, South Korea has broadly followed the Japanese lead (NIRA 1986).

One of the problems for South Korea has been, however, that in order to manufacture products that could compete on an equal footing in third markets with those from Japan, it has had to import not only production technology and know-how from Japan but also components and intermediate parts. The exact value of the Japanese input to South Korean economic development is difficult to evaluate. One Japanese MITI official has argued that the expansion of the South Korean economy derives from its successful expansion of exports; this export promotion policy, in turn, has been 'deeply entwined with the pattern of trade with Japan, most specifically Japan's one-sided technology exports and the flow of Japanese investment into the country' (Yamaura 1986 p.12). South Korean officials and economists, on the other hand, while admitting some beneficial inputs from Japan, argue that it has been becoming less and less helpful to South Korean economic endeavours . The following sections, in looking at flows of aid, trade, investment and technology between the two countries, will endeavour to throw more light on this question.

Persistent trade imbalances

Trade between Japan and South Korea has grown massively since the mid-1960s, particularly during the second half of the 1980s, but it has been characterised throughout by a trade surplus for Japan. This has been a persistent source of friction and has, on occasions, become notably politicised. South Koreans, of course, share many of the complaints of other Western and Asian trading partners of Japan about unbalanced trading relationships with Japan, but these are overlaid with the emotional resentment that Japan is once again exploiting them and not playing fair with them.

Bilateral trade was extremely limited until the normalisation of relations in 1965, when the total stood at only $211 million. By 1970 this had grown to $1.4 billion and by 1980 to $8.9 billion. Despite a certain amount of stagnation in the early 1980s, by 1991 this bilateral trade had reached $33.5 billion. Trade was particularly stimulated in the second half of the 1980s by the effects of yen-dollar-won exchange rate changes in the wake of the G-7 1985 Plaza Agreement and the industrial restructuring taking place in both economies. This trade has differing importance to the two countries, however. For Japan, in 1991, trade with South Korea represented only 6% of its total trade, but for South Korea, trade with Japan represented 22% of its total trade. This South Korean dependence is even more pronounced in terms of its imports, for in 1991 Japan supplied 26% of South Korea's total imports.

For both countries, the other country ranks along with the United States as part of a significant trade triangle. The normalisation of relations with Japan and the start of the South Korean export drive in the mid-1960s caused a switch whereby, for South Korea, Japan replaced the United States as its main source of imports and the United States replaced Japan as its main export market. This pattern has persisted ever since. With the exception of 1983, the United States has been South Korea's premier export market, with Japan, often well behind, in second place. Again, with the exceptions of 1982-3, Japan has maintained its position as South Korea's leading source of imports, with the United States in second place. More surprising, however, has been South Korea's rapid rise as a source of imports for Japan - from ninth place in 1985 to second place behind the United States in 1988-9 - though by 1990 it had slipped back down behind China and Indonesia.

The bilateral trade imbalance, despite the marked expansion of trade in the second half of the 1980s, has become significant and it has been persistently

Japan and Korea in the 1990s

in favour of Japan. As shown in Table 6.2, it has fluctuated around the $3-4 billion mark, but rose to nearly $6 billion in 1990 and it reached its highest level ever, $8.5 billion, in 1991. The first six months of 1992 showed a slight decrease over the same period in 1991, but the yearly deficit is still expected to be high.

Table 6.2: Japan's trade ($ billion)

	1985	1987	1988	1989	1990	1991
Exports to S.Korea	7.2	13.3	15.4	16.5	17.5	20.9
Imports from S.Korea	4.1	8.2	11.8	12.9	11.7	12.4
Trade balance	3.1	5.1	3.6	3.6	5.8	8.5

Source: IMF (1992)

In order to explain this persistent imbalance, it is necessary to examine further the structure of the bilateral trade and the linkages with the United States. Although the nature of the goods flowing between Japan and South Korea has changed over the years, the structure has remained remarkably similar. In the 1960s and 1970s, when South Korea was exporting textiles to the United States, it imported textile machinery and synthetic fibres from Japan. When South Korea moved into shipbuilding, it began by importing steel, engines and heavy electrical machinery from Japan. Now, its electrical and electronic consumer goods exports rely heavily on Japanese components and assembly-line equipment. Thus, while the share of South Korean imports from Japan held by chemicals and heavy machinery is now decreasing, that held by electrical and transport machinery is increasing. So, as South Korea moves up the technological ladder in terms of its exports, it still finds it necessary, for each product in turn, to rely on importing Japanese equipment or components.

To take the South Korean electronics industry as an example, in total around 60% of its domestic needs for components come from imports - but 36% of these domestic needs are supplied by Japan alone. For most of the major items imported, such as television parts, audio heads, computer parts and colour television tuners, Japan provides between 55% to 100% of all the imports (Bloom 1992 p.61). Even for those components which are produced within South Korea, foreign companies, through wholly-owned subsidiaries or joint ventures, supply about 40%; Japanese companies are involved here too (this aspect of Japanese FDI will be examined further below).

Amongst South Korean exports to Japan, labour-intensive industrial products, such as textiles, and agricultural and fishery products have predominated, and, thereby, helped to add a price differential by comparison with the higher-value products which South Korea has been importing from Japan. Although, in the second half of the 1980s, the cost-competitive Korean producers of consumer electronics began to make significant inroads, textiles, food and steel still provide the mainstay of South Korean exports to Japan. The imbalance in the machinery trade is particularly marked; according to South Korean figures, in 1991, South Korean machinery exports to Japan were only $600 million, compared with $7.6 billion of machinery imports from Japan.

On Prime Minister Nakasone's January 1983 visit to Seoul, economic assistance dominated the bilateral economic discussions for the last time. Since then the focus of discussion has been very much on trade and technology issues. The degree of South Korean frustration with the trade imbalance is exemplified by their habit, which still persists, of citing the trade imbalance figures not simply in annual totals, but in cumulative terms. For example, in 1985, the South Korean trade and industry minister cited the total deficit from 1965 to that year as being $30 billion. The Japanese, naturally, object to this unique manner of accounting.

In trying to correct this trade imbalance, two options have been open to the South Koreans: to reduce imports from Japan, by diversification, localisation or selective import banning, and to increase exports to Japan.

Attempts to restrict or completely exclude certain Japanese products from the South Korean market have represented the most long-standing policy approach. It is, for example, impossible to find the ubiquitous Japanese cars or advertisement hoardings for Japanese products on the streets of Seoul. Under a 1977 government directive, on the grounds of diversifying imports, 50 products from South-east Asian countries (Japan was not specifically designated but was the implied target) were subjected to import approval. In 1980 the list was expanded and the formal restrictions were applied to the country which had been the largest exporter to South Korea in the previous year (i.e. Japan); when, in 1982, Saudi Arabia became the largest import source, this qualification was changed to the largest import source over the past five years. This list has fluctuated in length, from 162 Japanese products subject to this system in July 1982 to a peak of 344 items in April 1988, before falling to a total of 258 in 1991. This list is regularly amended; in May 1991 30 items were removed and 20 items, including for example colour TVs with a screen of more than 25 inches, were added, while in October 1991 8 items were removed and 8 added. In late 1991-early 1992 the Korean government also moved to control the supply of special foreign exchange loans to enterprises which import machinery from Japan.

The problem for the South Korean government is to balance the needs of its own industries for key components and products from Japan against its fears that the Japanese would come in and dominate certain sectors of the domestic market if allowed complete freedom. Certainly, some Japanese companies may well have been induced to invest in joint ventures and technology transfer with Korean companies as a result of the import restrictions, but others can, just as easily, have been made more negative by such an approach. The Japanese feel that these Korean restrictions are introduced on a product once Korean manufacturers themselves begin producing that product. The Japanese government has protested regularly about these restrictions, which it regards as a violation of GATT principles prohibiting quantitative restrictions (MITI 1992 p.57), but has done nothing to retaliate. In part, this may well have been because, in practice, Japanese companies have been able to find ways around these restrictions.

In fact, it may well have been the South Korean decision to try to close one of these loopholes in mid-1991 that prompted the Japanese government to show the limits of its toleration. The South Korean government announced that, with effect from July 1991, new regulations on 'country of origin' certification of imported goods would be imposed. The main   intention, though not explicitly stated as such, was to limit Japanese goods coming in through South-east Asian, especially ASEAN countries. Not long after this announcement, the Japanese government informed the Korean government that it was considering lodging a suit with the GATT complaining that the earlier import restriction system contradicted the GATT principles of equal trade treatment. The South Korean government does not seem to have been impressed by this threat, arguing that the failure of the trade imbalance to improve would entail the system's retention until the mid-1990s at least (*Korea Times* 12 June 1991). There is a certain amount of bravado to this stance, since Korean economists outside government do admit that this 'discriminatory practice' is not sanctioned by GATT; if the Japanese were to press their case in the GATT, they would surely win. Political considerations - leverage in other issue areas - are, therefore, most likely to affect whether and when the Japanese appeal to GATT.

Although these restrictions on Japanese products were imposed in the name of diversification, a positive South Korean approach to seeking other sources of imported components and intermediate technology beyond the obvious alternative source, the United States, did not really begin until the late 1980s. President Chun's European tour in 1986 was accompanied by much rhetoric about 'looking to Europe' for components etc., but not until 1989, as a forerunner of President Roh's European visit, was a specific programme, under which 429 products were identified for importation from the EC, inaugurated. Nevertheless, this programme has not been very successful, for a number of reasons: European companies have not always been willing or able to supply the necessary products, 'political' considerations over the trade surplus with the United States have dictated a concentration on 'buy American', and existing production lines set up to utilise Japanese components cannot easily be changed to utilise other foreign products.

The South Korean government has also been nudging smaller firms to go into the parts business as part of a parallel 'localisation' policy. Domestic production, of course, reduces imports, boosts employment and consolidates the industrial base, but there are problems. As, indeed, in the case of Japanese parts producers, the Korean parts industry is very low value-added and the efficiency of capital is far from optimal. Localisation is, therefore, likely to be only a medium-term solution to the trade imbalance.

The other main element of the Korean response has been to try to increase exports to Japan. However, the Japanese market is a much more difficult one than, for example, the US and Canadian markets, where the South Koreans had notable export successes during the 1980s. The South Koreans, as indeed other NICs and Western exporters too, are faced with a sophisticated and variegated Japanese market, in which fashions change rapidly. In official negotiations, the South Korean side blames its difficulties on tariff and non-tariff barriers in Japan and the Japanese side's failure to sufficiently encourage - and, in one case, its open discouragement of - Korean imports.

The South Koreans, have, of course, asked the Japanese to improve market access for their products by reducing tariffs on marine and farm products and on light industrial goods such as leather and knitwear. When Korean Trade and Industry Minister Hahn Bong-soo visited Tokyo in June 1992 to meet his Japanese counterpart in the first ever official conference between trade ministers, he took with him a list of 16 Korean-made products from which tariffs should be removed, but in the final 'action plan' approved in July 1992 the Japanese only agreed to take up the tariff issue in the GATT Round context. Japanese tariffs in general have been reduced to the lowest level of any major industrial nation, but they are still kept at an above-average level for certain products which the South Koreans are particularly interested in exporting to Japan. However, this is not discrimination against South Korea alone, since other developing countries trying to export these goods to Japan suffer similarly.

The Koreans have also asked for an extension of the Generalised System of Preferences (GSP) to more Korean products. Japan introduced its GSP for all developing countries in 1971 and by the early 1980s South Korea already accounted for more than one quarter of all Japan's GSP-covered imports from developing countries (it has remained the largest beneficiary of the Japanese GSP system). The Japanese, however, like many Western governments, now feel that South Korea has effectively graduated from the class of developing countries. At the request of the South Korean government, the Japanese government did agree to renew the GSP privileges for a further ten years in March 1991, when they were due to expire, but it has been reluctant to widen these privileges any further. In fact, the share of South Korean exports to Japan which are covered by GSP has been steadily falling as South Korea has moved into increasingly sophisticated exports.

A marker for future tension between the two countries, however, has been laid by the Japanese response to increasing Korean competitiveness in some of these less technology-intensive sectors. In a remarkable mirror-image of past Western actions against imports from Japan, Japan itself has negotiated the first 'voluntary export restraint' (VER) with Korean manufacturers. As South Korean exports of knitwear, steel and cement to Japan grew, Japanese producers protested to the Japanese government. It was knitwear that was made the scapegoat, when formal action was precipitated by the decision in October 1988 of the Japanese Knitting Industry Association to lodge an anti-dumping suit against South Korean knitwear exporters (in January-August 1988, South Korean knitwear imports grew by 79% over the previous year's period, giving them around half of Japan's total knitwear imports).

Anxious to avoid a direct governmental-level confrontation, both governments encouraged negotiations between the industry associations. The result, in February 1989, was a VER agreement that South Korean producers would limit the annual growth rate of their exports to Japan to less than 1% for three years (*Nihon Keizai Shimbun* 2 February, 21 March 1989). The dispute had been a real headache for MITI at a time when it had been trying to show to the world that Japan was not protectionist and was encouraging imports; it had been reluctant to proceed with an anti-dumping action but was under strong pressure from industry. MITI was, however, relieved at the result and hoped that it might thereby act as a deterrent to South Korean producers of other products to moderate their exports. By encouraging a politically palatable solution, however, the Japanese government lost an opportunity to examine fairly an anti-dumping complaint under its new procedures, clarified in 1986 but never tested.

At the moment, however, the South Korean problems mainly revolve around the cost versus the quality of their products and the effect of the distribution system and other non-tariff barriers inside Japan. When South Korean goods succeed in the Japanese market, it is more because of cheapness than superior quality. According to a 1989 survey of Japanese consumers by the Korea Foreign Trade Association, 77% of those interviewed bought Korean goods because of cost considerations, compared with only 3% who cited quality. The rise and fall of Korean consumer electronics exports to Japan in the second half of the 1980s exemplifies this point. Until the mid-1980s, the bulk of South Korean consumer appliances entering Japan were limited to two categories: simple appliances such as humidifiers, which required little in the way of after-sales service, and appliances in which Japan had lost its competitive edge, such as radio cassette recorders. But in 1986 Jusco, a major supermarket store group in Japan, began to import video cassette recorders (VCRs) from Samsung and market them under the brand name of 'Samson'. In the same year, a rival supermarket group, Daiei, began importing electric fans, the following year VCRs, and, in 1988, colour TVs and refrigerators, from Lucky Goldstar and marketed them under the name 'Kolchina'. Some companies even set up 'NICs superstores' to sell exclusively products from South Korea and the other NICs. This policy came to be called kaihatsu yunyu (importing from developing countries) and was used to describe the manufacturing of products in the NICs to Japanese specifications in return for exclusive Japanese marketing rights.

From the Japanese side, the rapid appreciation of the yen after the 1985 Plaza agreement prompted this switch to cheaper Korean sources; Daiei's imports from Lucky Goldstar tended to retail at 30-50% of the cost of the major Japanese companies' rival products. The result was a rapid increase in the Korean sales of these electrical consumer goods in Japan. But by 1989, these sales had peaked and settled down to a smaller market niche than would have been expected two years before. Partly, this was due to the loss of competitiveness of the Korean producers, for high wage rises in South Korea in the 1987-89 period (around 20% per annum in the manufacturing sector) inevitably led to price rises. Partly, however, it reflected a determined move by some of the medium-sized Japanese makers, such as Funai and Crown, who had previously concentrated on exports, into the domestic market. Noting the Korean successes, for example, Funai began to sell VCRs domestically for the first time in 1987; within two years it had gained 7% of the domestic market, mainly at the expense of Korean products.

The Korean producers also suffered because the initiative in this new importing boom had come from Japanese companies. It was the Japanese who were providing the marketing strategy, the specifications (and even production line technology in some cases), and the after-sales care (Komaki 1991 pp.182-90). When rising costs in South Korea made it more cost-effective to import from cheaper sites elsewhere in Asia, then the Koreans were left exposed. The Koreans also complain against other non-tariff barriers which can impede imports from South Korea. For example, in 1987, Japanese complaints over the use of additives temporarily halted imports of instant noodles and kimchi. The Koreans have become more conscious of the need to overcome Japanese doubts about their products' quality and a large trade fair was held in Tokyo and Osaka in June 1992 under the title 'Korea for Quality'. Samsung reported a marked upward trend in its business suit sales to Japan in early 1991 after it started marketing Italian-designed Korean-made suits, which met strict Japanese tastes in materials and sewing.

The Korean companies have been too easily discouraged by the Japanese market's difficulties; Trade and Industry Minister Hahn actually described Korean companies as 'more or less negligent in attacking the Japanese market' (*Korea Times*, 21 June 1992). Nevertheless, the Korean companies do find it very difficult to operate within the Japanese distribution system on their own. The large chaebol do have offices in Tokyo and other Japanese cities but they still feel rather isolated. This is even more the case for the small and medium-sized Korean companies. In an attempt to reduce this problem, the two governments agreed in November 1990 that an official of the Small and Medium Enterprises Agency (attached to MITI) would be stationed in Seoul to assist these smaller Korean companies. The major Japanese trading companies themselves are reluctant to take on some Korean products. When South Korea began to produce quality steel at subsidised prices, some Japanese importers went down to the docks to remove 'made-in-Korea' designations, for they feared that, if their major Japanese suppliers had discovered they were importing Korean steel, they would have been black-listed.

Although trade disputes have primarily taken on the character of South Korean complaints about Japan, the Japanese do have a number of issues which they complain to the Koreans about. The import diversification programme, which restricts certain Japanese products from entering the Korean market, has been discussed above. In addition, the Japanese government feels concerned about the legal status of Japanese companies operating in South Korea and intellectual property protection.

All trading companies, whether Korean or foreign, must receive permission from the South Korean MTI in order to operate. However, the Japanese argue, when the South Korean subsidiary or office of a Japanese company applies to undertake trading in unrestricted products, then permission is difficult to obtain. Often these companies receive permission only to operate representative 'buying-only' offices, which handicap them from developing business. Since 1980 the Japanese government has regularly protested, but, after the November 1990 Japan-South Korean ministerial meeting, the South Koreans hinted that they would look positively at easing permission for Japanese sogoshosha to be involved in exporting back to Japan (thereby helping to improve the trade balance). The South Korean concern to protect its weaker Korean trading companies against its Japanese rivals has remained paramount. Indeed, the chaebol trading companies argue that the crucial question is not the scope of the Japanese companies' activities, but whether they should be let in at all. In the negotiation of the 'action plan', agreed by both governments in early July, the South Korean side gave ground on exporting access for the sogoshosha in return for a limited Japanese government involvement in a scientific and technological cooperative foundation.

In July 1987 South Korea introduced a patent system, after signing the relevant international agreements, but there were special exceptions for the United States, which was accorded retrospective protection for over 500 products. The EC strongly protested against this special treatment and when no agreement could be reached, in January 1988 suspended GSP treatment for Korean products. Only in September 1991 did the South Korean government agree to accord patent protection to over 350 European medical and chemical products. The Japanese government has protested against the South Koreans' discriminatory action (MITI 1992 pp.57-8) and, at the 1990 ministerial meeting, the South Koreans did agree that when agreement was reached with the EC then a similar treatment of Japanese products would be considered. This did not occur, and the dispute was left in abeyance until the Uruguay Round of GATT reached a conclusion on most-favoured-nation principles agreements. However, the painfully slow progress towards the GATT Round conclusion persuaded the Japanese to request, as part of the July 1992 'action plan' package, that bilateral negotiations on the issue begin later in the summer. The Japanese side has proposed developing exchanges between the patent agencies in both countries, but this idea has not yet been taken up. For the Japanese, as indeed for other countries, the issue of protection of intellectual property rights has an important impact on decisions to invest or participate in technology transfer, which will be discussed below.

Ending development assistance

When diplomatic relations were established in 1965, Japan promised $800 million economic assistance in order to settle property and other claims outstanding. The economic aid package, to be disbursed over a ten-year period, consisted of $300 million in grants, $200 million in long-term low interest government loans, and $300 million in commercial loans. The government loans were used for the construction of railways, motorways and dams; the grants were used to purchase equipment for developing the marine and agricultural sectors, textile, steel and machinery industries. The Japanese commitment of economic assistance strongly resembled the reparations given to a number of other East Asian countries in the 1950s and 1960s.

The first new loans to South Korea were extended in 1971. At first, commodity loans comprised the major part of Japanese ODA, but from the late 1970s yen credits became more prominent. These were used for project-based assistance, for export industries, agricultural development and multi-purpose dams. By 1980 Japan had provided 107 billion yen in grants and 317 billion yen in loans to South Korea. By that time the Japanese loans to South Korea were averaging around 20 billion yen per year. In 1981, when a new round of loan negotiations began, the Japanese initially offered to double the annual total to 40 billion yen on a five-year basis, making 200 billion yen or $1 billion. The South Koreans, however, asked for $6 billion, split between ODA funds and commodity loans. The final settlement enacted by Nakasone in January 1983, as shown in Chapter 2, was for $4 billion, spread over seven years (retrospectively from 1982), which would be divided into $1.85 billion yen-denominated ODA loans, $350 million yen bank loans, and $1.8 billion Export-Import Bank dollar-denominated loans (Kim, H.N. 1983 pp.95-6). This agreement marked a substantial new commitment and during the years 1982-84 Japanese ODA to South Korea grew by slightly less than 10% per annum, a rate far surpassing the average rate of increase in Japanese loans to other countries.

South Korea, therefore, became for a brief period in the mid-1980s the largest recipient of Japanese ODA, before it was overtaken by China. Initially, the South Koreans used the loans for urban infrastructural modernisation such as sewage and waste disposal facilities and for programmes of agricultural and marine research. The South Koreans, however, became increasingly interested in up-grading the technological level of their industries and, as such, their requests found difficulty in meeting Japanese ODA guidelines. They actually made no aid request at all in 1988 and agreement on the final tranche was only reached in early 1990 after the Japanese accepted the South Korean proposal for assistance in the Seoul underground system extension project. South Korea, therefore, has ceased to be a recipient of Japanese aid and the focus of bilateral interest has shifted to investment and technology transfer.

Investment patterns

Global foreign direct investment (FDI), since 1983, has been growing at a rate far exceeding that of world trade growth. FDI flows have been largely concentrated in the G-7 countries, but in the developing world the East Asian countries, including South Korea, have been important recipients. Japan is the largest single investor in the East Asian economies as a whole, although, on a cumulative basis, both the United States and the EC are the single most important FDI partners for some individual countries. After averaging around $10 billion per annum for the first half of the 1980s, Japanese FDI grew rapidly in the second half to peak at $67 billion in FY1989; by FY1991 the total had slipped to $42 billion.

Post-war Japanese investment in East Asia falls into four main categories: resource development, especially minerals and oil; import substitution, especially components and intermediate goods; export production for third markets using developing country bases; and the service sector. As far as South Korea is concerned, Japanese interest has been mainly focused on the second and third categories, but with the service sector becoming increasingly important. South Korea, by comparison with other East Asian nations, was extremely reticent about encouraging inward FDI, which it saw as a double-edged sword. South Korea financed its economic development through external loans (so much so that by 1984 it had become the world's fourth most indebted country) and preferred Korean firms to pursue technology through licensing agreements. The ballooning external debt and the realisation that certain high technology might only be available through associated FDI led the Chun administration to relax the rules. In 1984 new administrative measures reversed the previous approval system, so that all areas of the economy, except for a few specific sectors, were opened to foreign investment. The following year the beginning of the appreciation of the yen, after the Plaza agreement, started the rapid outflow of Japanese FDI. South Korea was to be an early target.

Although the South Korean market had been generally unattractive as a FDI location until the mid-1980s, the Japanese, nevertheless, had been the major investors. From 1965-70 the Japanese supplied 43% of an admittedly minute total amount of FDI, from 1971-80 the Japanese share rose to 51%, and from 1981-85 the share was 49% (partly caused by low levels of investment in 1981-82 when bilateral political relations were poor). But in 1985 the Japanese share began to rise notably, to 63%, and was to remain high until 1988 when it began to decline. According to South Korean figures, over the period from 1962 to June 1991 Japan accounted for 47% of the total cumulative FDI.

Table 6.3 Japanese FDI flows into South Korea

(FY basis, $ million)

1985	1986	1987	1988	1989	1990	1991	Total 1951-91
134	436	647	483	606	284	260	4398

As can be seen from Table 6.3, the amounts of Japanese FDI grew markedly from FY1985, reached a peak of $647 million in FY1987 and remained not far below that level for the following two years, before falling significantly in FY1990 to $284 million and further to $260 million in FY 1991. Although the amounts grew noticeably in FY1985-86, the share of total Japanese FDI actually remained relatively static, at around 2%. But, as overall Japanese FDI increased further during the later years of the 1980s, the share going to South Korea actually decreased and by FY1990 represented only 0.5% of total Japanese FDI. Therefore, Japanese FDI is far more important to the South Koreans than the South Korean sites are to the Japanese.

One characteristic of Japanese FDI into South Korea has been that, right from the early days in the late 1960s, the relative size of the Japanese investments has been small; in the number of cases by cumulative total from 1962 to June 1991 the Japanese represent 59%, well above their share by value. This is partly because much FDI is by small and medium-sized companies, which initially found it easier to move to the more culturally-similar Korea (and Taiwan) than elsewhere in Asia, and partly because joint ventures have been the predominant form of FDI. US and European companies have been more inclined to establish strongly majority-owned or even wholly-owned subsidiaries. The main motivation for Japanese companies has been production efficiency, moving labour-intensive processes aimed at exporting to third markets to South Korea, where production costs were lower. A 1987 survey of foreign companies operating in South Korea showed that out of 212 Japanese companies, 20 exported 100% of their products (compared with 8 out of 62 US firms and none out of 34 European firms) and a total of 130 exported more than 70% of their products (Jung 1989 pp. 69-74).

The corollary of this kind of investment, however, has been that as labour costs began to rise in South Korea (the annual wage rises in the manufacturing sector averaged 20% over the 1987-90 period) and labour relations deteriorated (the number of strikes increased significantly in 1987-89) causing shipment delays, Japanese companies began to look elsewhere, particularly in South-east Asia, for production sites. Asics Corporation, a major shoe company which had sourced nearly 40% of its total sports shoe production from its Korean factories, decided in 1989 to begin shifting its production to Indonesia for these very reasons. In a few cases, the 'runaway shop' style of certain Japanese companies in stopping their operations has brought confrontation with workers demanding compensation. When Sumida Electric Co. decided to dismiss all its workers and close down, without any warning, in October 1989, a prolonged campaign for compensation involving sit-ins and hunger strikes followed. Although, by 1991, the South Korean government had brought wage rises under control and the number of labour disputes had decreased significantly, there were few signs of a recovery in Japanese interest in FDI. With the general outflow of Japanese FDI, anyway, now slowly declining, South Korea is unlikely to again become a major destination for Japanese FDI during the next few years.

South Korean FDI is a more recent and far smaller phenomenon than Japanese FDI. Although a few examples of natural resource FDI occurred during the 1970s, not until the mid-1980s did South Korean FDI become important. In 1987 South Korean FDI reached $333 million, compared with a cumulative total of $633 million for the whole period from 1962 to 1986. From the mid-1980s the share of South Korean FDI which went to exploiting natural resources in developing countries decreased. Instead, manufacturing FDI both in South-east Asia (for export to third markets by utilising cheaper labour costs) and within the United States itself (as defensive investment to hold on to market share which otherwise might have been lost by import restrictions) became just as important (Taniguchi 1990 pp. 83-91; Jung 1990 pp. 183-96).

FDI into Japan has been limited, reaching only a cumulative total of 76 cases by the end of 1989. Although the South Koreans do appreciate the size and sophistication of the Japanese market and the technology and balance of payments advantages of investing in Japan, the number of investments is growing only slowly. Some Korean companies are beginning to see the advantages of joint ventures in Japan. In June 1991 a major Korean construction company, after finding that its Tokyo branch established two years earlier was doing little business, decided to enter into a joint venture with an Osaka-based medium-sized Japanese construction company, Saimon, with the intention thereby of entering not just the housing construction business but also the Kansai international airport project. Nevertheless, the current trend to invest either in South-east Asia or the United States (and increasingly Europe) is likely to remain predominant for the coming few years. As such, the investment imbalance issue, while clearly a second order one compared to the trade imbalance issue in Korean eyes, may well rise in importance as a source of tension in the bilateral relationship in the medium term.

Technology transfer

However, for the immediate future, the South Koreans will be most concerned about the technology transfer aspect of Japanese FDI. In its early years of industrial development, South Korea, like other similarly developing East Asian countries, suffered from inadequate research infrastructure and a shortage of technically-skilled manpower. Many new industries, therefore, were created and, subsequently, up-graded through the use of foreign technology. This technology input came through a mixture of technology licensing, sub-contracting, original equipment manufacturing (OEM) and joint ventures/joint development. Also included under the Japanese definition of 'industrial cooperation' would be transfers effected through wholly-owned subsidiaries operating in South Korea. In the South Korean case, joint ventures predominated in the early technology transfers. In the electronics industry, for example, in 1976 over half of all employment was in foreign-owned or joint-venture companies.

The acquisition and absorption of foreign technology involves both government and private sector efforts. In the 1980s, the South Korean government became keen to improve the foreign technology transfer climate. Revisions to the technology transfer system were made in 1984 and 1988 to liberalise the process. Having concluded a science and technology agreement with the United States in 1976 (renewed in 1988), the South Korean government tried to reach similar agreements with other advanced countries, including Japan. Efforts were made to encourage Korean scientists, many of whom were involved in research in the United States, to return home (Bloom 1992 p.94), although the Chun administration's efforts to strengthen research and development capacity by amalgamating two research institutes into the Korean Advanced Institute of Science and Technology for these researchers to use failed to work effectively.

Corporate approaches have differed. Hyundai has generally avoided joint ventures, preferring to employ foreign technicians, purchase foreign machinery and equipment and license the relevant technologies from overseas. From its formation in 1967 until 1984, Hyundai Motor Co. licensed a total of 54 technologies from eight different countries; a group of contracted British technicians were instrumental in developing the Pony car during 1974-77, but then a technical assistance agreement was reached with Mitsubishi Motors in 1981. Lucky Goldstar has taken the opposite approach, setting up independent joint venture companies by hiving off promising sectors from the original parent company. It joined with Hitachi Cable in 1969 to convert its own company division into a new joint venture, Goldstar Cable; others, such as Goldstar Electric with NEC and Goldstar Instrument and Electric with Fuji Electric, followed in the early 1970s (Bloom 1992 pp. 90-3).

The United States and Japan have been the principal suppliers of foreign technology to South Korea, but with Japan as the major contributor in terms of number of cases but not in value. According to South Korean figures, from 1962 to June 1991 the Japanese supplied 3,683 technologies (or 51% of the total imported technologies), valued at $1.5 billion (or 31% of the total). However, despite this strong Japanese record, the South Korean government has regularly complained since the early 1980s about the lack of a positive Japanese approach to technology transfer and the particular reluctance to transfer the latest technologies. The Japanese government has consistently argued that this is a question for the private sector and that Japanese companies make their decisions on commercial grounds rather than as part of a concerted 'political' campaign against the Koreans; instead, the onus lies on the Korean government and Korean companies to create a climate more conducive to technology transfer.

There is some truth in both sides' arguments. Certainly, there is a perception amongst many Japanese companies that the 'boomerang phenomenon' would work to their disadvantage - aiding potential rivals would lead to a loss of their own domestic or third markets. Some also feel that the Koreans do not place a sufficiently high monetary value on the technology and that, once the contract is finished, the Korean side is quick to reinterpret production agreements or ask for additional technology free of charge. Not all joint ventures have proceeded smoothly as a result; Sanyo left a joint venture with Samsung in 1983, Ishikawajima Harima left Samsung Heavy Industrial Co. in 1984 and NEC withdrew from Goldstar Electric in 1987.

Yet, although some Japanese companies clearly feel threatened or dissatisfied, the fact that 333 cases in 1990 alone were contracted suggests that there are many Japanese companies who see benefits from technology arrangements with Korean companies. In some instances, too, advanced technologies have been transferred. In July 1989, Hitachi, which has had a long relationship with Lucky Goldstar, controversially decided to sell its 1 megabit DRAM semiconductor technology to that company; this was followed in June 1990 by an agreement on 4 megabit DRAM technology. While moving ahead into the development of 16 megabit semiconductors, Hitachi can expand its production capability for the 1 and 4 megabit DRAMs through Goldstar's OEM export. Another consideration for Hitachi was the belief that if they had not supplied them then some other foreign rival would have sold the technology.

The South Koreans, on occasions, have succeeded in inducing Japanese technology by making the most of the possibilities of playing the Japanese off against other competitors. The Japanese decision to get involved, despite the initial antagonism of the Japanese steel industry, in the second Pohang Steel (POSCO) plant was spurred by the wish to prevent European competitors gaining the contracts. Similarly, in the current bidding for the major contracts on the planned Seoul-Pusan high speed railway, the Koreans are making technology transfer a key component in deciding whether it will be the Japanese, French or Germans that succeed.

An early example of what may become a new form of technology transfer can be seen in the April 1992 agreement between Fujitsu and Samsung. They signed a five-year cross-licensing agreement to give each firm access to the other's semiconductor technology, but, owing to the disparity in value of the two companies' patents, Samsung would also pay $30 million to Fujitsu (*Nihon Keizai Shimbun* 22 April 1992). This agreement shows that the Japanese feel that, with Korean technology advancing, a costly 'patent war' needs to be avoided, but that the Koreans realise that a 'free ride' on technology is not possible and that it is sometimes necessary to pay - even pay heavily - for top-class technology. Similar negotiations are reportedly also now occurring between other leading Korean and Japanese companies in these sectors.

The Japanese government has tried to avoid direct involvement in technology transfer issues, but in 1983 did agree to establish a joint Japan-South Korean industrial technology cooperation committee at the working officials' level. The main result has been to encourage Japanese government support for training and technical assistance. In 1984 it did introduce a new system for training Korean technicians and, by the end of 1989 a total of 910 Koreans had spent periods on attachment to Japanese factories. Also, from the same time, around 50 Japanese technicians a year have been sent to Korean companies and research organisations. In 1991 the system was revised to give special emphasis to small- and medium-sized Korean enterprises; about 50 Korean training staff were received and about

30 experts sent as result. Cooperation between national research institutes began in 1973, but, under strong pressure from the South Korean government, a Science and Technology Cooperation Agreement was signed in December 1985 which strengthened the joint research and personnel exchange programmes. A total of 99 research themes were decided on, covering subjects from acid rain prevention to diesel fuel engine systems to compound metals (Matsumoto 1991 pp. 34-7). Not all personnel exchanges are made under official schemes; during the 1980s, Korean companies often recruited Japanese engineers for post-retirement jobs or weekend moonlighting contracts!

The negotiations for the 'action plan' during the first half of 1992 saw considerable differences of opinion over the Korean proposal to set up a joint foundation which would help finance Japan's technology transfer to Korea. The Koreans initially proposed a $160 million capitalised foundation, with Japan putting up three-quarters; the government refused and the Keidanren offered $40 million. The Koreans tried to up the ante, but as the deadline approached they were forced to slash their requests. In the end, it was agreed that each side would set up an $8 million foundation, primarily from private sector sources but with a small annual input from the two governments, a disappointment to the Korean negotiators, and as such not likely to have much short-term impact.

One of the ironies of the Korean approach and the Japanese response has been that, although the South Koreans are driven by the desire to reduce both their trade deficit with and their import dependence on Japan, their concerted efforts to obtain Japanese technology (by implication, increasing their technological dependence on Japan, at least in the short run) have actually helped to do the opposite, to increase them. Although not true of all sectors, certainly in many cases the introduction of technology from Japan has resulted in factory lines and production systems which closely resemble their Japanese counterparts and which rely on (imported) Japanese components and intermediate materials. This has aggravated rather than improved the trade balance.

Competition or cooperation in third markets

As suggested earlier in this chapter, the Japan-South Korean economic relationship is closely bound in with the United States. Both Japan and South Korea are strong rivals in the US market but both have been able to find significant market shares. Just as they first found it possible for them both to take shares in cutlery and textile goods, now they find it the same for cars and VCRs. During the 1980s, the South Koreans followed the Japanese into the United States (and, indeed, the EC) offering a similar mix of products but trying to undercut them. They had some initial success, but found that the appreciation of the won against the yen in the late 1980s, concerns about quality and after-sales service (by comparison with the Japanese), and anti-dumping actions handicapped them. Nevertheless, Japanese companies do find cause for concern in continued Korean attempts to undercut them on the American market. Samsung has now overtaken its Japanese rivals to take the number one slot in supplying 4-megabit DRAM semi-conductors to US industry (*Nihon Keizai Shimbun* 7 May 1992).

While the competitive element has been predominant, there are a small but increasing number of cooperative ventures which involve US companies. Often the Americans are responsible for the design, development and marketing, the Japanese for the sophisticated production and components, and the Koreans for the simple production and assembly of the final product. Taiyo Yuden's ceramic condensers and Shin-etsu Chemical's silicon resin are the result of this approach; Isuzu Motors is cooperating in a tripartite venture to obtain South Korean ignition coils and other electrical parts (Fukagawa 1987 pp. 14-15). Tripartite cooperation is no longer limited to American companies either, as Europeans and Koreans get to know each other better. Hyundai Precision & Industrial Co. now makes parts for the BK117 helicopter, developed jointly by Japan's Kawasaki Heavy Industries and Germany's Deutsche Aerospace. There has also been a growing number of cases where Japanese companies have secured contracts in third countries but procured their basic materials from South Korea. These various kinds of cooperative work are beginning to encourage a new division of labour between the two countries.

There are also signs that companies and organisations from the two countries could well develop their exchanges in the broader sub-regional context of the opening up of the Japan Sea (or East Sea as the Koreans call it). This, of course, involves China, the Soviet Union/Russia, and North Korea. It will, therefore, be discussed below in the context of North Korea's own economic development and relations with Japan. Another emerging form of cooperation may be seen in the agreement in May 1992 between the Export-Import Banks of Japan and South Korea to exchange information about exports of industrial plant to Third World countries.

North Korean economic problems

North Korea, like its southern counterpart, has managed to transform a backward economy ravaged by war into a predominantly industrial one. However, since North Korea ceased publishing comprehensive economic statistics in the mid-1960s, it has become difficult to measure and compare the progress of its economy with the South's. The World Bank stopped giving estimates of North Korea's GNP growth and per capita GNP in the late 1970s; the South Korean National Unification Board estimates that the North's GNP was $23 billion in 1990, compared with the South's $237 billion the same year (Rhee 1992 p.58). Recent Soviet estimates suggest that the North's per capita GNP figure could be as low as $ 400-500 (compared with over $5,000 in the South). Other estimates, while not showing as great a disparity as those figures, do nonetheless suggest a large gap and one that is growing, since North Korea not only averaged probably only around 2% GNP growth in the 1980s (well below the South Korean average of 9%), but also almost certainly recorded negative GNP growth in 1990 and 1991.

The North Koreans initially patterned their economic system closely on the Soviet model of central planning, but although this played a positive role in the early stages of industrialisation, the economic costs of a heavily 'statist' mode of development have become increasingly apparent (Chung, J.S. 1983 pp. 164-96). Industrial growth has been affected by the inability of the energy and mining industries to provide reliable and sufficient supplies of power and raw materials; transportational infrastructure remains inadequate; grain crop yields have fluctuated; and foreign currency shortages and an inability to repay outstanding debts (estimated by the end of 1991 to have reached around $6 billion) have restricted the import of Western technology and plant. The 1980s opened with 'ten long-range economic goals' for the decade; these have been subsumed into the current Seven-Year Economic Plan, due to end in 1993, and subsequently have been quietly down-played in public mention. Clearly reliance on revolutionary zeal and exhortation, such as the 'speed of the eighties' and, more recently, the '200 days struggle' campaigns, has not produced the desired results.

Whereas other socialist countries, with China's 'open door' and 'four modernisations' in the van, began to incorporate market elements into their economies during the 1980s, North Korea, if anything, strengthened the role of central planning. Not just through his 'on-the-spot guidance' but also through his arbitrary interference in plans already made, Kim has the final say (Foster-Carter 1992 pp. 12-16). Any significant change in economic policy poses presentational problems, for unlike Deng Xiaoping in China and Mikhail Gorbachev in the Soviet Union, who could claim to be pursuing new policies in order to overcome the (partial) failures of their predecessors, Kim Il-sung does not want to undermine the prestige which he has invested in earlier policies.

North Korean economic planners have to walk a delicate tightrope between the two goals of self-reliance and modernisation, if the latter can only be achieved with modern technology from abroad. So, in recent years, for all the rhetoric, self-reliance in its practical application, not least in the area of foreign trade, has displayed a certain amount of flexibility. Indeed, the current Seven-Year Plan put particular emphasis on foreign trade, but North Korea remains heavily dependent on China (now that trade with the former Soviet

Union has slumped) as its main trading partner and, with Western countries still inhibited by North Korean debts outstanding from the mid-1970s, it is doubtful whether targets can be met. Total foreign trade actually fell in the years 1989-90. According to Japanese estimates it also fell again by as much as 24% in 1991, although IMF figures, which do not include data on Soviet trade with North Korea (which did drop drastically during the year), actually show a slight increase in trade in 1991. In 1984 North Korea introduced a joint venture law, modelled on earlier Chinese practices, but it has been far less successful than its Chinese counterpart in attracting overseas investment. By the end of 1990 only 135 joint ventures had been announced, over 70% of them with Korean residents of Japan, 20% with China, the former Soviet Union and the former socialist bloc, and a handful with Western and Third World companies.

Japan has been by far the largest non-socialist economic partner of North Korea, though by comparison with the growth in South Korean-Japanese and even Sino-Japanese economic interactions the record has been poor (Shin, J.H. 1987 pp. 275-93; JETRO 1988-91). Trade remained at a low level from its beginnings in the mid-1950s until the early 1970s. Then, however, economic interactions surged as North Korea launched its new Six-Year Economic Plan (in 1971) which was predicated on inducing in Japanese industrial equipment and technology. At the same time, the Japanese government eased its trading restrictions as part of a general mood of detente in North-east Asia, and a comprehensive trade agreement was signed between the Japanese Dietmen's League for Friendship with North Korea and the (North) Korean Committee for the Promotion of International Trade. This mirrored the post-1962 'Liao-Takasaki memorandum trade' carried on between Japan and China (Radtke 1990 pp. 131-47). Japan became North Korea's largest non-socialist trading partner, a position it has held ever since.

In the second half of the 1970s trade slowed again as North Korea found itself in difficulties over paying its debts. After fluctuating slightly throughout the 1980s, total trade by 1991 was still only $496 million. Trade with North Korea, far outshadowed by trade with South Korea, has been of minimal importance to Japan as a whole, representing 0.1% of its total trade. But, it has been of far more significance to North Korea, accounting during the 1980s for approximately 15% of North Korea's total trade. With the collapse of North Korea-Soviet trade in 1991, Japan in 1992 will become the second largest trading partner of North Korea after China. From 1971 onwards North Korea ran a trade deficit with Japan, but in the second half of the 1980s as debt repayment problems mounted, the North Korean government deliberately reduced imports from Japan and pushed its exports, so that since 1987 it has recorded a small surplus in trade with Japan.

Given that the export of Japanese high technology products to North Korea is prohibited under Cocom regulations, the bulk of Japanese exports to North Korea consists of general and electrical machinery and transportation equipment, with textile machinery and materials, designed for use in the newly-established joint ventures, growing in importance in the late 1980s. North Korean exports to Japan are primarily base metals and marine and agricultural products (such as crab, squid and ginseng), but with textiles growing in importance.

Pro-North Korean residents of Japan have been the most enthusiastic overseas participants in joint ventures, with the number of deals agreed rising from 4 in 1986 to 34 in both 1988 and 1989. In all, 87 joint ventures with Japan have been agreed, of which 51 were in operation by the end of 1990. About half of these ventures were in mining, manufacturing, construction and transportation. The total value of these proposed joint ventures had reached 13 billion yen ($98 million), which testifies to the small size of these operations (JETRO 1991 p.125). In September 1992 Nissho Iwai did send engineers to investigate the possibilities of jointly redeveloping an iron mine, using Japanese drilling machines, but the major Japanese companies remain cautious.

Although at periods in the past, notably in the mid-1960s and the early 1970s, the degree of bilateral economic interaction was significantly affected by changes in the political climate in the relationship, during the 1980s trade growth has been handicapped more by economic problems themselves, specifically on the North Korean side, than by political ups and downs. For example, diplomatic sanctions imposed on North Korea by the Japanese government for a period after the 1983 Rangoon bombing and again after the 1987 KAL airliner destruction had little direct impact on trade.

Instead, the Japanese business community has been discouraged by the unreformed and inflexible nature of the North Korean economic system, the unattractive produce of North Korea (with the exception of certain marine and mineral products), and, above all, by the North Korean failure to repay their outstanding debts. Convoluted negotiations between the North Koreans and the Japan-(North) Korea Trade Association, representing Japanese creditors, had led to a rescheduling agreement in 1983, but this soon broke down and since 1987 there have not even been any direct negotiations on the issue. The outstanding debts to the Japanese are estimated to have reached around 70 billion yen. The Japanese have not been impressed by North Korean offers such as that, in 1986, to repay them in fish! Another debt rescheduling agreement, therefore, will have to be part of the settlement of relations between Japan and North Korea.

For the Japanese business community as a whole, to use the words of a Keidanren official, the North Korean market has very little 'charm'. A large Japanese business delegation, including representatives of the major trading houses and banks for the first time, visited North Korea in July 1992, but the participants generally came back prepared to conduct further feasibility studies on possible joint ventures, but reluctant to commit themselves to any serious deals yet. Indeed, trade has been almost a North Korea-ethnic (North)

Korean trade, for an estimated 80% of the total Japan-North Korean trade is actually handled by North Korean-related companies and organisations based in Japan. As such, the Japanese government does not feel itself under any pressure from the business community to push for an early establishment of diplomatic relations.

Regional and sub-regional cooperation

Although the concept of East Asian or broader Pacific economic cooperation can be dated back to the Pan-Asian ideas of the early part of the twentieth century or even to the Japanese wartime 'Greater East Asia Co-Prosperity Sphere', it was the mid-1960s that saw the first real flowering of ideas of regionalism as the establishment of the EC began to impact on international trade and investment. However, unlike the EC, which has developed both a high degree of intra-regional trade and investment and also economic and political arrangements which entail subordinating sovereign rights, the East Asian region is still only at the embryonic stage of regional economic, let alone political, integration. Apart from the South Pacific Forum, which involves primarily the small Pacific islands, only ASEAN has developed to any degree as a sub-regional organisation. In North-east Asia, there has been no progress towards sub-regional organisational integration.

A Japanese academic, Kiyoshi Kojima, floated the idea of a Pacific Free Trade Area in the mid-1960s. His intention, that the five most advanced Pacific nations, including Japan, should form this grouping, was neither politically nor economically acceptable at the time, but it did stimulate thinking in the region and indirectly led to businessmen in these five countries setting up the Pacific Basin Economic Council (PBEC) in 1967. This business grouping has met regularly since, but its influence has been limited. The next stage of cooperative discussions began in the late-1970s, with Japanese Prime Minister Masayoshi Ohira's study group on Pacific Basin cooperation, a major US Congressional report on the same subject and an Australian initiative to hold an international conference on the subject. The result was the creation of the Pacific Economic Cooperation Conference (PECC), which has met bi-annually since 1980; the characteristic of this organisation is tripartite business, academic and unofficial government delegations (Drysdale 1988 pp. 204-28). Both Japan and South Korea became founder members of PECC, but the participation of socialist states has always been a problem, so North Korea has not become a member. Indeed, not until the 1988 PECC Conference in Osaka, did it begin to even acknowledge the PECC's existence and to make tentative soundings about possible observer status.

Until the late-1980s the running on regional cooperative ideas had been made by academics and businessmen, with governments giving only covert support. However, the third phase of regional integration initiatives began at the governmental-level, with Australian Prime Minister Bob Hawke proposing, and hosting in November 1989, an Asian Pacific Economic Cooperation (APEC) conference. Japan and South Korea were founding members; indeed, the original idea had developed from a discussion between Hawke and President Roh earlier in 1989 (Cotton 1990 pp.171-3). Three subsequent conferences have been held, and at the November 1991 Seoul conference the 'three Chinas' (China, Taiwan and Hong Kong) were admitted. The form of institutionalisation (the establishment of a small secretariat was agreed upon at the 1992 conference) and direction in which its policy debates proceed will affect the future of region-wide economic cooperation. There is certainly the possibility that APEC could move to something equivalent to the OECD ministerial meetings (Harris 1991 p. 310). However, whatever form APEC takes, there is no likelihood of North Korean membership in the near future.

Both the Japanese and South Korean governments were positive about APEC, once it had become clear that the United States, originally excluded from the Australian plan, would be a full participant, but they have been far from positive about an initiative by Malaysian Prime Minister Mahathir Mohammed, made in December 1990. Mahathir proposed an East Asian Economic Grouping (EAEG), which deliberately excluded both the Australians and the Americans and was conceived as a regional counter-weight to the emerging North American Free Trade Area (NAFTA) and the EC's 1992 programme. The Japanese and South Koreans had their doubts about the exclusion of the United States and themselves came under strong US pressure to try to forestall this grouping. Some other South-east Asian countries also had reservations and, in the autumn of 1991, Mahathir watered down his proposal into an East Asian Economic Caucus (EAEC), which could meet on an *ad hoc* basis (*Far Eastern Economic Review* 25 July 1991). This was less objectionable to the Japanese and South Koreans, but in practice it meant that the Malaysian initiative was being slowly talked into the ground. Whether or not the EAEC becomes institutionalised - and the odds are that it will not - North Korea is once again not being considered as an early member.

PBEC, PECC, APEC and even EAEC have all been seen in terms of broader regional institutions. At the sub-regional level, the complex and diverse political and economic systems of the countries of North-east Asia have prevented any serious discussion of organisations equivalent to South-east Asia's ASEAN further north. A few academics and businessmen have talked about formal economic cooperative linkages between Japan, South Korea and Taiwan, sometimes including China, occasionally even the Soviet Union/Russia and North Korea, but they have not received much support. Similarly abortive have been ideas about an East Asian version of

Comecon, which would link China and North Korea with the Indochinese countries, and an Asian NICs-grouping (suggested by Singapore Prime Minister Lee Kuan Yew to President Roh in 1988).

However, recently, interest in the concept of Japan Sea Rim cooperation has begun to grow, spreading slowly from academics and business groups to governments in the region. This concept derives from the apparent complementarity amongst the countries bordering the Japan Sea: the coal, natural gas, mineral, timber and fishing resources of the Soviet Far East, the agricultural and mineral resources and labour forces of China and North Korea, and the capital, technology and managerial skills of Japan and South Korea. The Japanese have been acting as the catalyst in the initial exchanges and discussions. The geo-political changes in the region in the late 1980s - the spread of perestroika to the Soviet Far Eastern provinces, the establishment of Soviet-South Korean diplomatic relations and the development of Sino-South Korean economic relations - provided the stimulus for local governments and business circles in the Japan Sea coast cities and prefectures, who had long felt unhappy with the relative imbalance in economic development between their side and the Pacific Ocean side of Japan, to try to better utilise their geographical advantages.

Central governments have now begun to be drawn in, particularly into one concrete proposal for cooperation, the Tumen River project (Valencia 1991 pp. 263-71; Sugimoto 1992 pp. 1-17). The basin of the Tumen River, which borders the Soviet Primorskiy (maritime territory), the Korean autonomous region of Yanbian in North-east China, and North Korea, is now being considered as a site for the multilateral development of port and other transport infrastructure and industrial facilities. Starting from a Chinese proposal in mid-1990, a preliminary conference involving North Korea, South Korea, China and Mongolia was held in Ulan Bator in July 1991, under the auspices of the United Nations Development Programme (UNDP). This was followed by a further conference, involving additionally Japan and the Soviet Union, in Pyongyang in October 1991, which considered an initial UNDP feasibility study.

The UNDP survey suggested that around $30 billion would be needed to finance a twemty-year development programme, but that the region had strong potential as a site for regional industrialisation and as a hub for transportation from North-east Asia to Europe, via Mongolia. Two scales of development zones were considered: a smaller one centred on North Korea's Najin port to China's Hunchun to the Russian port of Posyet, and a much larger one stretching from North Korea's Chongjin port to China's Yanji city to the Russian port of Vladivostock. The Pyongyang conference itself decided to fund a detailed 18-month feasibility study and to give priority to the North Korean proposal to create a special economic zone in the Najin-Sonbong area (in December 1991 the North Korean government formally decreed the Najin-Sonbong SEZ). In November 1991, representatives of interested governments (including Japan and the two Koreas) also met with officials of the United Nations Industrial Development Organisation to discuss a plan to create a free economic zone on adjacent Russian territory, centred on Vladivostock.

The North Koreans view the Tumen river development as a way of revitalising their economy, but, at the same time, keeping 'capitalist elements' strictly confined to one small area. It could also be a way of inducing in Japanese capital and 'economic assistance', under a UN umbrella, which might not be so forthcoming on a directly bilateral basis. The South Koreans want to cast the project as a regional, not a purely inter-Korean, cooperative venture, which could solve some of their emerging labour shortage problems as well as provide access to the huge potential market of North-east China. Nevertheless, the South Korean government's suspicion of North Korean objectives meant that during 1991-2 its attitude to Korean companies' involvement in the projects blew hot and cold depending on the state of the North-South dialogue, and, particularly, of the nuclear inspection issue.

For Japan, the project provides access to cheap labour and abundant resources, but Japanese business-men will need to factor in the costs of infrastructural inadequacy, unskilled labour, bureacratic inefficiencies and political uncertainties. The Japanese Foreign Ministry also argues that ODA cannot be given to North Korea, even indirectly through the UNDP, without diplomatic relations first being established. For the moment, the Japanese attitude is very much one of caution. The Russians, Chinese and Mongolians have different objectives and varying degrees of enthusiasm as well; the Russians are becoming more interested in a 'Great Vladivostock Free Economic Zone' which would adjoin but rival the Tumen plan, while the Chinese wish to see Hunchun rather than Najin as the focal point. As such, the implementation of the plans will be slow and probably contentious.

Nevertheless, this kind of sub-regional cooperation, which mirrors ideas of 'growth triangles' in South-east Asia (one, involving Singapore, the Malaysian state of Johore, and the Indonesian Riau archipelago, is already very active [Lee, T.Y. 1991]), is more likely than inter-governmental institutionalised structures to point the pathway to economic cooperation.

However, particularly for Japan, but also to a lesser extent for South Korea, the commitment to this kind of sub-regional economic cooperation or even to the broader East Asian economic cooperative movements has to be balanced against involvement, and occasionally conflicting ties, with the global economy. The flows of trade, FDI and aid show some complex patterns of interdependence, both within and beyond the East Asian region. The 1980s saw a major increase in the absolute size of trade, FDI and even aid flows between Japan and South Korea, but, in terms of a relative share of external flows, the data is less clear cut. For both Japan and South Korea trade with the other has declined slightly in relative importance during the 1980s. For both, indeed, trade with extra-regional partners (in particular the

United States, but increasingly the EC too) has grown relatively more important than trade with East Asian regional partners. On the investment side, Japanese and South Korean FDI has gone predominantly to the United States and countries outside the region. During the 1980s, Japan ceased to give aid to South Korea and rebalanced its global ODA distribution to enhance slightly the share of non-East Asian developing countries. South Korea itself became an aid donor, to both regional and extra-regional countries. So, for both countries, there has been over the 1980s and into the 1990s a growing global - rather than merely bilateral or even regional-economic interdependence and integration (Shibusawa, Ahmad and Bridges 1991 pp. 4-34).

7 Culture, Korean Residents and Reconciliation

The volume of international transactions has grown rapidly over the past few decades. The numbers of actors involved in international contacts have expanded in both kind and quantity. The closer contacts between peoples and nations become, however, the more important are international cultural relationships and, for that matter, cultural frictions (Hirano 1988 pp.143-64). In the case of Japan and the two Koreas, their cultural and geographical closeness has been overshadowed by the historical patterns of interaction which still today influence the degree of sensitivity over popular interchange.

The 1965 Japan-South Korean treaties attempted to cover the problems of the Korean residents in Japan as well as cultural properties and cultural exchanges. Neither issue was settled, and the following years have seen a politicisation of the issues which has done little to speed their resolution. Recent years have seen a surge in Korean - both South and North - attempts to push Japan into reconciling its past with the present. However, there is great complexity in the issue of reconciliation and there is certainly no easy relationship between it and compensation.

Korean residents in Japan

Korean emigration to Japan has a long provenance and its origins, back in the early centuries, have generated controversy. Japanese historians, particularly those writing in the late Meiji period, asserted that first Japanese gods and later Japanese emperors/kings had ruled Korea in antiquity. This was used as justification for the theory of identical ancestry and, by extension, the Japanese right to rule Korea again. Since the Second World War, however, a number of Japanese and Korean historians have adduced evidence for the theory of the 'horseback rider origin of the Japanese state', which argues that people from either Koguryo or Puyo in present day Manchuria/northern Korea crossed to Kyushu in the fourth century A.D. and established what the Japanese have called the Yamato kingdom (Lee, C-s. 1985 pp. 151-63).

Recent excavations in both the southern part of Korea and in Japan have produced artifacts of remarkably similar construct. Much remains to be done in the archaeological and historical research of the origins of the Japanese state, but, undoubtedly, people of Korean origin played significant roles in the early political and intellectual life of Japan.

Yet that was by no means the end of Korean influence, for over the following millennium, Korea served as a bridge for the transmission of Chinese culture to Japan, as a succession of Korean priests, artists, scholars and scientists introduced elements of Chinese, and Korean, civilisation to Japan. Inevitably, some stayed on in Japan. However, the first enforced emigration came at the end of the sixteenth century, when Korean craftsmen, including potters and weavers, were taken back to Japan during Hideyoshi Toyotomi's destructive, but ultimately unsuccessful, campaigns in Korea.

Even when the Japanese annexed Korea in 1910 the number of Koreans living in Japan was only a couple of thousand. The Japanese occupation changed the status of Koreans, whether living in Korea or in Japan, into that of Japanese nationals (though, significantly, not into Japanese citizens). Some Koreans crossed over to Japan in search of work, but found themselves in lowly-paid and harsh conditions. Also, in the aftermath of the 1923 Great Kanto Earthquake, a nation-wide anti-Korean hysteria, which was covertly encouraged by the Japanese government, led to vigilante mobs hunting down and killing Korean residents. Estimates vary, but probably around 6,000 were killed. Nevertheless, in the worsening economic conditions in southern Korea in the 1930s, farmers who defaulted on loans and lost their land to Japanese banks crossed over to Japan for work in increasing numbers.

The numbers of Korean residents in Japan grew to 660,000 in 1936 and 1,470,000 in 1941. But after 1937, as the Japanese economy and society moved onto a wartime footing, the Japanese began to import Korean labourers under contract (in practice, conscripted) for work in Japanese mines, building sites and factories. After December 1941, Japan conscripted Korean men and shipped them overseas to fight. The Japanese government acknowledges about 22,000 Korean deaths in battle and at least 100,000 Koreans missing in action, but Korean organisations claim the total number of soldiers and civilians killed is 440,000. By early 1945 there were probably as many as 2,400,000 Koreans in Japan, of whom about half would have been forced labourers and their families (Wagner 1951; Weiner 1989; Lee and De Vos 1981).

The defeat of Japan, the liberation of Korea and its subsequent division into two created a complicated legal situation and an ambiguity which has still not been resolved. Spontaneous and, later, officially-sanctioned repatriation reduced the numbers of Koreans in Japan to around half a million by the early 1950s. However, in 1947 they had been forced to register under the new Alien Registration Law and in 1952, under the terms of the San Francisco Peace Treaty, they were officially designated as 'foreigners'. Most of them came from the earliest Korean immigrants and had offspring born and raised in Japan. Although the question of their legal status became one of the key issues of the protracted Japan-South Korean negotiations leading up to the 1965 treaties, the Japanese government did agree, under strong internal pressure, in 1959, to enter into an agreement with North Korea which resulted in the repatriation of around 85,000 Koreans to the North over the following decade (KMK 1984 pp. 519-22). As the reality of the North Korean situation has become better known to those pro-North Koreans in Japan, enthusiasm for actually repatriating to the North to live, as opposed to visiting or sending money and goods, has dissipated; a mere 140 people were repatriated during the whole of the 1980s (Sato 1991 pp.167-76).

The 1965 Japan-South Korean accord allowed those Koreans, and their families, who had resided in Japan prior to the Pacific War, to apply for permanent residence and attendant educational and social welfare benefits. This covered the majority of Korean residents, although, in practice, this status was only granted to those willing to hold South Korean nationality. By the deadline of 1971 approximately 350,000 Koreans had registered (leaving around 300,000 in the pro-North Korean and thereby effectively 'stateless' category). In 1981 the Japanese Immigration Law was changed to allow a form of general permanent residency under which the North Korean residents qualified. As the Korean community has become polarised between support for the two Korean governments, so this numerical split has remained relatively constant ever since. According to Japanese Justice Ministry statistics, at the end of December 1989, 326,318 Koreans held permanent residency under the Japan-South Korean treaty arrangements and 268,320 under the general permanent residency provisions.

Most Koreans do in fact qualify for naturalisation under Japanese law, but the emotional costs involved in so doing (not least in the 'Japanising' of the family name) often militate against so doing. The designation under the Japanese koseki (family register) includes the word shin (new) against the Japanese nationality of those naturalised Koreans; this is distasteful to them and brings back memories of the pre-war forced assimilation. Consequently, only a few thousand each year (approximately 1% of the Korean population) do naturalise, thereby roughly off-setting the natural birth increase and keeping the size of the Korean community to around the 680,000 mark now.

The two Korean governments operate through, and heavily subsidise, their respective support organisations amongst the Korean community in Japan. Chongnyon, founded in 1955, is backed by the North Koreans and, indeed, the long-standing chairman of its Central Committee, Han Dok-su, is a duly elected member of the North Korean Supreme People's Assembly. It has an extensive but centralised network of branches and schools and even one university (Lee and De Vos 1981 pp. 112-23). The number of schools has grown to 153 and it is estimated that about one-quarter of the children of pro-North Korean families attend these schools (*Korea Times* 30 June 1992). There has been a 'two-way' flow of funds, but, in recent years, this has predominantly been from Japan to the North. By December 1990 North Korea had given a declared cumulative total of 41 billion yen to Chongnyon for its educational activities, but the North Koreans have themselves received far more significant collections from amongst Chongnyon supporters. The North Korean authorities apparently asked Chongnyon to collect 50 billion yen ($400 million) in 1988 alone for the 40th anniversary of the KWP's founding and a further 10 billion yen in 1989 for the World Youth Festival held in Pyongyang (Sato 1991 pp. 165, 191-2).

Mindan, formed in 1946, has a much looser structure and is less well focused than Chongnyon. Although membership is limited to those who have registered as South Korean nationals, the South Korean government attitude towards it has been less committed than its northern counterpart's support for its rival (Lee and De Vos 1981 pp. 123-7). Indeed, not until after the 1965 normalisation did the South Korean government give direct funding and by the mid-1980s the South Korean Embassy in Tokyo and the various consulates around Japan actually seemed to be taking over some of Mindan's roles in ministering to the Korean community. There are only four schools specifically for the pro-South Korean community (two of them financially supported by the Seoul government) and only an estimated 1% of the eligible children actually attend them. As with Chongnyon, there tends to be a two-way flow of money, for Mindan-endorsed organisations raised 54 billion won (US $75 million) towards the 1988 Seoul Olympics (Pyon 1991 p. 8).

Paralleling their two home governments on the peninsula, these two organisations have been at great pains to keep themselves apart. In 1988 a Korean resident intellectual suggested to the two organisations that they cooperate in the movement to abolish the Alien Registration Law and in festivities to commemorate the August 15 liberation of the Korean peninsula. Although the proposal was generally well-received by the Korean community, both organisations ignored it. In mid-1990, the two organisations did actually begin discussions about sending representatives to a planned Pan-National Conference in Panmunjom, but the plan fell through. As a result of this manifest and sustained competition, one characteristic tendency amongst the Korean community during the 1980s has been a gradual reduction in interest in and commitment to the ideological activities of the two organisations; in practice the 'neutrals' may now actually be in the majority (Colbert 1986 pp.285-6). Ironically too, in spite of the fact that the general international socio-political climate has encouraged ethnic groups elsewhere to campaign for and win greater privileges from dominant states, commitment to the cause of the Koreans in general may not be growing greatly. A 1986 survey of Korean residents reaching adulthood showed that 83% did not know how many Koreans there were in Japan.

Since the mid-1970s the South Korean government has become more active in pressing the Japanese government to improve the legal status of the Korean residents, by eliminating regulations which distinguish them from Japanese citizens. The most resented has been the Alien Registration Law's requirement for the Koreans to carry identification cards at all times and to be finger-printed every five years (just like other 'aliens'). In the early 1980s objections to the indignity of the finger-printing provisions became more vocal from other non-Japanese and from some Japanese intellectuals and opposition politicians. Some of these joined a few Koreans in refusing to renew their finger-prints and were either arrested or fined. By the end of 1985 nearly 7,000 foreigners had refused or were late in renewing their finger-print records.

A few overseas politicians, most notably the US Democrat Jesse Jackson, also picked up this issue and urged the Japanese government to alter its regulations. This broadening of support helped the South Korean government and the Korean community in their campaign. The Japanese Justice Ministry and the police, who were interested in keeping checks on potential North Korean terrorists or criminals, strongly resisted modification or abolition of finger-printing (and, ironically, received some sympathetic support from their South Korean counterparts - including the Korean security agencies - who were also concerned about surveillance of pro-North Korean activists). However, pressure from other ministries, especially the Foreign Ministry, and from certain progressive city and prefectural governments (particularly those with large Korean populations) increased.

A number of minor amendments were made: in 1985 colourless ink was substituted for the black ink previously used, and in 1988 the necessity for a renewal of the finger-printing every five years was removed. In the late 1980s, as the protests and court cases became more acrimonious, however, the Japanese government moved first to grant an amnesty to all finger-print refusers (after the death of Emperor Hirohito) and then entered into intensive negotiations with the South Korean government on this issue. This led to an agreement in April 1990, on the eve of President Roh's visit to Japan, that the Japanese government would exempt third generation Koreans (those born to Koreans who themselves had been born in Japan since 1971) from the finger-printing regulations and would consider alternative ways to identify them (*Nihon Keizai Shimbun* 1 May 1990). The South Korean government requested that these changes also be applied to first and second generation Korean residents as well.

Consequently, when Prime Minister Kaifu visited Seoul in January 1991 he agreed that a special exception to the Alien Registration Law would be allowed, so that all Korean residents should be exempt from finger-printing (*Nihon Keizai Shimbun* 11 January 1991). The Japanese government agreed to introduce the necessary legislation so that the system could be abolished during 1992. Instead, a family-based registry system, using photographs and signatures to replace finger-prints, would be established. Mindan welcomed the abolition of finger-printing, but noted that the Koreans were still required to carry the alien registration cards at all times; Chongnyon described the intended replacement family registration system as a ruse to increase the surveillance of Korean residents (*Japan Times* 11 January 1991).

Further examination of the issues involved in framing the necesary legislation led the Justice Ministry to conclude, in mid-1991, that the finger-printing regulations would have to be abolished not just for Korean residents but for all non-Japanese nationals resident in Japan as well. However, in December 1991, the government reversed this decision under strong pressure from the National Police Agency which was concerned about a further boost in the already growing number of crimes committed by foreigners and of illegal foreign workers entering the country. The final version of the legislation, approved by the cabinet in February 1992 and passed by the Diet in April 1992, was a compromise. The finger-printing requirement was ended for the Koreans, Taiwanese and other permanent foreign residents (about 40,000 in that last category), but not for the other, approximately 320,000, foreign nationals who have lived in Japan for more than a year (*Japan Times Weekly* 27 April 1992). Although finger-printing for the Korean and other permanent foreign residents would be dropped with effect from January 1993, the finger-printing of other foreigners resident in Japan seemed likely to continue for a further one to three years.

Of course, the operation of the finger-printing regulations has been only one, though the most symbolic, of the many legal and social dimensions in which the Korean residents in Japan have tried to improve their status (Onuma 1986). In fact, the inter-governmental negotiations, from late 1988, over the status of the 'third generation' Koreans became the focus of South Korean attempts to improve the status of all Korean residents. The 1965 Japan-South Korean Treaty granted permanent residency to those Koreans who came to Japan before and during the war and their children born between 1945 and 1971 ('first generation') and to the children of these Koreans ('second generation'), but with a provision that a settlement of the 'third' and subsequent generations should be reached by January 1991.

By early 1990 at least four children had been born who fell into that 'third generation' category and the problem had become urgent. President Roh, indeed, hinted that he might even postpone his trip to Japan if the negotiations were not speeded up. The South Korean government presented a list of nine demands, covering not just automatic permanent residence for the newly-born Korean residents, but also, for the sake of all Korean residents, the abolition of finger-printing and re-entry visa regulations and the opening up of local government and teaching posts. The Japanese government did make concessions over the finger-printing and permanent residency, as well as over re-entry visas for Korean residents, which were extended to five years (*Korea Times* 25 May 1990). However, arguing that it needed to consider the position of all non-Japanese in general, the government was not willing to move on the other contentious points.

Restricted employment opportunities have been a major grievance of the Koreans. While they are able to earn degrees from Japanese universities, Koreans often find it difficult to gain employment - and later promotion - with major Japanese corporations, to start their own businesses in some sectors (such as fishing, shipping, telecommunications, and mining where Japanese nationality is a legal prerequisite), or to enter public service. The traditional nationality clause which prohibits non-Japanese (and, thereby, Korean residents) from becoming teachers or local government officials has gradually been abolished in recent years by a number of metropolitan and prefectural governments (by mid-1990, by 14 out of 47 such bodies), including Tokyo and Osaka. Yet, resistance by the Education Ministry and some prefectural governments has been strong. Foreign Ministry officials, indeed, resorted at one stage to arranging meetings with prefectural officials pitting the more 'progressive' prefectures against the more 'conservative' ones in order to try to speed up this process of opening up local government to the Korean residents. By mid-1990 only about 40 Koreans had become teachers at public schools.

At the local level, a number of city councils, such as Kawasaki (which, in 1985 became the first city to formally defy a Justice Ministry memorandum to report finger-print refusers to the police), have taken a very active part in trying to promote the rights of Koreans, but they still remain the exception rather than the rule. The nationality ruling also affects the various Korean schools established in Japan, which are usually designated as 'special' by the Japanese Education Ministry. This has hindered, for example, the sports teams from these schools competing in national competitions. When, in July 1990, a Korean high school's volleyball team won Osaka's prefectural title, it was barred from participating in the national championship (Pyon 1991 p.9).

The Korean residents tend, as a result of the difficulty of entering 'normal' companies, to gravitate towards three forms of business: high-interest money-lending, restaurants, especially for yakiniku (Korean barbecue), and pachinko (pinball) parlours. With parlours operating in every town and city in Japan, pachinko has become the major Japanese urban leisure entertainment; well over half of the parlours are owned by Koreans, many of whom are believed to be pro-North Korean. In the autumn of 1989 a minor political scandal arose over revelations that pachinko operators had been giving donations to both the JSP and the LDP (*Japan Economic Journal* 12 October 1989). The donations, which in the JSP case included purchasing tickets to a party celebrating Takako Doi's inauguration as party leader, were not illegal, but, nevertheless, helped to confirm the popular Japanese perception of Koreans being involved in somewhat shady activities.

As foreign nationals, Korean residents cannot vote in national or local elections. On the other hand, they are required to pay taxes, so many Koreans feel that the right to vote is their fundamental right. Japan joined the UN Human Rights Convention in 1979, the UN Refugee Convention in 1981, and enacted an Equal Opportunity Law in 1985, but still has not carried out all these human rights commitments in practice at home. Inter-marriage with Koreans is legally tolerated, but many Japanese do not like to see it and the indefatigable investigators of intended spouses' backgrounds are still responsible for the calling off of weddings. The Nationality Law was changed in 1984 to allow Japanese nationality to be passed through the female of a mixed-nationality marriage, so that, for example, the child of a Japanese wife and a Korean husband could be Japanese. But anecdotal evidence suggests that the Korean surname cannot be used and only the Japanese maiden name can be. Consequently, the Koreans' complaints now tend to be less about the nature of the laws than their application.

Undoubtedly, the legal situation of the Koreans has improved since the mid-1980s, but the problem is not just one of legal technicalities but of the conciousness and attitudes of the Japanese as a whole (and, to a lesser extent, how the Koreans perceive themselves). In fact, the Japanese attitude towards the Korean residents can be seen as a test-case of the real 'internationalisation' of Japan, or uchi naru kokusaika (internationalisation from the inside).

The Japanese tend to represent Japan to the outside world as a basically homogeneous nation free of the minority group problems found in most other countries. Senior politicians and officials, such as Prime Minister Nakasone in his notorious 1986 comparison of the social problems of the mixed-race United States with the ethnically homogeneous Japan, have perpetuated this approach. Nakasone's remarks actually echoed a deeply-held conviction amongst many Japanese that they are 'unique' and that, consequently, non-Japanese can never be accepted as full citizens (Lee and De Vos 1981 pp. 354-60). Yet, minority groups probably account for around 4% of the total population of Japan. These can be classified as indigenous (the burakumin 'outcasts'), foreign (the Koreans and a few Chinese), aboriginal (the Ainu, found mainly in Hokkaido), and conquered (around 1 million Okinawans) (De Vos and Wetherall 1983 p. 3). The traditional Japanese governmental approach has been one of assimilation, but the popular attitudes have been disparaging towards even those Koreans who have tried very hard to become assimilated.

The reactions of the Korean residents, therefore, can be grouped into three categories: those who seek to 'pass' as Japanese, those who strongly assert their ethnicity, and those who seek an accommodating middle ground. Now, of course, more than 75% of the Koreans resident in Japan have been born in Japan. For many they know only the life in Japan, they speak Japanese fluently and have a poor knowledge of Korean. While those Korean children attending the pro-North Korean schools are drilled on North Korean society, history and literature, almost all the other Korean children are being educated in the ordinary Japanese education system. A 1986 survey of Korean residents visiting immigration offices to apply for re-entry visas showed that over 90% wished to continue living in Japan and that around 75% were using Japanese only or Japanese predominantly in their daily lives. Another survey the same year, of Korean residents reaching adulthood, showed that less than half of them could actually exchange simple New Year greetings in Korean (*Korea Herald* 24 May, 27 July 1986). Almost all Korean residents in Japan have a deep appreciation and love for Korean cooking and drinks, but most feel more at home reading Japanese novels and newspapers and watching Japanese films than Korean ones.

The dilemmas and, indeed, contradictions of the life-styles of the Korean-Japanese are not easily resolved. In a competitive, achievement-oriented society such as Japan, minority ethnic groups such as the Koreans have difficulty in keeping up (Lee and De Vos 1981 pp. 354-83; Hyon 1983 pp. 70-131). They often find themselves undertaking marginal occupations, which are not reflective of their real educational levels. There is a relatively high rate of juvenile delinquency amongst Korean youth and the 'toughness' of the Japanese underworld yakuza gangs has appeal - and a degree of acceptability - for some. The more individualistic character of the Koreans makes it more difficult for them to make the emotional commitments of loyalty and dedication to the company that is implicitly expected by the Japanese. In the worlds of professional sport (such as baseball or sumo) or show business, it is possible for Korean-Japanese to reach the top, but rarely other than by determinedly passing themselves off as Japanese. Not until 1986 was an ethnic Korean, Arai Shokei, who was born in Japan, became naturalised in 1966 and is married to a Japanese, elected to the Diet. His opponents, including some within his own party, the LDP, such as Ishihara Shintaro, alleged that his ethnic background made his loyalty suspect (*Straits Times* 8 September 1986), but his popularity amongst the constituency voters was clear from his re-election in the 1990 election.

In trying to become more integrated into Japanese society, the Koreans face a difficult problem of acculturation - they must give up some of their Korean identity in order to take on those very social characteristics (Japanese) which are disparaging towards Koreans. Marriage between Koreans and Japanese can transcend the social barriers, but the children of such marriages often find themselves with even more complicated identity problems. Koreans who become naturalised Japanese can find themselves fully accepted neither by the Japanese they have 'joined' nor by the Korean community which they have 'left'.

The Sakhalin Koreans

Although the status of the Korean residents has been a predominantly bilateral problem between Japan and South Korea (with North Korea only partially involved), the status of one particular group of Koreans, those in Sakhalin, has become a more complicated diplomatic issue. As discussed above, during the Second World War Koreans were forced to serve in the Japanese military as either soldiers or forced labourers. In August 1945, when the Soviet forces occupied the southern part of Sakhalin island (the Soviet Union had controlled the northern part since 1905), there were about 43,000 Koreans (of whom about 12,000 were women and children) living there. Under agreements between the Allied Occupation forces in Japan and the Soviet Union, in 1946, and between Japan itself and the Soviet Union in 1956, all Japanese nationals and prisoners-of-war (and those Koreans who were married to Japanese) were repatriated to Japan. But the Koreans remained.

There are now about 60,000 Koreans residing in Sakhalin. Most of them are second or third generation, since many of those Koreans who went there in the early 1940s have died of old age. Probably only about one-third of these residents are able to converse in Korean. The majority of the original Koreans came from the southern part of Korea, mostly from Taegu and Cheju-do. They, and their children, refused permission to emigrate by the Soviet authorities, have generally accepted Soviet nationality or even North Korean nationality in order to qualify for reasonable treatment. Figures vary, but of the present inhabitants probably about 70% now have Russian (superseding Soviet) nationality, and most of the remainder have North Korean nationality; a minute number are stateless. Those stateless Koreans, who have refused to adopt either Soviet/Russian or North Korean nationality, have done so because they strongly wish to return to South Korea, but because of their age their number has shrunk to only around 750 people, according to an April 1989 survey (*Korea Herald* August 1989; Arai 1990 pp. 20-5).

As a matter of policy, the Japanese government in 1946 refused to accept the Koreans in Sakhalin as Japanese nationals, and it has subsequently argued that the 1952 San Francisco Peace Treaty has given legal validity to its claim not to have responsibility for these Koreans. Despite a 1961 court case which backed up the Japanese government's claims, there are a number of inconsistencies in its arguments, which leave it open to doubt whether the official Japanese line can really be sustained under international law (Chough 1987 pp. 711-37).

The South Korean government first raised the issue of those Koreans in Sakhalin who wished to return to South Korea (this group was assumed to include an indeterminant number of Koreans with Soviet/North Korean nationality as well as the stateless Koreans) with the Japanese government in 1959, but even when the 1965 treaties were signed this question was left unresolved. The Japanese government did raise the question intermittently with the Soviets, but with no response whatsoever. However, in 1973, after appeals through the Red Cross, the Soviet government agreed to treat the Koreans under the same regulations as those applying to Soviet citizens who wished to emigrate, though these were subject to extremely strict and time-consuming procedures. In 1976, the Japanese government agreed to issue limited-period entry permits to Sakhalin Koreans who had lived in Japan prior to the Second World War and who would be allowed entry into South Korea. Four Koreans qualified and applied, but bureaucratic tardiness prevented them leaving and three were eventually to die in Sakhalin. By the end of 1976, the Soviets had ceased any consideration of permission for Koreans to emigrate (by then around just over 400 had applied).

Throughout the late 1970s and early 1980s the Japanese government's regular enquiries were met by a Soviet refusal to accept it as a subject for Soviet-Japanese discussion. The Japanese government had been under little pressure from Japanese political parties, but in 1983, Kusakawa Shozo, a Komeito politician who has taken a deep personal interest in this question, became the first Japanese Dietman to visit Sakhalin since the end of the war. The Sakhalin authorities told him of their fears that any returning Koreans would be utilised for US propaganda purposes, but did agree to allow temporary reunions of Koreans holding Soviet nationality with relatives, on Japanese soil (from 1984-88 around 80 Koreans achieved these brief reunions) (*Tokyo Shimbun* 2 August 1983).

The arrival of Gorbachev as Soviet leader brought about a further change in the Soviet approach. In 1986, the Soviet government switched to arguing that it had to consider the North Korean position, but, after a loosening of the general Soviet regulations on travel outside the Soviet Union in 1987, permission was given for one Korean, in mid-1988, to return to South Korea, via Japan, to live permanently. Unfortunately, being nearly 80 and in poor health, he died barely two months after reaching South Korea. On the Japanese side too, political interest in the issue grew. The Foreign Ministry moved to a more positive mode than its previous over-cautious 'step-by-step' approach, and allocated a small part of its budget to covering some of the costs of the reunions. In July 1987, at Kusakawa's initiative, a supra-partisan Dietmen's group, headed by Hara Bumpei, an LDP politician, was launched. Significantly, in April 1990, Foreign Minister Nakayama for the first time specifically expressed Japan's 'regrets' for forcing the Koreans to go to Sakhalin during the war (Arai 1990 pp. 25-34; Takagi 1990 pp. 51-224).

The Seoul Olympics in 1988, of course, marked the beginning of the warming of Soviet-South Korean relations which was to result in September 1990 in the establishment of diplomatic relations. In January 1989, Soviet permission was given for individual elderly Koreans to return to and younger Koreans to visit South Korea via Japan. In February 1990, a KAL airliner was allowed for the first time to fly to Khabarovsk to collect a group of Koreans wishing to visit South Korea. In July 1990, for the first time, a joint Japanese-South Korean Red Cross team visited Sakhalin to assist in facilitating these visits. With the establishment of Soviet-South Korean diplomatic relations, the passage of Koreans back to South Korea has become easier (though, ironically, North Korea, in retaliation, has refused to allow Sakhalin Koreans with North Korean nationality to visit there so easily). It is estimated that nearly 1,000 Sakhalin Koreans were able to make temporary visits back to South Korea during the course of 1990.

However, the cost of these reunions did become a problem, as the Sakhalin Koreans themselves were not allowed to convert enough rubles into foreign currency to pay the travel costs to Seoul. A variety of support associations, founded in both Japan and South Korea, therefore helped to meet some of the costs involved. Both the South Korean and Japanese Foreign Ministries began to include special funding in their budgets. However, some opposition politicians in South Korea in 1989 began to demand compensation from Japan, to the tune of $5 billion, for the displaced Koreans. The Korean Foreign Ministry's attitude has been that the Japanese government bears moral and political responsibility for the fate of the Sakhalin Koreans, but it has avoided a direct demand to the Japanese government for compensation as such. However, in late 1989, the Koreans did propose setting up a joint fund to meet some of the costs involved in the reunions and resettlement. The Japanese response, however, has not been positive.

The collapse of the Soviet Union has complicated the arrangements for the Sakhalin Koreans. Russia has inherited the Soviet legacy in many respects and has endeavoured to encourage South Korea to continue the developing relationship. The treatment of national minorities in the post-Soviet Commonwealth of Independent States (CIS) has already become a key issue; as such the successor Russian government is likely to be more open to contacts between the Sakhalin Koreans and South Korea. Symptomatic of this change of attitude has been the Soviet/Russian authorities' permission for South Korean language textbooks and printing equipment for the Korean-language local newspaper to be imported. On the other hand, the very process of disintegration and decentralisation in the former Soviet Union has allowed a greater voice to smaller, autonomous regions. As the Japanese have found in their discussions with the Russians over their disputed 'northern territories', the role of the Sakhalin government has become an additional complicating factor. So, too, the Sakhalin administration is set to become a more important player in the diplomatic manoeuvring over the fate and freedom of the Sakhalin Koreans.

Korean A-bomb victims

In August 1945 the atomic bombs dropped on Hiroshima and Nagasaki caused massive devastation and loss of life. The Japanese survivors of those two attacks have been suffering and slowly dying from the side-effects of their exposure to radiation ever since. Known as hibakusha, they have been supported by Japanese government health and welfare provisions on a regular basis. However, at the time the bombs were dropped there were an estimated 70,000 Koreans in Hiroshima and 30,000 in Nagasaki who were working, under Japanese wartime forced labour regimes, or living in the areas of the two cities. Although the figures for deaths and survivors are subject to some dispute, approximately half of these Koreans were estimated to have died. Of the survivors, about 25,000 were estimated to have returned to South Korea at the end of the war, while the rest remained in Japan.

A survey completed in August 1991 recognised 2,300 Korean atomic bomb survivors still alive in South Korea. 89% of those identified suffered from health problems relating to the bomb blast; 67% had suffered physical injury (about one-third of whom were disabled) and 46% reported difficulties in making a living due to health problems (*Korea Newsreview* 26 October 1991). About three-quarters of those identified were registered with the Association of A-bomb Victims, a support group in South Korea, but the actual number of survivors is unofficially thought to number close to 20,000. The health facilities and welfare support available to these victims are extremely limited. There is only one clinic, at Hapchon, in southern South Korea, which is actually funded by private Japanese sources, devoted to the care of the victims.

Some of the victims, therefore, have tried to travel to Japan to get diagnosis and treatment there, but the hospitalisation and transport costs involved have become the subject of diplomatic exchanges. In 1968, with encouragement from some LDP and DSP politicians, a joint Japanese-Korean committee was set up to raise funding for both Koreans still in Japan and those back in South Korea to come to Japan to get proper medical care as well as for Japanese doctors to visit South Korea. The Japanese government's attitude was that, with the reparations paid on the establishment of Japan-South Korean diplomatic relations in 1965, government obligations had ended. Nevertheless, some officials within the Japanese Ministry of Health and Welfare did begin to take an interest in the issue in the mid-1970s and, finally, in 1981, there was an inter-governmental agreement, for five years, for victims in Korea to be financially assisted in coming to Japan for treatment. Around 350 victims visited Japan under this programme, but the Korean government, which argued that all those victims most in need of treatment had already been to Japan and that the standard of medical care in South Korea was now more than sufficient, did not push for an extension to the programme (Ichiki 1990 pp. 30-3).

In 1987, the Korean Association of A-bomb Victims for the first time asked the Japanese government for a specific amount of compensation, $2.3 billion, a calculation based on the Japanese government's annual allowances for individual Japanese victims, the number of Korean victims, and the number of years that had passed since the end of the war. In response, in May 1988, the Japanese government sent an investigation team to South Korea, and in November 1989 handed over to the South Korean Red Cross 42 million yen for helping the Korean victims; the same amount was transferred in 1990. In May 1990 Prime Minister Kaifu agreed with the visiting President Roh that the Japanese government would, in future, provide support for the medical expenses incurred.

The plight of these victims has not been eased by the tensions within the Korean community in Japan, and the tendency to politicise what should be a humanitarian problem is pronounced. Even the issue of a memorial to the Korean victims became an intra-Korean tussle. In April 1970 the Hiroshima branch of Mindan, the pro-South Korean group, built a cenotaph on the edge of the Hiroshima Peace Memorial Park, following a municipal ordinance which prohibited the construction of additional cenotaphs within the park. Complaints against this discrimination continued, until finally in May 1990 the Foreign Ministry and the Hiroshima city government agreed to have the monument relocated within the Peace Park. A dispute then broke out between Mindan and the pro-North Korean Chongnyon representatives on the organising committee. Mindan opposed a proposal to change the wording on the cenotaph from kankoku-jin, used primarily to indicate people from South

Korea, to victims from the 'Korean peninsula' (*Japan Times* 13 July 1990).

To Koreans, and concerned Japanese, the Japanese government attitude to the A-bomb victims is symptomatic of a refusal to squarely address the past. While grateful for the financial support provide since 1989, they feel that the Japanese government simply chose a figure out of the air, without doing sufficient study of the numbers of people involved. The Japanese, on the other hand, have themselves been traumatised by the events of Hiroshima and Nagasaki and cannot understand why the Korean victims pick only on them and make minimal requests for compensation to the US government, which had after all actually dropped the bombs.

Wartime conscripts

The survivors of the atomic bomb attacks are not the only groups in South Korea to want compensation from Japan. In recent years, demands by representatives and bereaved relatives for compensation for those Koreans drafted into military or civilian work, or prostitution, during the war have become increasingly vocal. The Japanese have reacted defensively.

The numbers of Koreans involved in forcibly working for the Japanese during the wartime period are unclear, but South Korean studies suggest that as many as 1.2 million Koreans were drafted as military personnel, civilian workers, and 'comfort women' for Japanese soldiers. The Korean Association for Bereaved Families of Victims of the Pacific War estimates that more than 150,000 Koreans were either killed or missing in action with the Japanese Army. The Japanese government has been reluctant to pursue the details of these draftees. In 1948, the remains of 7,643 Koreans were due to be handed over to South Korean officials at the port of Pusan, but the level of quay-side protests from Koreans demanding the return of survivors led to a confused situation which has still not been adequately explained. According to the Japanese Ministry of Health and Welfare, the remains were handed over; according to families of the bereaved, the remains were abandoned at sea off Pusan after the two ships failed to dock (FBIS-EAS-90-094, 15 May 1990). After the normalisation of relations in 1965, the remains of a further 21,919 soldiers and civilian workers were handed over to South Korea.

The Japanese government thereafter consistently maintained that it had no details on the draftees available and that the financial package associated with the 1965 normalisation treaties had covered all claims for compensation. The Korean association for the bereaved families, though not recognised officially by the South Korean government, nevertheless continued to press for compensation and later enlisted the support of the JSP in Japan. Eventually, in April 1990 the Japanese Ministry of Health admitted for the first time that

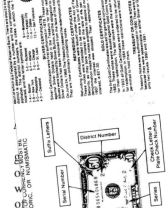

drafted into the Japanese military during the
ed to hand over the list or detail the numbers,
rmine whether the people were dead or alive.
filed a lawsuit demanding that the Japanese
llion yen ($1.7 million) in compensation for
Japanese wartime service (*Mainichi Daily*

o recently raised claims against the Japanese
inals. After Japan's defeat in 1945, a number
from the major Tokyo War Crimes Trial -
tries. Among the 4,403 people found guilty
, 23 of whom were sentenced to death. Most
ar criminals were not soldiers, but gunzoku,
ese Imperial Army who were assigned to
var in Thailand, Malaya and the Dutch East
ted on charges of brutality to prisoners and
pplies, but they claimed that, as conscripts,
e orders of the Japanese military.
eans (six who had served prison sentences
and   had been executed) presented claims to the
Japan se government totalling 136 million yen ($1 million). They argue that
the Japanese government has a responsibility to compensate them. The
Japanese government, however, while acknowledging that they were still
'Japanese' when they were arrested in 1945, claims that since they lost their
Japanese citizenship under the terms of the 1952 San Francisco Treaty it has
no obligation to compensate them (*Asahi Evening News* 9 November 1991).

The final, but in many ways the most traumatised, group of Koreans
trying to obtain compensation from the Japanese government is the former
'comfort women'. These were women who were forcibly drafted into sexual
service for the Japanese troops throughout East Asia during the period
1937-45. They were described by the Japanese as teishintai (literally corps of
self-devotion), but have become known euphemistically in English as
'comfort women'. After the outbreak of the Sino-Japanese War in 1937, the
Japanese army began drafting young unmarried Korean women, but as the
war zones expanded to South-east Asia it undertook wider 'slave hunts',
taking married women as well. These Korean women were then distributed
to Japan and other war zones, where they were subjected to horrifying sexual
demands.

Numbers and details are still subject to controversy, but according to the
submission made by the Korean support group to the United Nations Human
Rights Commission in March 1992, it is estimated that between 100,000 and
200,000 women were drafted as military 'comfort women', of whom around

80% would have been Korean (the remainder came mainly from Taiwan and the Philippines) (Yun 1992). With the defeat of Japan, many 'comfort women' were killed by the Japanese army or committed suicide rather than return to face humiliation in Korea; others soon succumbed to various diseases that they contracted. Those that did return to South Korea went to great pains to hide their experiences and tried to start a new life.

Only in the late 1980s did some Korean women's groups begin to try to establish the true facts of these wartime activities. In November 1990 an umbrella organisation, the Korean Council for Women Drafted for Sexual Service by Japan, sponsored by these women's groups, began to actively campaign to raise public awareness of the issue. The Council demonstrated in front of the Pagoda Park during Japanese Prime Minister Kaifu's visit there in January 1991. It was difficult to find any women, still living in Korea, who would come forward publicly to say that they had been drafted, but, eventually, in December 1991, three former 'comfort women' filed a suit in the Tokyo district court seeking Japanese government compensation of 20 million yen ($156,000) per person (in May 1992 a further nine filed suits in Tokyo).

The Japanese government's initial response to this campaign was that private businesses or individual brokers had been responsible for the recruiting, transporting and employing of the women. However, during the early months of 1992 academics and Japanese opposition party researchers discovered a series of documents in official repositories, including the Defence Agency archives, which proved the wartime government's involvement. Some elderly Japanese, who had been involved in the securing of Korean women, also began to give public testimonies.

Aware of the build-up of public concern in the South, and some rumblings even in the North Korean media, the South Korean government gave notice that it would raise the problem as a diplomatic issue during the January 1992 visit to Seoul by Japanese Prime Minister Miyazawa. Miyazawa was greeted by street demonstrations and a strident media campaign on this issue. In his speech to the Korean National Assembly, therefore, he expressed his 'acute distress' over these past Japanese actions. During his visit to Seoul, he also promised to investigate the circumstances and appeared to edge close to the idea of compensation (*Japan Times* 18 January 1992). However, Chief Cabinet Secretary Kato Koichi almost immediately afterwards stated that, although 'some sort of measures' should be taken to show remorse, compensation would not be considered as all claims from the Korean side had been settled by the 1965 treaty (FBIS-EAS-92-013, 21 January 1992).

The South Korean government, which had not raised the question during the 1965 negotiations and which had been rather lukewarm to the beginnings of the protest movement, changed tack. It set up an inter-ministerial task force to gather documents and testimonies in order to put in a full claim for compensation to the Japanese government later in the year. However, many 'comfort women' did not want to suffer the agonies of revealing their past, which most had tried hard to keep concealed from families and friends. By early July 1992, only the names of 155 had been discovered, of whom less than 100 had registered at the special unit established to receive reports. The timing of the South Korean push on this issue seems to have been affected not only by the emotional media coverage within South Korea, but also by the failure of the South Koreans to make much progress with the Japanese over the trade imbalance - the key issue of the Roh-Miyazawa talks - and the signs of activism on the North Korean side on the 'comfort women' issue.

At the sixth round of Japan-North Korean normalisation negotiations, in late January 1992, the North Korean side did raise the issue (and, indeed, actually supported the South Koreans' claims for compensation), and the Japanese negotiators apologised and repeated the pledge to investigate. At the late February 1992 North-South Korean prime ministers' talks, the North side also raised the question, arguing for joint action against the Japanese. The South, however, argued that it was already in bilateral discussions with the Japanese, so the need for joint action was obviated (*Korea Times* 1 February 1992; *Nihon Keizai Shimbun* 3 March 1992).

The North will use the issue to up its own demands for compensation from Japan for colonial era sufferings (see Chapter 8). The South will also use it as a diplomatic lever, but more with the intention of unsettling the Japanese into making concessions in other areas of bilateral contention. Nevertheless, now that it has been brought onto the diplomatic agenda, both South Korea and Japan will have to take the matter further. In early July 1992 the Japanese government published its report, accompanied by an apology, in which it admitted that the wartime governments had systematically recruited (though no evidence was found that forced recruitment took place) women for front-line brothels (BBC-SWB, FE/1427, 8 July 1992). The South Korean government welcomed the report but felt that it did not go far enough. Its evidence, incorporated into a white paper published at the end of July, showed that the Japanese government had used coercion to secure women.

The diplomatic tussle over responsibility and, crucially, compensation is, therefore, likely to continue. The Japanese are likely to maintain the position adopted by Foreign Minister Michio Watanabe in mid-February 1992 that the government cannot compensate individual women (*Nihon Keizai Shimbun* 20 February 1992), something that must await the result of a no doubt long drawn-out legal process. But they may well instead suggest some form of 'humanitarian' aid, such as funds for a medical centre.

The comfort women, in pressing for apologies and compensation, stress that they are not motivated by a desire for money. Rather, they are trying to 'reclaim the spirit' of the Korean people. As in other areas of the Japan-Korea relationship, the Japanese find the past coming back to haunt them. Once again, the need to face up to that past openly confronts the Japanese.

Cultural imperialism

The domestic society of any country provides essential non-economic resources for its foreign policy. Society supplies not only attitudes and actions which can reinforce or undermine a country's international policies (an issue touched on in Chapter 3), but also links with other societies which can cross-cut those policies (Tugendhat and Wallace 1988 pp. 82-103). The increasingly interdependent world, in both economics and politics, has led to increasing cultural interconnections and influences. Yet, many countries, in trying to assert their national independence and sovereignty against this trend of interdependence, have been forced into stressing their cultural and national values and to work hard to protect and promote them.

Countries wish to resist outside cultural influences, but like Japan in the Meiji era, they may well find themselves forced to borrow ideas and institutions from outside (in the Japanese case, the West) in order simply to resist. But cultural borrowing is a complex action. Non-Western countries, for example, have found it impossible simply just to input only Western technology. The very dynamics of this form of cultural borrowing lead on to the borrowing of legal and educational elements, which in turn can affect traditional values (Hirano 1988 pp. 147-9).

In the case of Korea the influx of foreign ideas and influences during this century has been heavily distorted by the Japanese role. In a reversal of the historical flow of Chinese culture through the Korean peninsula to early Japan, which gave it a Paekche flavour, Korea has received Western things with a distinctive Japanese accent. Forcibly during the colonial period and more peacefully subsequently, Japan has introduced into Korea, particularly South Korea, many facets of Western industrial civilisation. There has been, however, a Korean reaction of hostility and regret about foreign influences that dates back to the opening up of the country in the mid-nineteenth century. This has become particularly pronounced in a post-1945 determination in both Koreas to exclude Japanese influence and to prevent the ravages of Japanese 'cultural imperialism' returning again.

These tensions feed into domestic debates within South Korea about how to treat the Japanese occupation period in history books and how to deal with the more visible legacies of that period such as buildings constructed by the

Japanese. On the Japanese side, there has been a continuing debate about how to describe, particularly in history textbooks (as detailed in Chapter 2), the Japanese actions in Korea in the first half of this century.

Representative of the internal tensions on the South Korean side over these issues are the cases of the old Capitol building in central Seoul and the reception of satellite broadcasts from Japan. In 1926, the Japanese colonial administration built a massive granite and marble building for its use, right in front of the main royal palace in Seoul. The building, known as Chungang-chong (but called the Capitol building by foreigners because of its similarity to the home of the US Congress), was used as an administrative centre by post-1945 Korean governments too, until in 1983 President Chun decided to convert it into the National Museum. However, over the last few years, calls for it to be totally removed have increased. Advocates of removal argue that the country now has the technology and funds available to remove this colonial eyesore designed to subjugate the Korean national spirit. Opponents, however, argue that the money would be better spent on welfare projects than on this emotionally-laden undertaking; moreover, its presence will be a necessary reminder of the country's tragic past. The Culture Ministry did begin a ten-year project to restore the Kyongbok palace, by removing all traces of Japanese influence, but the final fate of the Chungang-chong building next to it has not yet been resolved.

In the early 1980s, the South Korean government became very concerned about Japanese television satellite broadcasts being picked up in South Korea after the launch of a new Japanese satellite. Some parts of southern Korea, especially around the Pusan area, have long been able to pick up Japanese television broadcasts, but the diffusion of satellite dish technology threatened to bring Japanese programmes to a much wider audience. The South Korean government tried both to persuade the Japanese to alter the 'footprint' (the area covered by a particular satellite) further away from South Korea and to discourage Koreans from buying satellite dishes. It has not been successful in either respect. One Japanese businessman who worked on a project in a country area in South Korea recently has recalled that the Korean joint venture partner actually installed a satellite dish so that the Japanese staff could watch Japanese television and not feel too homesick. The South Korean government is now planning to launch its own satellite by 1995; that could well cause problems the other way if anti-Japanese programmes were to be beamed down into Japan.

Cultural exchanges

After liberation from Japan, the South Korean government tried to expunge elements of Japanese literature, art, music and even architecture. Performances of traditional Japanese arts, seen by Koreans as being associated with the imperial tradition, were prohibited for decades. Not until the 1980s was a slight loosening of restraints allowed, and through the sponsorship of the Japan Foundation, the first post-war performances by visiting Japanese theatre groups were arranged: noh in 1983, bunraku in 1985, kabuki in 1988, and kyogen in 1989.

Japanese songs have continued to be banned from South Korean radio and television, and the Japanese folk singer Kato Tokiko, who became the first Japanese 'pop' star invited to perform in Seoul, in 1990, came in for considerable criticism for singing in Japanese as well as Korean and English when she performed. Until 1987, when democratisation brought a lifting of bans on 'problematic' popular songs, a number of Korean songs which were considered to be written in a Japanese style were also banned from being broadcast. Indeed, between 1961 and 1987 a total of 253 Korean songs were banned on the grounds that they 'emit a Japanese flavour'. Yet, the influence of Japanese popular music styles on Korean popular music is unmistakable. There is a considerable underground circulation in South Korea of cassette tapes and videos of Japanese popular music.

Japanese films have continued to be banned in South Korea, although a number of illegally-duplicated videos of Japanese films are on sale. Even cartoon films, produced in Japan, are subject to the ban on broadcasting (and video tapes) if they are deemed to carry a Japanese flavour. Controversy arose in early 1991, for example, over the import and public showing of a cartoon adventure, 'The Wild Boy', from Hong Kong (all the dialogue was in Chinese), which was initialled approved by the Culture Ministry, but later found to actually be a copy of the Japanese Toho company's 'Akira' cartoon. In recent years, the pressure from Japanese film companies and Korean film importers for a liberalisation has increased. But the Culture Ministry has not yet relaxed the general ban on Japanese films. As a result, the only place in Seoul that it is possible to legally view Japanese films in public is at the Japanese Embassy's Cultural Centre. The Ministry, however, in January 1991 did give permission for the production of joint Korean-Japanese films based on historical fact. One of the first products of this new collaboration was 'Monja, Akiko, Sonya' (which also involved Russians), which was released to critical acclaim in the spring of 1992.

The Korean film industry developed during the Japanese colonial period. Directors such as Na Un-kyu used their films to subtly portray the resistance to Japan and to stimulate feelings of Korean nationalism; Na's 1926 silent movie, 'Arirang', is a classic of this type (Ahn 1989 pp. 47-50). The immediate post-liberation period saw a burst of dramatic feature films depicting the Koreans' struggle for freedom, but since then anti-Japanism, or rather, depiction of Japanese as the 'bad guys' in Korean films has become only one of many themes covered by Korean directors.

The Japanese, while accepting that anti-Japanese themes will be inevitable in Korean films and on television, have nevertheless been unhappy at the way these themes are sometimes picked up. In April 1992, the Korean television station MBC started a serial called 'Kingdom of Wrath', which included in its opening episode a story about the attempted assassination of the Japanese Emperor and included actual film footage of Emperor Akihito's enthronement parade. The Japanese government were upset as what they saw as *lese majeste* and protested to the Korean government (*Korea Newsreview* 18 April 1992).

Cultural exchanges in the opposite direction have been less sensitive, but still relatively limited (Sato 1983 pp. 72-87). From the 1950s, traditional Korean dance, theatre and music groups visited Japan two or three times a year, but in the mid-1980s these performances increased noticeably; in 1987 25 different groups visited Japan. Since the early 1980s, Korean popular singers have also had some success in Japan, led by Cho Yong-pil's 'Pusan-ko e kaere' (Return to Pusan port), which broke all records for a foreign singer in the Japanese pop music market. Prompted by Cho's success, Japanese talent scouts scoured South Korea to recruit singers who might appeal to the Japanese. A number of Korean singers have signed recording contracts, but none have been able to repeat the success of Cho. It is, however, symptomatic of the suspicion between the two countries that, at the time of Cho's success, some Korean officials actually questioned whether the Japanese had deliberately made his song into a hit in order to allow them to ask for reciprocal opening of the Korean music market!

North Korea, lacking diplomatic relations with Japan, has been handicapped in the extent to which cultural exchanges, other than through sympathetic Korean residents or opposition politicians and supporters' groups, could be carried out. Nevertheless, the North has tried to raise the banner of 'cultural exchange' as a way of enhancing its influence in Japan, even though the results were meagre. The clearly idolatrous treatment of Kim Il-sung in the performances of North Korean music has not helped their broader appeal in Japan (the 'reunification' concerts of the Korean State Symphony Orchestra in Japan in May 1992 were typical of this tendency). The North has been as determined to exclude Japanese cultural imperialism as the South, but, in January 1991, for what was believed to be the first time in either Korea, a Japanese movie was shown on (North) Korean national television.

Education and tourism

One of the global characteristics of the 1980s has been the tremendous increase in the flows of ordinary people across national boundaries, particularly as tourists and students. This trend has been clear also in the case of Japan and South Korea.

South Koreans travelling to Japan have grown considerably in numbers during the 1980s, in particular after the South Korean government began loosening its restrictions on overseas travel after 1987 (abolishing them finally with effect from January 1989). From just under 200,000 in 1979 the number had risen to 806,000 by 1989 and their share of all visitors to Japan had risen to 27%. Two trends which emerged at the end of the 1980s were for an increasing number of under-thirties to visit Japan and, amongst those still at school or college, an ever increasing majority were making their first visit to Japan. As most of these younger people were going for tourism rather than business, by 1989 tourism had replaced business as the main objective for the Koreans as a whole (*Nijuisseiki* 1991a pp.5-9). More disturbing for the Japanese authorities, however, has been the tendency for some Koreans to visit Japan on tourist visas and then disappear into the growing illegal labour market; as of mid-1992 an estimated 30,000 Koreans were thought to be illegally working in Japan. As the Japanese youth become less inclined to do the dirty and dangerous jobs, the attractions for small companies in employing foreigners such as the Koreans grows.

Japanese visitors to South Korea have been steadily growing in numbers over the past 20 years, but they also have grown noticeably since the mid-1980s. In 1989, the number passed the million mark for the first time, reaching 1,113,000. South Korea, therefore, has become the second most popular destination for Japanese travellers after the United States. According to Korean figures, Japanese now account for well over 50% of all visitors to South Korea. However, compared to the usual pattern of Japanese overseas travellers, those going to South Korea show an unusually high percentage of men, who tend to be mainly in the late thirties to early fifties age group (*Nijuisseiki* 1991a pp. 10-15). The attractions of the 'sex tours' have barely dimmed.

Until April 1991, Japanese nationals retained in their passports the caveat that it was valid for all countries except North Korea. This did not prevent Japanese from visiting North Korea through China and, as in the case of the various JSP delegations, often quite senior politicians visited openly. But the numbers have been very small; in 1984, for example, 798 Japanese visted the North (additionally, 5,645 Korean residents in Japan also went) and 167 North Koreans visited Japan. The beginning of the Japan-North Korean negotiations has brought about more interest amongst the Japanese in the

North, but even then only 1,090 Japanese signed up for tours to the North in 1991. Although a January 1992 agreement allowed for charter flights between Japan and North Korea, only three took place in the first half of the year and tourist numbers barely exceeded the previous year's rate. The high costs and the limited facilities and sight-seeing sites are likely to ensure that the numbers remain small.

Although the marked increase in Japan-South Korean flows is to be welcomed as a way of bringing more people into direct contact with the other country, there are doubts as to the quality of these visits. It is clear, for example, that the package tours avidly used by Japanese men are rarely concerned with Korean historical or cultural interests. Even the very recent trend for Japanese newly-weds to spend their honeymoon in Cheju-do island has more to do with the semi-tropical nature of its climate and scenery than an intrinsic interest in Korea.

More encouraging, however, is the gradual, but steady, increase in the number of students, scholars and scientists visiting each other's country. Tours of South Korea by Japanese high school students began in 1975, but increased noticeably after President Chun's 1984 trip to Japan led to a formalisation of the youth exchange programme. At the initiative of the South Korean side in early 1988, a joint '8,000 persons exchange programme' (800 to be invited each way each year for five years) was begun. The number of Korean students studying at Japanese universities and colleges has grown rapidly from 4852 in 1987 to 9,483 in 1991, second behind the Chinese as the largest group of foreign students (22% of all foreign students). Japanese students studying in South Korean universities are far fewer, numbering only 572 in 1989 (of whom about half may well be ethnic Koreans brought up in Japan), but the number is slowly increasing.

Another important indicator of the degree of cultural interchange is the development of language studies. After liberation, the South Korean government halted study of the Japanese language, for understandable reasons given the way in which it had been forced upon the Koreans during the colonial period. Not until 1961 did any Korean university introduce a Japanese language course. In 1973, as part of President Park's revision of the school curriculum, Japanese was allowed to be taken as the second foreign language at high schools. By the end of 1991, Japanese was being taught at over 900 high schools and colleges.

Yet, the diffusion of Japanese studies remains controversial. In the spring of 1992, Korea University (one of the two leading private universities) set up the first ever course on the Japanese economy, but the most prestigious Seoul National University (SNU), which a few years before rejected a proposal to establish a Japan studies centre, decided to remove Japanese from the list of foreign languages eligible for use in its entrance examinations from 1994.

SNU's dean for academic affairs commented: 'We think Japanese is a useful tool in daily life, but less worthy of academic research' (*Japan Times Weekly* 4 May 1992).

Korean studies in Japan are even more limited, though the extent is slowly expanding. Only five Japanese universities offer degree courses in the Korean language and a further 76 colleges teach Korean as a second foreign language option. As of 1988, only 14 Japanese high schools offered part-time or extra-curricular language tuition in Korean. However, in May 1992, Osaka city education authorities decided to recruit the first full-time high school teacher of Korean language anywhere in Japan. A number of local community groups arrange Korean language lessons, but these tend to be by and for ethnic Korean residents. After years of controversy over the exact title to be used (for the two words mostly commonly used in Japanese for the Korean language - kankokugo and chosengo - implicitly displayed support for one or other of the two Koreas), NHK radio and television finally began a Korean language course in 1984, under the title of 'Annyong hassimnika' ('hello, how do you do'). In the Kanto region, these courses have recorded higher audiences than NHK's French language courses, but it is argued that many ethnic Korean residents, who do not know Korean but wish to learn it, make up the audience.

Other forms of exchanges are growing too. Sports associations have developed links; 1991 saw the first ever match between baseball teams chosen by the Korean and Japanese professional leagues. Twinnings have increased markedly; the proclamation of Seoul and Tokyo as sister cities on the eve of the 1988 Olympics was the most significant, but now over 40 cities and prefectures have twinning arrangements. The two governments agreed in February 1988 to establish a private sector '21st Century Committee' to examine all levels of bilateral exchanges. Headed on the Japanese side by Sunobe Ryuzo, a former ambassador to Korea, and on the Korean side by Koh Byong-ik, formerly SNU president, the Committee issued a report in January 1991 which outlined a number of ways in which more constructive exchanges between the two countries could take place.

The general picture from all these Japanese-South Korean cultural, educational and other exchanges is one of growth, but from a low base and often on a lop-sided basis. Japan-North Korean exchanges barely exist by comparison, though will inevitably expand after relations are normalised. Nevertheless, for the two Koreas and for Japan the higher degree of interest in each other needs to be accompanied by steps to rectify the still imperfect knowledge of each other. Greater efforts on this often forgotten item on the agenda can do much to ease the tensions and transitions in other aspects of the bilateral relationships.

8 Normalising Japan-North Korea Relations

Japan's policy towards North Korea cannot easily be separated from either the inter-linkages with the Japan-South Korean and the North-South Korean relationships or the close Japan-US relationship. Throughout the post-war era, Japan has adhered to its policy of non-recognition of North Korea and placed its policy priority on maintaining close ties with South Korea, as the best way of ensuring stability on the peninsula. This has meant that, despite considerable tension in the Japan-South Korean relationship at times, Japan has not really progressed beyond a slow expansion of economic and cultural links with the North. North Korea has tried to push Japan into adopting an 'equidistant' policy through recognition of the North. However, although the Japanese did occasionally, such as in the early 1970s, waver towards the North, the Japanese concept of balance towards the two Koreas has always come down as a tilt towards the South.

However, the degree of tilt and the way in which it has been pursued have caused considerable controversy, both within Japan and between Japan and South Korea. Any signs of Japanese shifts towards the North have inevitably been controversial within South Korea. Chapter 4 examined the major trends in Japan-North Korean relations through to the end of the 1980s. This chapter considers the dynamics and characteristics of the current third phase of prospective Japan-North Korean detente, which began in the autumn of 1990.

North Korean concerns

North Korea had been badly shaken by the traumatic international events of 1989. Its closest Asian socialist ally, China, had been riven by a student democracy movement which culminated in the massacre at Tiananmen Square in June 1989, and its other close ally, the Soviet Union, under Gorbachev, had decided to allow the East European democratic domino movement to run its course. One by one, the former East European friends of North Korea recognised the South during the winter of 1989-90. However, by the spring of 1990, encouraged by Chinese solidity, the North Korean leadership had recovered some of its composure.

But then, North Korean ideological isolation was to take a turn for the worse in the summer of 1990, as Roh flew to San Francisco for a dramatic summit meeting with Gorbachev, who was then visiting the United States. The Soviets, out of consideration for the North Koreans, deliberately tried to keep the meeting informal and low-key, but the two presidents did agree to promote commercial and cultural relations and, despite Gorbachev's vagueness about the timing of full recognition, that step was clearly anticipated. Soviet-North Korean relations became increasingly irritable and when Soviet Foreign Minister Eduard Shevardnadze visited Pyongyang in early September 1990 to explain that the Soviet Union would be recognising the South, Kim Il-sung pointedly refused to see him.

For political reasons, to compensate for the deepening isolation in which he found himself and to get back at the South, Kim decided to turn towards Japan. But he also had compelling economic reasons. By 1990 North Korea's economic difficulties were beginning to mount. Energy and food shortages were growing and the leadership had to resort to the '90-day struggle' campaigns to encourage greater productivity (JETRO 1991 pp. 1-21). Possible sources of help were few. The Soviet Union faced considerable economic difficulties itself (later in 1990 it informed the North Koreans that they would have to pay hard currency for oil from January 1991), China was going through a period of economic retrenchment, the Europeans were - both East and West - preoccupied with the costs of integration and restructuring in Europe, and the Americans were in no mood to offer anything concrete. Japan, then in the midst of what was to become its longest post-war economic boom period, offered the most likely, indeed the only possible, source of economic assistance and resources needed.

In Japan, the LDP had revived itself from the set-backs of the July 1989 Upper House election to secure a working majority in the more important February 1990 Lower House election. North Korea, which during 1989 must have had some expectation that a coalition headed by the pro-North Korean JSP would come to power, was forced back into the reality of having to deal with the LDP. In July 1990, therefore, the North Koreans approached the JSP to arrange a joint JSP-LDP visit to Pyongyang.

Japanese domestic environment

The Japanese response and follow-up in the next few months displayed the complexities of the Japanese foreign policy-making process. The politicians, the bureaucrats and the business community had differing perspectives on relations with the North. The shifting power balances and alliances within the decision-making process helped to bring tensions and, occasionally, inconsistencies.

The Foreign Ministry has always considered itself the guiding hand of foreign policy towards South Korea and, despite the absence of diplomatic relations, North Korea too. A strong core of 'Korea experts' has been built up within the Ministry, even though inevitably their language training and diplomatic experience has been only in the South. The director-general of the Asian Affairs Bureau until mid-1992, the head of the Korea desk throughout most of the first year of the negotiations, and the chief negotiator with the North Koreans had all served previously in Korea-related posts.

However, with the increased complexity of international relations, the Foreign Ministry has found that in policy towards North Korea, as elsewhere, the number of ministries involved in policy inputs has grown steadily during the 1980s. The Foreign Ministry has worked closely with the Defence Agency on aspects of security and defence policy. There is considerable suspicion within the Agency about North Korea's military and, indeed, nuclear capabilities and it, therefore, acts in a cautionary role against too rapid development of ties with North Korea.

The Foreign Ministry's traditional rival in foreign economic policy areas has been MITI. However, unlike its role in the late 1960s-early 1970s in encouraging trade with China prior to the Sino-Japanese normalisation of relations, MITI has not acted as a strong supporter of developing economic contacts with North Korea. The Finance Ministry was heavily involved in discussions over loans to South Korea and will be again as the negotiations with North Korea extend into detailed discussion of economic cooperation. However, given the growth in other aid commitments, especially to the Middle East, Eastern Europe, Cambodia and the Rio Earth Summit, coupled with a growing feeling of resentment that Japan is being expected to be the 'treasury' for 'bailing out' operations around the world, the Finance Ministry will inevitably try to bargain down the level of assistance.

The LDP, or rather certain factions and individuals, are involved in North Korean affairs. Nevertheless, by contrast with the deep involvement of the Nakasone and Fukuda factions in the pro-South Korean lobby, contacts with the North have been sporadic and superficial. For decades, few LDP politicians of any standing took an interest in North Korean affairs, and the main line of communication - the Dietmen's League for the Promotion of Japan-North Korean Friendship - was left in the hands of a little-known LDP politician from the Tanaka faction. It was only during 1990 that senior LDP politicians began to take an interest in developing relations with North Korea and the visit to Pyongyang discussed below became feasible.

Given the absence of formal relations and the low profile of the LDP, at least until 1990, the key channel for communication with North Korea has been the JSP. The JSP, therefore, has acted as a constant lobbying force for better trade and cultural relations as well as arguing, ultimately, for diplomatic relations with North Korea. This has not been an easy furrow to plough, at least until 1990, when it began to find support from within the LDP itself.

The Japanese business community can be considered a heterogeneous player; the interests of the leaders of the major economic organisations, the industry sectoral groups and individual corporations are different and competing. Japan is North Korea's largest non-socialist trading partner, but the bilateral trade is miniscule compared to Japan-South Korean trade. Japanese business has been keen on trade and investment in the South, but has shown little sustained interest in the North's market. The brief flurry of interest in the early 1970s in plant and machinery exports turned to concern, and, at times, despair about securing repayment for the debts dating from that period.

In the period immediately before the normalisation of relations with China, in 1971-72, Japanese business leaders accelerated the change of political climate within the LDP and helped realise the formation of a cabinet committed to a new policy towards China. Although some companies are interested in the long-term prospects for the North Korean market and even a 'Japan Sea economic zone' which would have to include North Korea, there is no pressure from business leaders in any way comparable to the earlier China case.

Kanemaru's visit to North Korea

The Japanese government responded favourably to the North Koreans' mid-1990 initiative, but with the proviso that the release of two Japanese seamen from the Fujisan-maru, held in North Korean custody since 1983, be expedited.[1] The North Koreans wanted to attract an influential LDP politician but one not in an official post (Ishii 1991 pp. 58-64). Kanemaru, a former deputy prime minister and co-head of the powerful Takeshita faction, was chosen to join with Makoto Tanabe, vice-chairman of the JSP, in leading the delegation.

During a series of meetings, including one involving Kanemaru and Kim Il-sung alone, the North Koreans surprised the Japanese with the speed and direction in which they wished to move. The subsequent joint declaration by the LDP, JSP and KWP, issued on 28 September, stated that Japan should 'fully and officially apologise and compensate' North Korea for 'the enormous misfortunes and misery imposed on the Korean people for 36 years and the losses inflicted on the Korean people in the ensuing 45 years'.[2] Kanemaru had, in fact, handed over to Kim a letter from Kaifu apologising for Japanese pre-1945 colonial rule, but it had been written in the latter's capacity as president of the LDP. In addition, the two governments were urged to initiate diplomatic talks in November 1990 for the establishment of diplomatic relations as soon as possible.

Although not incorporated into this declaration, it was also agreed that the two Japanese seamen would be released; this was done in October 1990 when another LDP-JSP delegation went to Pyongyang to attend the 45th anniversary of the KWP's founding (Ishii 1991 pp.179-92).

The change in the North Korean attitude and the sudden push for full normalisation of relations with Japan caught not just Kanemaru but also the Japanese and South Korean governments off-balance. The North Koreans explained their policy shift as being due to the rapid changes in the international situation and to the reluctance of some Japanese officials to make reparations to North Korea unless diplomatic relations had been established. Influential were Eduard Shevardnadze's visit to Pyongyang, after which the establishment of Soviet-South Korean relations was clearly imminent (it followed on 30 September), and Kim Il-sung's own visit to Shenyang in mid-September to meet Chinese Party Secretary-General Jiang Zemin. Aware of which way the wind was blowing, Kim Il-sung evidently decided to make the most of the opportunity of Kanemaru's visit, to appeal to his vanity as a politician and hopefully secure a deal which the Japanese government would find difficult to repudiate.

Kanemaru's commitments in Pyongyang were criticised by both the Foreign Ministry and parts of the LDP, who felt that he had gone too far in his 'personal diplomacy' by agreeing to pay compensation for the post-1945 years. The Foreign Ministry felt aggrieved that accompanying Foreign Ministry officials had been deliberately excluded from the drafting stages of the final communique. A former foreign minister, Ito Masayoshi, commented that Kanemaru was not well-suited to diplomacy (*Bungei Shunju* January 1991). Yet, Kanemaru's actions were not without precedent in Japanese diplomacy, for, in the past, LDP politicians have on occasions played a key part in developing relations with socialist countries. Kono Ichiro's mission to Moscow in May 1956   similarly played a crucial role in expediting Japan-Soviet negotiations for normalisation (Hellman 1969 pp.139-41).

The Foreign Ministry, however, found the autumn of 1990 a particularly hard time in terms of its relations with the LDP, for major disagreements arose over relations with the Soviet Union (where again Kanemaru was amongst those trying to push the Ministry further than it wanted to go) and the response to the Gulf crisis, in particular the abortive UN Peace Cooperation Bill.

The Japanese government also came under pressure from both the American and South Korean governments. Kanemaru, in fact, visited Seoul in early October to meet President Roh and explain his intentions; he argued that the expression about post-war compensation was made for political reasons and did not mean that the Japanese government would actually pay such compensation. Roh asked through Kanemaru that the Japanese accept 'five principles' in its dealings with North Korea (these were later confirmed through regular diplomatic channels and during the Roh-Kaifu meeting in January 1991). While basically not opposing the improvement of Japan-North Korea relations, Roh asked that:

(1)   Japan should consult extensively with South Korea about the negotiations;

(2)   Japan should not give economic assistance to North Korea until after formal diplomatic ties are established and this aid should not be used by North Korea for military purposes;

(3)   Japan should pay attention to the state of the North-South Korean dialogue;

(4)   Japan should press North Korea to sign the nuclear inspection agreement with the International Atomic Energy Agency (IAEA); and

(5)   Japan should encourage North Korea towards openness and reform (*Korea Times* 9 October 1990; BBC-SWB FE/0891, 10 October 1991).

The US government also discussed the normalisation issue with Japanese officials and with Kanemaru himself. Amongst the US cautionary advice to the Japanese, the issue of IAEA nuclear inspection clearly figured as the most important; indeed, at the end of October, Assistant Secretary of State Richard Solomon described 'nuclear proliferation on the Korean peninsula as the number one threat to stability in East Asia' (FBIS-EAS-90-202, 18 October 1990; *Korea Times*, 1 November 1990). The Japanese Foreign Ministry itself, of course, wanted to try to water down the Kanemaru commitments and gain control of the negotiations with North Korea, but its naturally cautious attitude was reinforced by external pressure from the United States and South Korea.

Opening negotiations

Preliminary talks on the agenda and negotiating arrangements were held three times in Beijing in November and December 1990, before the full negotiations opened in Pyongyang at the end of January 1991. In total, seven rounds of negotiations have been held, the second one in Tokyo, and all subsequent ones in Beijing. The eighth round of negotiations, after much postponement, is due to take place in November 1992.

The negotiations can be divided into two broad phases. Firstly, the first three meetings, in January, March and May 1991, when both sides barely got beyond stating their basic positions and no real negotiating took place. Secondly, after an interruption, the more regular and more substantial negotiations held since August 1991.

The delegations were led by Ambassador Noboru Nakahira, former ambassador to Malaysia, on the Japanese side and Chon In-chol, vice-foreign minister, on the North Korean side. The Japanese suffered from the poor and insecure communications between Pyongyang and Tokyo, so it was agreed that from the third meeting onwards Beijing would be the site of all future negotiations. The North Koreans tried hard to bully and bounce the Japanese into an early recognition. At the third meeting, in May 1991, when the negotiations were sticky, the North Koreans even proposed moving to an early solution of basic issues, including diplomatic recognition, and then discussing more complicated issues such as compensation later, but the Japanese were not to be drawn.

The Japanese Foreign Ministry's aim was not only to regain the negotiating initiative from Japanese politicians but also to slow down the negotiations to their own pace. On being appointed as the chief negotiator, Nakahira commented that the negotiations might take two years (*Nihon Keizai Shimbun* 22 December 1990). This was not intended to be an official target date, but it did symbolise the Ministry's propensity for caution.

After the January 1991 meeting, when the cool Japanese stance became clear, the North Koreans tried to revert to political pressure. Kim Yong-sun, the KWP secretary for International Affairs, led a delegation to Tokyo in February 1991. He met Kanemaru, who felt under some obligation to try to help promote relations and also offered to act as an intermediary between North Korea and the United States, Tanabe and even Kaifu, the first occasion for a Japanese prime minister to meet a senior North Korean official (*Nihon Keizai Shimbun* 24 February 1991). However, the Japanese Foreign Ministry was finding it easier to resist pressure from the politicians. Cooperation between the LDP and the JSP on the North Korean issue suffered because of a sharpening of the conflict between the two parties during the winter of 1990-91 over the abortive UN Cooperation Bill. Moreover, during the spring of 1991 Kanemaru's own political influence waned slightly because of a political set-back in his home prefecture and the death of his wife. The North Koreans, noting that decline, turned to Takeshita and invited him to North Korea; well aware of how that would incense the South Koreans (for he was head of the Japan-South Korean Dietman's League as well as a former prime minister), Takeshita declined.

The preliminary talks had failed to clarify the issues of compensation and nuclear inspection and these two problems dominated the first three meetings.

The North Korean side argued that compensation was the most important problem; since the tripartite declaration of September 1990 had delineated the Japanese responsibility for both the colonial period and the post-war period, only the exact formula and the amount was left to be settled. The Japanese replied that the tripartite declaration was not binding on the Japanese government and that, under international law, Japan had never been at war with North Korea; compensation for the post-war period was not conceivable (FBIS-EAS-91-021, 31 January 1991).

The Japanese, on the other hand, urged the North Koreans to sign the nuclear safeguards agreement attached to the Nuclear Non-Proliferation Treaty and allow inspection of its nuclear facilities. North Korea, at the urging of the Soviet Union, had signed the NPT in 1985, but it failed to sign the additional nuclear safeguards agreement within the statutory 18 months. During 1989-90, however, US and South Korean intelligence officials became increasingly concerned that North Korea might actually be trying to develop a nuclear weapon at its facilities at Yongbyon, 50 miles north of Pyongyang. In the aftermath of the Kanemaru visit, the United States became disturbed at the prospect that financial assistance from Japan might be diverted into nuclear weapon development programmes. Michael Armacost, the US ambassador in Tokyo, hurriedly called on Kanemaru and requested that inspection of North Korean nuclear facilities by the International Atomic Energy Agency (IAEA) be a prerequisite of normalisation. A Central Intelligence Agency military specialist, stationed in South Korea, was sent to Tokyo with satellite intelligence of the North Korean site; he explained that the North could be capable of producing nuclear bombs by 1995 (*Mainichi Daily News* 22 November 1991). With the post-Gulf War revelations of the Iraqi secret development of nuclear weapons, the US attitude to the non-proliferation of nuclear weaponry hardened even further.

The North Korean response to the Japanese demands was that it was not an issue to be discussed in these bilateral negotiations, but that anyway North Korea had neither the intention nor capability to produce nuclear weapons. The North would sign the nuclear safeguards agreement, but only if the US nuclear threat (from nuclear weapons stored on South Korean soil) were removed (*Nihon Keizai Shimbun* 17 March 1991; FBIS-EAS-91-021, 31 January 1992).

A number of other issues were raised, such as the terms of an apology from a Japanese leader to the North Korean people, permission for the Japanese wives of North Koreans (estimated to be about 1,800 women) to visit Japan, a guarantee of rights for pro-North ethnic Koreans resident in Japan, and admission of North (and South) Korea to the United Nations. But the third round of negotiations, in May 1991, was brought to a complete impasse by the Japanese request for information on a missing Japanese. She was Taguchi Yaeko (known in Korean as Yi Un-hye), who, Japanese police alleged, had been kidnapped to the North to act as a language teacher for Kim Hyon-hui, who had later impersonated a Japanese and planted the bomb which destroyed a KAL airliner off the coast of Burma in 1987 (*Nihon Keizai Shimbun*, 26 May 1991). The North Koreans, who did not want to admit to having anything to do with any terrorist action, reacted strongly to this enquiry and dismissed it as being irrelevant to the ongoing negotiations.

The North Koreans no doubt thought that the Japanese had deliberately raised the Taguchi problem to be obstructionist. The Japanese had been pushed into raising it at that particular time by the South Koreans, who persuaded Kim Hyon-hui to reiterate publicly her previous revelations about her language instruction (Foster-Carter 1992 p.72), but there is evidence that the Japanese police had only recently succeeded in working out the actual identity of the teacher. Anyway, there then followed a long period of behind-the-scenes diplomatic manoeuvring before both sides could be brought back to the negotiating table for the second phase.

The North Koreans acted the more desperately. They tried to mobilise Japanese political support by again approaching Kanemaru with an invitation to visit Pyongyang, but not only did he turn them down, but Tanabe actually wrote to the North Korean leadership explaining that unless they were more cooperative little progress could be expected. The North tried to play the American 'card': on 21 May, the very day when the third round of negotiations ground to a halt, the North Korean media called for the US-North Korean talks, which had been held intermittently a dozen times over the past three years between junior diplomats from the respective embassies in Beijing, to be up-graded to a more senior level. Despite a disappointing US response, the North Koreans followed up in mid-June by returning the bodies of 11 US servicemen missing since the Korean War (*Korea Times* 25 June 1991).

The North Koreans were undoubtedly trying to play on the underlying but unfounded Japanese fear that, following the awful precedent of the sudden US move towards China in 1971, they might once again be caught napping by the Americans. The Americans, however, reassured the Japanese that, while not totally ruling out a slow improvement of relations with the North (and the Bush administration made it clear that it would not veto the North Korean application for UN membership), they had no intention of recognising the North yet, especially while the nuclear issue was unresolved.

Far from being able to use leverage on the Japanese, the North Koreans actually found their diplomatic position weakening during the late spring and summer of 1991. The formation of an informal 'coalition' of countries concerned about the North Korean nuclear threat gathered pace. Despite the outburst by the South Korean defence minister about a pre-emptive strike against the Yongbyon reactor (discussed in Chapter 5), the military option was not considered seriously, but the possibility of imposing sanctions or appealing to the UN Security Council for action was. However, the main effort was put into sustained persuasion and pressure. Not just the United States but several West European states that the North Koreans aproached made it clear that there could be no relations without IAEA inspection. The Soviets suspended technical assistance to the North and the Japanese were surprised at how easy it was to persuade Gorbachev to agree to a reference to the need for outside inspection of the North's facilities in the communique at the end of his trip to Japan in April 1991. Even the Chinese, while warning the West against putting excessive pressure on the North, quietly encouraged the North to be more realistic about inspection.

Chinese 'quiet diplomacy' was effective in two respects: at the end of May 1991, North Korea abandoned its long-standing objection to separate UN membership for the two Koreas and decided to apply for independent membership, and also announced the resumption of talks with the IAEA about a safeguards agreement. In July 1991 the North initialled an inspection agreement with the IAEA and proposed the resumption of the North-South prime ministers' talks, which had been suspended since December 1990 because of North Korean displeasure over the annual springtime US-South Korean 'Team Spirit' exercises. A visit in the same month to Pyongyang by a Japanese Foreign Ministry official and an academic managed to secure a way out of the Taguchi problem, whereby the North Koreans agreed to discuss it, but in a separate sub-committee which would operate in parallel to the main negotiations.

The second phase

Encouraged by what they saw as slight signs of North Korean flexibility, the Japanese entered the second phase of the negotiations prepared for more detailed discussions. The subsequent rounds of negotiations have been held in August and November 1991 and January and May 1992. Although the fourth meeting, in late August 1991, became acrimonious over the Taguchi problem (the North Koreans refused to admit that in the July informal discussions they had agreed to investigate her whereabouts), the Japanese were able to detect in that round some signs of recognition on the North Korean side of the realities of the negotiating process.

The two sides have been conducting the negotiations under four headings: basic problems (recognition etc.), compensation (economic assistance), nuclear inspection, and miscellaneous issues (Taguchi case, missing Japanese wives, 'comfort women' etc.). On the basic question of recognition of North

Korea and its area of sovereignty, the admission of the North into the United Nations in September 1991 as a separate entity undoubtedly made it less easy for the North Koreans to object to a definition of its sovereignty confined to only the northern part of the peninsula. However, the North Koreans continued to argue for an apology from Japan for the colonial period to be included in the draft treaty. The Japanese, wary of the precedent of the 1965 Japan-South Korean Basic Treaty which contained no such apology, have been arguing for a separate 'political statement'; they feel that this is likely to be accepted eventually by the North Koreans.

On the compensation issue, the North Koreans have gradually dropped the formal demand for post-war compensation and the discussion has focused on the terms of the compensation for the colonial period. The Japanese have conditionally acknowledged the North's right to seek property damages linked to colonial rule, but have asked for documentary evidence to back up the claims (something which, the North Koreans rightly argue, it is difficult to find after 50 years). Discussions of the actual amounts involved - and the provision of a lump sum by the Japanese as economic assistance to cover all potential claims - has, therefore, been confined to the informal discussions in the margins of the negotiating sessions. The final treaty will, no doubt, contain some reference to the question of compensation.

On the miscellaneous questions there has been little progress. The separate sub-committee discussing the Taguchi case has merely re-covered old positions, but, given that the Japanese police now have reason to believe that she is already dead, the issue may well be left to one side if the other issues in the negotiations can be resolved. As for the wives issue, at the November 1991 meeting the North Koreans did provide a short list dealing with the whereabouts of 20 missing Japanese women, but the Japanese considered that only a token first step because what they really wanted was permission for all the wives to visit Japan. In April 1992, during a visit to Pyongyang by LDP and JSP politicians to attend Kim Il-sung's eightieth birthday celebrations, however, Kim did seem to indicate that some easing of travel restrictions might be possible.

At the January 1992 round of negotiations, the North Koreans raised the fate of the 'comfort women' forced into prostitution for the Japanese armed forces (an issue that had also been raised diplomatically by the South Koreans earlier the same month). The Japanese side referred to Prime Minister Miyazawa's apology for these past actions but pointed out that no compensation could be paid. The North Korean side clearly wish to use this newly-emerged issue to boost up their claims for compensation, and the Japanese, who finally produced a report of their own investigations on this issue in July 1992, will find it difficult to avoid treating the two Koreas equally.

Nuclear inspection

However, the most contentious issue has proved to be the inspection of the North's nuclear facilities. Japan, as the only country to suffer from attack by nuclear weapons, has a particular sensitivity to nuclear development. This has led, in the past, to concern not only about the nuclear arsenals of the two superpowers, but also about the nuclear arming of either Korea. A normalisation of relations with a nuclear-armed or potentially nuclear-armed North Korea might well encourage South Korea, which suspended its own nuclear weapon development programme in 1979 under intense US pressure, to re-open its own programme. Japanese officials argue that they need to prevent a nuclear arms race in North-east Asia at all costs.

The complexity of the nuclear issue has been increased by the linkages with US and South Korean policy. During the summer of 1991 US intelligence activities, together with the interrogation of a defecting senior North Korean Foreign Ministry official, heightened concerns about the speed and direction of the North Korean nuclear programme. In May, the Japanese were given details of the nuclear fuel reprocessing plant apparently under construction at Yongbyon and in September a CIA official briefed them on the shortened estimates for North Korean use of these facilities.

As discussed above in Chapter 5, the North Koreans also backtracked on their commitments to the IAEA and in September refused to sign the nuclear safeguards agreement on the date agreed. The response of the United States and South Korea, with their shift of emphasis to a more complex carrot-and-stick approach including the removal of nuclear weapons from South Korea, initially surprised the Japanese. But, at the same time, the US officials made it clear that there would not be any diminution of their commitment to South Korea. US Secretary of State James Baker visited Tokyo in November 1991 and told Miyazawa and Foreign Minister Michio Watanabe of the need for the United States, Japan, South Korea and China to join forces to put pressure on North Korea. Watanabe assured him that Japan would not compromise on this issue. At the November 1991 round of negotiations, the Japanese expressed concern at the reports of the reprocessing plant construction by North Korea, but did not specifically ask for its dismantlement.

Kim had succeeded in securing one of his long-standing aims, the removal of US nuclear weapons from South Korea, but he had not gained the diplomatic recognition from either Japan or the United States which would allow economic inputs for his struggling economy. As international diplomatic pressure mounted and it became clear that the only way out was compliance with inspection demands, Kim turned to the South. In December 1991, the North and South Korean prime ministers signed an agreement on reconciliation and exchanges, followed on 31 December with a de-nuclearisation agreement. On 31 January 1992, the North Koreans did sign the IAEA nuclear safeguards agreement; they ratified it in early April and allowed a preliminary inspection of their nuclear facilities by the IAEA in May 1992.

The Japanese, who have been concerned at the slow pace of North Korean implementation procedures, have welcomed the beginning of IAEA inspections. A letter from Miyazawa to Kim Il-sung, handed over by a LDP delegation visiting Pyongyang in mid-April 1992, had specifically asked North Korea to alleviate international concern over its nuclear programme (BBC-SWB, FE/1356, 15 April 1992). The Japanese are now awaiting fuller details of the IAEA findings and follow-up visits by IAEA teams later in 1992, as well as waiting to see whether the two Koreas can come to agreement on mutual inspection procedures.

Characteristics and prospects

The two years since the Kanemaru visit to Pyongyang have seen remarkably little progress in the negotiations, but it is possible to establish a few trends from their troubled course.

Firstly, the Japanese Foreign Ministry has succeeded in slowing down the negotiations to its own pace. Since the autumn of 1991, the North Koreans appear to have become reconciled to an approximately two-month interval between the two rounds. The seventh round originally set for March 1992 was only delayed by the unexpected death of the chief North Korean negotiator, Chon In-chol, and the North Korean preoccupation with the run-up to Kim Il-sung's eightieth birthday celebrations in April. Following on its eventual meeting in May, however, the next round has been repeatedly postponed for niggling reasons on both sides and is now planned for November 1992.

Secondly, the Foreign Ministry now feels under less pressure from party politicians. The JSP has continued to attempt an intermediary role - Tanabe personally wrote to Kim Il-sung about the outstanding issues in the negotiations in mid-1991 and he led a large JSP delegation to Pyongyang for Kim's eightieth birthday celebrations in April 1992 - but the JSP's influence has suffered from its declining popular support. Kanemaru's influence too has declined and he decided not to participate in the LDP delegation sent to Pyongyang in April 1992; moreover, in late 1991 he sent a personal message to Kim explaining that diplomatic relations would not be established without nuclear inspection. The exposure in the autumn of 1992 of his involvement in a corruption scandal is likely to further reduce his role in the contacts with the North.

Thirdly, there are two major points of contention - compensation for the post-war period and IAEA nuclear inspection - with two other points, the fate of a Japanese woman abducted to North Korea, which brought the third meeting to an impasse, and compensation for the 'comfort women', raised by the North Koreans at the sixth meeting, likely to be short-term irritants rather than long-term obstacles.

As Nakahira has repeatedly emphasised in the negotiations, the Japanese government refuses to compensate North Korea for post-war losses; the North Koreans seem to be gradually putting less emphasis on this point, so that as the negotiations progress the focus is shifting to the amount of economic assistance to compensate for the colonial period alone. Opinions amongst Japanese officials and politicians differ about the amount of economic assistance that should be given to North Korea. The North Koreans apparently initially wanted $10 billion, but $8 billion, which would be roughly equivalent to the $800 million given to South Korea in 1965 after adding interest and inflation, is reported to be the current North Korean target. But there is still considerable doubt as to whether the Japanese government would agree to such a large amount, partly for budgetary reasons and partly because North Korea would come within the confines of a new policy, announced in March 1991, which makes overseas aid more conditional on whether the recipient nation is involved in arms exports or nuclear weapons development. Moreover, as in the case of large aid packages given to China and South Korea during the 1980s, the amounts would be spread out over a period of five or six years, which may, in practice, do little to solve the immediate economic problems of North Korea.

Japan, because of its past experience under nuclear attack, remains particularly sensitive to the nuclear issue. By the time the full negotiations began, a North Korean agreement to allow IAEA inspection of its nuclear facilities had become a Japanese precondition for normalising relations. The Japanese position was, of course, supported not only by the South Korean government, which has been reassured by the firmness of the Japanese arguments, but also by the Americans, who have gone to some lengths to provide additional intelligence information. The nuclear weapon threat is one of the few 'cards' that Kim Il-sung holds and he has been prepared to use it to keep the Japanese, and the Americans and the South Koreans, on edge and to lever out US nuclear weapons from South Korean soil.

The Japanese, while encouraged by the signs of some North Korean flexibility over the nuclear inspection issue, continue to be cautious about pushing ahead with normalisation until the proper inspections actually take place. They have also been upset by the North Korean counter-attack in January 1992 about the dangers of Japan's own nuclear fuel reprocessing programme (BBC-SWB, FE/1293 1 February 1992). The Japanese response is that their own nuclear programme is under complete IAEA inspection and is clearly for domestic electricity power generation purposes, whereas the North Korean projects are not linked to any domestic power lines and are not yet under full IAEA monitoring. This new North Korean approach, heralded at the December 1991 meeting, when the North Koreans started complaining about Japanese ambitions to again become a military power, is, however, being taken by the Japanese as at least being a step forward in one sense. It is implicit recognition by the North that Japan's concerns over nuclear inspection are not being made simply at the behest of the United States or South Korea, but being voiced for 'very real Japanese reasons' (Kakizawa 1992 p. 62).

Following consultation with the South Koreans, who argue that their own inspections due to take place when the   December 1991 North-South de-nuclearisation agreement is implemented can be more extensive than those of the IAEA, the Japanese have now also begun to argue that not just IAEA inspection but South Korean inspection is desirable. However, they have not yet made South Korean inspection an absolute precondition before the establishment of Japan-North Korean diplomatic relations. Instead, the Japanese have made clear their need for inspections, ideally by both the IAEA and the South Koreans, which are 'thorough and rigorous enough to dispel international suspicions and concerns' (Kakizawa 1992 pp.63-4).

The North Koreans, always sensitive to any discussion which would highlight their involvement in terrorist activities, denied any knowledge of the missing Japanese language teacher, Taguchi. Japan will not withdraw its enquiry, but, given that Taguchi is now believed to be dead, the issue has been effectively shelved - by the process of setting up a separate sub-committee to consider the issue - in order to continue the main negotiations.

The issue of the 'comfort women', forcibly taken from Korea to act as prostitutes for the Japanese army during the 1937-45 period, had become a diplomatic issue between South Korea and Japan when Prime Minister Miyazawa visited Seoul in January 1992. At the sixth Japan-North Korean negotiations later the same month, the North Korean delegate openly supported the South's attempts to obtain compensation from Japan, and, at the next North-South prime ministerial talks, in February, the North proposed joint action against Japan over this issue. The South did not agree to this idea, saying that the issue was already under active bilateral discussion, but the North's actions suggest that this issue is likely to be incorporated into its general demands for 'upping' its compensation from Japan.

Fourthly, although the Japanese government has been maintaining close contact with the South Korean government, some of the five principles have become blurred. Nakahira himself, on his three visits to Seoul during the course of the negotiations, and other Japanese diplomats and officials have reassured the South Koreans that they are firm on the nuclear inspection issue. Japan certainly has played its part in trying to persusade North Korea to sign and implement the IAEA nuclear safeguards agreement. It has proved difficult to find concrete ways of opening up North Korean society during the process of negotiation, although that should be the end effect of normalisation. The South Koreans have been strongly against any 'interim payment' of economic aid - assistance should be forthcoming only after establishment of relations - and any diversion of the eventual aid to military purposes (a point forcibly emphasised by Defence Minister Lee Jong-koo to visiting Director-General of the Defence Agency Ishikawa in December 1990). However, Japanese officials feel that whenever finally Japanese economic assistance is given, in practice it will be hard to ensure that some of it is not used for military purposes; tied loans or project-based loans would only be given after joint feasibility studies, but grants would be less easy to monitor.

The most important point, however, has been subtle differences in interpretation of the linkage between Japan-North Korean negotiations and the North-South dialogue. For the South Koreans, Japan-North Korean relations should not be normalised before 'meaningful progress' has been made in the North-South dialogue. After the North-South prime ministerial dialogue was suspended by the North Koreans in January 1991, however, the Japanese argued that the Japan-North Korean normalisation process should help to re-open the North-South dialogue; Nakahira did, indeed, use the formal meetings to urge the North Koreans to return to talking to the South. Although the North-South prime ministerial meetings began again in the autumn of 1991 and culminated in the December accords on reconciliation and exchanges, the logic of the Japanese position is that even if the North-South dialogue should again lapse, the Japan-North Korean normalisation process should continue.

Fifthly, the North has had few cards to play, apart from the nuclear threat, which Kim has been using to maximum effect. Kim Il-sung clearly takes a close interest in the development of relations with Japan and has been prepared to meet Japanese politicians and give interviews to Japanese newspapers in order to achieve his goals. In the general negotiations with the Japanese, the chief Foreign Ministry negotiator has been allowed a minimal amount of flexibility; on the nuclear issue, however, everything has to be referred back to Kim. The role of his son, Kim Jong-il, is less clear. He has had responsibility for overseeing the work of the Foreign Ministry since 1985, and there have been occasional hints in the North Korean media about his involvement in directing the negotiations with Japan. Nevertheless, not until the LDP and JSP delegations visited Pyongyang in April 1992 did any of the visiting Japanese politicians or officials get to meet him; even then, there was no serious discussion with him. The older Kim may well be trying to direct some of the credit for the eventual establishment of relations to his son - to help consolidate the latter's position. But, in practice, Kim Il-sung is relying mainly on the Foreign Minister Kim Yong-nam and Kim Yong-sun, the influential KWP secretary for International Affairs, who has been active in the party-to-party diplomacy with the Japanese political parties.

The South Koreans remain suspicious of North Korean intentions and tend to argue that the North is trying to use the resumption of its dialogue with the South as a way of showing its 'reasonableness' and, therefore, helping to encourage Japan to move faster. Japanese officials, however, are more sceptical as to whether the North actually links the two sets of negotiations in such a way. Indeed, it seems probable that in the autumn of 1991 the North moved towards the South not because of a tactical desire to prod the Japanese into moving faster but because it had realised that Japan could not be prodded into faster action. Kim Il-sung's visit to China in October 1991 must have had a salutary effect on him; the Chinese not only explained that there was very little that they could do economically to help him but they also will have pointed up the unlikelihood of early Japanese inputs. Kim, therefore, turned to the South as the country best able and most likely to give economic cooperation, provided that he also made some concessions. The result was the December 1991 accords and the January 1992 visit to the North by the Daewoo Chairman, Kim Woo-chong, who discussed a number of joint ventures and cooperative projects. Progress since then has been less marked - and the South Korean government actually put a damper on Daewoo's plans until the implementation of the nuclear inspection agreement occurred - but for Kim, the South holds more promise than Japan in terms of short-term inputs. In the medium term, however, Japan's economic assistance will prove the greater incentive to Kim.

Symptomatic of the new North Korean approach has been the attempt to join forces with the South against Japan. This was particularly the case in the February 1992 North-South prime ministers' meeting, when the North suggested that the two Koreas get together both to coordinate their demands for Japanese repentence and compensation for using Korean 'comfort women' and to criticise and prevent the Japanese development of a nuclear programme, with nuclear fuel reprocessing, which could lead on to the development of nuclear weapons. The South was not enthusiastic about either idea. The South Koreans argue that the 'comfort women' issue is already being pursued bilaterally and that, whatever concerns they may have over Japanese conventional arms expansion, they do not believe that the Japanese are developing nuclear facilities (which, anyway, are under the supervision of the IAEA) for any purpose other than domestic energy supply.

Nevertheless, the Japanese have noted with concern that one by-product of a slow amelioration of tension between the two Koreas may well be a greater propensity to act together against Japan.

Sixthly, the United States has acted as a kind of 'shadow participant' to the negotiations, primarily over the nuclear issue. North Korea has been endeavouring to go through Japan to secure its long-standing objective of the removal of US nuclear forces from South Korea by putting that as a condition of its agreeing to the Japanese demand for IAEA inspection. At the very first round of the negotiations, in January 1991, Chon In-chol urged the Japanese to advise the Americans to enter into discussions with the North about removing the nuclear threat to the peninsula (*North Korea Quarterly* Spring 1991). The North Koreans have undoubtedly succeeded in removing US nuclear weapons from South Korean soil, although during the spring-summer of 1992 they continued to demand the right to inspect US bases in South Korea to check that this was so. What they have not succeeded in doing is to totally remove the US nuclear umbrella from the South, since the North could be targeted by US sea-launched missiles.

On the other hand, the Americans, reasoning that only Japan has any real leverage over North Korea at the moment (because of the North Korean need for Japanese aid), have been trying to go through Japan to ensure the non-proliferation of nuclear weapons. Post-Gulf War inspections of Iraqi facilities have shown that signature of both the NPT and the IAEA safeguards agreement does not prevent a state from conducting undeclared nuclear activities. The disintegration of the Soviet Union has raised questions about the fate of the nuclear warheads held in the individual countries of the CIS. These two developments have heightened US concern about the North Korean case, which, increasingly, is being seen as a test-case of the NPT/IAEA regime's effectiveness in the post-Cold War environment (Simpson and Howlett 1991 pp.483-91).

The Americans have talked to the Russians and the Chinese about putting pressure on the North Koreans, but they recognise that the Russians now have little leverage and the Chinese have reservations about pushing too hard. Consequently, the Japanese would seem to have the greatest leverage, in so far as any country has leverage over North Korea. The Japanese, themselves, seem less sure of how much they can influence the North, but the closeness of the Japan-US security dialogue helps to enhance their position. Indeed, the North Koreans probably underestimate the degree to which there is close tripartite consultation between Japan, South Korea and the United States on this particular issue.

Before the Kanemaru visit, some Japanese diplomats had actually expected US-North Korean relations to develop faster than Japan-North Korean relations. That is clearly no longer a prospect - even if the North Koreans occasionally wish to hint that it is - for the American response to repeated North Korean overtures has been very measured. President Bush, on his visits to South Korea and Japan in January 1992, made it clear that the United States had absolutely no intention of going behind the backs of these two countries. Increasingly preoccupied with domestic affairs, including the impending presidential elections, the Americans felt no need to rush into anything with the North. Japanese moves are likely to keep them a step or two ahead of the Americans, but not much more than that.

Towards normalisation

The May 1992 round of negotiations was once again marked by only slow progress, but the Japanese did come away with the feeling that the North Koreans were becoming a little more realistic in their negotiating demands. The road ahead seems to be a difficult one, with an early normalisation of relations unlikely. Much will depend on the North Korean attitude towards inspection of its nuclear facilities by the IAEA and by South Korean officials. The IAEA followed up their initial May inspection with a further inspection in July, but it still wishes to make a more extensive inspection. South Korean inspection has yet to take place, despite a timetable (under the procedures worked out after the December 1991 North-South agreement) which required one by June. Implementation of these inspections - and the absence of any North Korean weapon producing facilities (though the North Koreans would have had time to remove any evidence to other locations) - should prove the key to solve the other complications in the negotiations. Whenever those inspections take place - more likely in 1993 than later in 1992 - then Japan-North Korean relations would be established soon after.

As both South Korean and Japanese diplomats fear, the establishment of Japan-North Korean relations will, in the short term, make the Japan-South Korean relationship more difficult to handle. An unreformed North Korea can clearly try to exploit its new 'equality' with South Korea. Even a partially reformed North Korea will undoubtedly endeavour to play off Japan and South Korea, particularly in offering commercial opportunities. However carefully the Japanese government may proceed, some party politicians and interest groups will inevitably try to play off the two Koreas to Japan's advantage. In the medium and longer term, however, South Korea can draw consolation from the change that greater Japanese involvement will bring to the closed North Korean society. The irony for North Korea will be that, in calling in Japanese assistance to bolster its existing system, North Korea will have to open the door to the kind of 'undesirable influences' that will ultimately undermine that very system.

Notes

1. In October 1983, Min Hong-gu, a North Korean soldier, stowed away aboard the frozen-fish freighter Fujisan Maru No.18, then in the North Korean port of Nampo. Min was handed over to the Japanese authorities when the boat reached Japan, but when the boat returned again to North Korea in November the five-man crew were arrested. Three sailors were released in early 1984, but the captain and chief engineer were imprisoned. Min was released by Japanese immigration authorities in late 1987 and, in retaliation, the two seamen were sentenced by the North Koreans to 15 years labour on charges of espionage.
2. The full text of the agreement is in *Korea & World Affairs* Winter 1990 pp. 784-6.

9 Conclusions

Near neighbours usually have a checkered history of contacts, with emotions shifting between amity and enmity. Japan and North and South Korea are no exceptions to the rule. The challenge for the coming years is to see how far leaders in all three countries can overcome negative images and experiences, derived from past conflicts and tensions, in order to pursue positive relationships beneficial to their national interest.

As the opening years of this decade have shown, economic development in the Asian Pacific region is continuing to proceed at a pace that other regions cannot compete with. Yet, at the same time, the region finds itself becoming increasingly interdependent with, and exposed to, global trends, whether in the international trading environment or in the changing context of post-Cold War political and security alignments. Japan and the two Koreas, inevitably, find themselves forced to fashion a new triangular relationship against the background of these broader patterns of growth and interdependence.

Coping with the past

Both Japanese and Koreans share the tendency to link the present with the remote past in relations between peoples. They take for granted that the present cannot be understood apart from the past. However, there are differences in approach between the two. The concept of han, difficult to translate into English but representing a combination of resentment, regret and renewed suffering, governs how most Koreans look back on their past. Koreans, both South and North, therefore, feel a compulsive emotional need to anchor their policies in the memory of past Japanese misdeeds. It does also stimulate a desire to revive these memories, on occasions, as calculated bargaining postures that target Japanese business and government.

The Japanese, on the other hand, in their relations with both Koreas, as in their relationship with the Chinese, would prefer not to dwell too much on the past - indeed, every hint or insinuation about their past makes the Japanese wince - but concentrate on building a new relationship. The

Japanese tend to dismiss Korean references back to the past as either a tactic to secure concessions or an irrational obsession with the past, without realising the degree to which Koreans genuinely feel that the Japanese have not owned up to their past aggressive behaviour in the way that the Germans have done over Nazism and the Holocaust.

The Japanese, through imperial statements or prime ministerial speeches, have moved towards some degree of reconciliation with the two Koreas, but, as the recent case of the Korean 'comfort women' has shown, tend to take two steps forward and one step back. Compensation for the 'comfort women' has now become a diplomatic issue not just between Japan and South Korea but also between Japan and North Korea. Japanese insistence that all such claims for compensation were settled in the 1965 Japan-South Korea treaties may be technically correct under international law, but does little to settle the psychological traumas involved or improve the state of the relationship. Until Japan is prepared to go further than just legal niceties and really face up to, and apologise for, its past actions against Koreans, the relationships will continue to be strained by these kinds of issues.

One of the most evident signs of the past is the presence of the Korean community within Japan. Ideologically polarised and societally discriminated against, the Koreans in Japan have found it difficult to become full members of Japanese society. Intra-community tensions and frictions between ethnic Koreans and Japanese still remain, despite the passing of years. While the Japanese government is slowly improving the legal position of the Korean residents, the wider problem of altering the social attitudes of Japanese towards them is inevitably going to be a much longer process.

Economic intertwining

A best-selling book in Japan in 1986 by the nationalistic author Hasegawa Keitaro, entitled *Sayonara ajia (Goodbye Asia)*, depicted a gleaming sky-scraper (Japan) rising out of the rubbish dump of Asia. He saw the possibility of only one other smaller building emerging, South Korea. While Hasegawa's peremptory dismissal of the potential of the rest of Asia is not shared by all Japanese, it is certain that most Japanese do see South Korea as their nearest economic rival. South Koreans too, after regarding North Korea as their competitor in the early years, have now clearly taken on Japan as the target to catch up with.

Certainly, the pace of South Korean economic development over the past two decades has transformed the shape and strength of the South Korean economy, enabling it to catch up with Japan in certain sectors. In the mid-1980s there was a debate in South Korea about whether that country would become a 'another Brazil', characterised by a shaky economy and vicious cycles of authoritarianism and democracy, or 'another Japan', which was seen as having a working democracy and a prospering economy (Ahn 1987 p.16). Koreans, as always, will want to do it their own way, but they are edging much closer to the Japanese alternative in this formulation. Nevertheless, it is clear that Japan, while now moving at a slower pace, is still well ahead in terms of industrial, technological and financial strength.

However, neither side has found it easy to cope with rebalancing the relationship to take account of the new realities of South Korean economic progress. Japan has acted, in the past, as a model as well as a mentor, which, inevitably, compounds the difficulties for either side to adjust to a more equitable economic relationship.

The trade deficit remains a potent source of friction, but the structural nature of the problem makes early resolution of the problem unlikely. The July 1992 'action plan' agreed between the two countries will make little immediate difference. If anything, the China-South Korean rapprochement of August 1992 will accentuate the problem, as South Korean business, at least temporarily, turns away from exporting to Japan to what is seen as an easier market in China. In the medium term, therefore, it will need continued efforts by the South Koreans to diversify and localise their industries away from dependence on Japanese components and to both use the technology from the Japanese and other countries to better effect and devote more resources to new research and development.

It will also need the South Koreans to avoid simply taking Japan as scapegoat for economic setbacks to the Korean economy as a whole. In the second half of 1991, for example, President Roh's personal remarks on the trade deficit with Japan sharpened noticeably, mainly because he himself was under considerable pressure to do something to alleviate the general dissatisfaction with the slowdown in the Korean economy. Just as Japan cannot be blamed for all the problems of the Korean economy, neither can technology transfer from Japan alone be the panacea.

The Japanese, on the other hand, need to recognise that, although their market is now more open than at any time in the past, there are a few tariffs and some more nebulous but nonetheless important non-tariff barriers which hinder Korean exports to Japan. These issues are being discussed within the context of the multilateral GATT Uruguay Round talks, the conclusion of which Japan says it is waiting for, but more sensitivity to the Korean viewpoint can bring an easing of bilateral tension. Japanese companies, who varied between condescension and fear - depending on the sector - when they viewed South Korean competitors, are now slowly coming round to see the advantages of cooperating, particularly where the costs and scale of technological development and production demonstrate the need for partners.

The coming years, therefore, are likely to see more cooperative ventures and agreements between the leading Korean and Japanese companies, but the old suspicions will inevitably make some of them seem like hard work.

It is not yet clear whether the increased commercial contacts between Japan and the Korean peninsula (and also with other neighbouring countries) will lead on to solid economic cooperative organisational structures. Efforts towards broader regional cooperation, which include Japan and South Korea (and conceivably North Korea, should it reform), have not had a good record. Even APEC itself, while slowly broadening its membership, developing data-sharing capabilities and establishing a small secretariat, is still some way from substantative policy-making. The European example suggests that companies have moved faster than governments, that industrial and commercial decisions have led political decisions in the creation of a single market. Now, in the Asia-Pacific region too, commercial attractions are pushing business ahead of formal inter-governmental structures. In specifically North-east Asia, the commercial contacts across the Yellow/West Sea and the Japan/East Sea are developing well ahead of inter-governmental agreements. However, full-scale EC-style economic integration is unlikely, even in the medium term, not least because no state is yet prepared to accept arrangements that would entail subordinating sovereign rights. The turbulence in the European currency markets in September 1992 has also done little to encourage ideas of EC-style currency linkage or even a 'yen bloc' in the Asian Pacific region.

Political complementarities

Solid and sustained partnerships require a basis of shared interests. They do not need to be identical, but they should at least be complementary and compatible. They should also be interests which give a medium to longer-term underpinning. Countries do find shared interests in cooperating against a common threat or difficult neighbour, such as, conceivably, North Korea in the case of South Korea and Japan, but partnerships that arise solely as a distinction from a third country are more vulnerable to turbulence and to change within that country.

Although, at the height of the Cold War, the United States had dreams that the Japanese and the South Koreans could work together in an anti-communist bloc, mutual antipathies dictated otherwise. Nevertheless, Japan and South Korea have been linked together by the varied security problems of North-east Asia, even if their perspectives have differed.

The Japan-South Korean political and security dialogue has been far less advanced than the economic interactions. South Korea has been preoccupied, understandably, by the North Korean threat, whereas the Japanese have been equally fixated on the Soviet threat. Historical legacies have precluded any real security cooperation or dialogue; only under the 'neutral' banner of RIMPAC exercises have their armed forces worked together. Only since the Nakasone visit to Seoul in 1983 has high-level political dialogue become common; even then, meetings were focused on areas of contention rather than shared interests.

However, the ending of the Cold War and the disintegration of the Soviet Union, coupled with heightened suspicions that the North Koreans were trying to develop a nuclear weapon, has brought the Japanese closer to South Korean perspectives. Shared concerns, though of differing degrees of intensity, have become more apparent. Although the Japanese remain concerned to settle their own particular problem of the 'northern territories' issue with Russia, both they and the South Koreans wish to see stability emerging from the Russian scene and the emergence of a Russia which plays a positive role in the Asia-Pacific region. The Japanese worries about the North Korean nuclear programme have encouraged a considerable degree of consultation with the South Koreans and the Americans. The nature of a post-Kim Il-sung North Korea remains unknown. China remains a potentially volatile force, particularly when the power struggle after the death of Deng Xiaoping occurs.

Yet, ironically, one by-product of the end of the Cold War has acted as a force in the opposite direction, to push the two apart again. The apparent lessening of the US commitment to the region because of a perceived reduction in rivalry with the Soviet Union/Russia and increased US demands on other regional powers to take up some of the slack have fed into the broader debate within Japan about its role in the world. The catalytic effect of the 1990-91 Gulf crisis pushed Japan into, eventually, passing legislation to allow limited Japanese participation in UN peace-keeping activities, but this step once again revived fears in South Korea about how Japan will operate in the newly emerging world order. Internal constraints are unlikely to allow the Japanese to advance much further into a military role in the coming few years, but those steps that they do take need to be carefully explained beforehand to neighbours such as South Korea. The problem at the moment is that the only thing that is certain is that the Japanese are uncertain about how they should play a more active role. The absence of a clear sense of direction does not help to dispel the concerns of South (and North) Korea; it only provides another reason for the South Koreans and the Chinese to get closer together.

One way of reducing Korean anxieties about Japan's future military role (and, for that matter, as is discussed further below, Japanese concerns about a reunified Korea) is for multilateral regional security structures to be developed which would both constrain any adventurism and build more positive cooperative habits. International (or multilateral) security is not a prerequisite for national security, but it does contribute towards it. However, bilateral alliances rather than multilateral structures have been the pattern for the Asia-Pacific region, and nowhere is that truer than in North-east Asia. Ideas for a new politico-security architecture floated during 1990-91 by two relatively peripheral states, Australia and Canada, who were inspired by the intense European debate, failed to evoke a positive response from regional powers.

However, in 1992 the mood has begun to change. The Japanese, while still resistant to an Asian version of the European CSCE, are beginning to promote embryonic ideas of a security 'multiplex' (IISS 1992 p.218) which will add multilateral efforts to already existing bilateral arrangements. American officials began to suggest a Korean/North-east Asian version of the successful '2 + 4' meetings which helped to manage German reunification. President Roh, when addressing the United Nations in September 1992, revived an idea that he had first floated four years earlier, for a consultative conference of the interested powers in North-east Asia. South Korean policy planners, while arguing that it is still premature for a collective security system for the region, nonetheless are considering a seven-power regional security structure as a medium-term foreign policy objective. Consultation rather than coordinated security activities will have to be the first step. While there is still a long way to go, the probability of some form of regional security organisation emerging later in the 1990s is growing stronger.

Changes in the domestic political polities of the three countries have helped to add uncertainties to the inter-relationships in the past and, as the period of transition is by no means over, will continue to do so. South Korea has had the most troubled transition so far, as President Roh has attempted to manage, not altogether successfully, the changeover from authoritarianism to democracy. The March 1992 elections showed that the public is by no means enamoured with his efforts to create through the DLP an equivalent of the long-lived Japanese LDP. Under the present constitution, Roh cannot stand for a further term as president. Although Kim Young-sam has been chosen as the DLP's candidate for the December 1992 presidential elections, intra-party feuding is by no means over and the proliferation of candidates from newly-emerging parties seems likely. Kim Young-sam, who seems likely to win provided that the DLP does not fragment, will be unlikely to change the basics of policy towards Japan significantly, but should Kim Dae-jung be returned he is likely to take a more abrasive approach, not least because he will want to know more about the Japanese involvement in his own kidnapping from Tokyo in 1973.

Despite the succession of political scandals in Japan, the LDP's hold on power does not seem threatened. The July 1992 elections provided an opportunity for it to reclaim some lost ground in the Upper House and the opposition suffers from being implicated in the scandals as well. Miyazawa, not least because there is no agreement within the LDP about who might be his successor, will remain as prime minister until the expiry of his current term as LDP president, in October 1993. He is unlikely to make any serious change to existing policies towards the two Koreas and, if Kanemaru's political fortunes continue to wane, there will be little new pressure from politicians to advance the normalisation talks with North Korea.

North Korean political succession, however, remains the wild card. Kim Il-sung has already handed over elements of decision-making to his son, but he must still take a firm control of the key decisions. His death or incapacitation - he is already 80 - could, however, have the most marked impact on the triangular relationship. His son's leadership capacities remain subject to doubt and he may end up more of a transitional figurehead before either a military or technocratic leader emerges. The potential for a serious post-Kim power struggle within North Korea is clear. Whatever form of leadership emerges, economic necessity will require courting of Japan; reformist leaders would be more flexible than the current Kim approach.

The North Korean factor

Japan's relationship with South Korea, difficult though it has been and, indeed, still is, is much deeper and broader than Japan's relationship with North Korea. One of the two most potent signs of the beginning of change in the North-east Asian area developing from the winding down of the global Cold War has been the opening of negotiations to end the frigid state of 'non-relations' between Japan and North Korea (the other sign was the Soviet-South Korean rapprochement).

In reality, for all three protagonists the Japan-North Korean normalisation process has great significance. For Japan, it represents not just the closing of one of the last chapters of its imperialistic and militaristic past but also the opening of a new one of Japan's higher profile in political and diplomatic affairs. For the North, it is a test of how the necessity, for purposes of regime survival, of having to turn for help to one of its former enemies can be both justified and controlled to avoid an undesirable impact domestically. For the South, it is a test of its self-confidence and maturity vis-à-vis both the North and Japan.

Although ideological variants of communism survived in Asia beyond its collapse in Eastern Europe and the Soviet Union (most notably, of course, in China), North Korea was left politically and diplomatically isolated, but also with few sources of help with its economic problems. In the early 1960s, as President Park sought to strengthen South Korean economic and political capabilities to compete with the then superior North, he turned to Japan for inspiration and practical assistance. Ironically, two and a half decades later the roles are reversed (Park 1992b p.332). Now, the North, losing out in its economic and diplomatic competition with the South, has been forced to turn to Japan, one of its old ideological and historic enemies, as the only answer. The negotiations since late 1990, however, have not been as easy or as fruitful as the North Koreans initially anticipated.

North Korean attempts to bounce the Japanese into early recognition and financial hand-outs failed as the Japanese government negotiators, having regained control from certain LDP politicians, exuded patience and the North Koreans proved obstinate over the two key issues: Japanese apologies and compensation and assurances on the North Korean nuclear programme. Although there has been some movement on the first issue (the North Koreans are quietly dropping their demand for compensation for post-1945 Japanese actions, while the Japanese are begining to think in more concrete terms about the level of economic assistance), the North Koreans have displayed foot-dragging and truculence over the nuclear inspection issue. Coupled with a number of smaller but nonetheless contentious issues, there remain plenty of problems in narrowing the gap between positions of the two sides.

The key sticking-point actually is the nuclear issue. Full North Korean implementation not just of IAEA inspections but also of South Korean inspections will speed up the process of negotiations considerably. If, as seems probable, the North Korean economic situation continues to deteriorate, then North Korea will have to be more forthcoming later this year over the inspection issue. Concessions on the inspection issue will be followed by the normalisation of relations with Japan. This could happen in early 1993.

The South Koreans, for all their encouragement of Japan-North Korean contacts in President Roh's July 1988 speech, have remained suspicious of Japan's underlying policy towards the North. The Japanese are certainly well aware that one of the costs of the 'new' relationship with the North might be an impaired relationship with the South. Considerable efforts have been put into trying to reassure the South. These will not prevent the triangular relationship becoming more awkward in the short term once Japan-North Korean relations are established. North Korea will inevitably try to play off Japan and South Korea, not just in political terms but also in tempting in commercial enterprises, but the scope for doing this will depend on the degree to which North Korea itself undertakes economic - and political - reform. The Japan-South Korean relationship, despite its tendency to veer from warm to chilly and back again, is now mature enough to withstand these tensions in the medium term. Indeed, the opening up of the so hermetically-sealed society in the North, under the influence of Japanese trade, aid and people flows can only be to the advantage of the South. As the Japanese price is certain to include reasonable measures to ensure that North Korea is not developing a nuclear bomb, that too will be to South Korea's benefit.

Some South Koreans fear that a Japanese rapprochement with the North would lead to trade and investment inputs that would prop up and even strengthen North Korea in its struggle against the South. Yet, significant Japanese investment is unlikely to take place in North Korea without at least partial reform of the economic system there. The Tumen River project could become a self-contained centre for such investment, but there would be little trickle-down benefit to other parts of the North Korean economy nor would the Japanese be tempted into other areas under an otherwise unreconstructed system. Genuine economic reform, as opposed to limited playing with capitalism in geographically-isolated enclaves, in the North, whether under Japanese influence or not, would make the North a less dangerous place for the South to deal with.

Reunification

The problem, however, in the longer term is whether reunification of the two Koreas will be hastened or handicapped by the Japan-North Korean normalisation. The current mood in South Korea has shifted noticeably from the euphoric days of 1989, when it naively seemed possible that the Korean peninsula could follow quickly on the German model, to one of caution about reunification. Here, at least, there is currently some measure of tacit agreement amongst North and South Koreans. The North fears 'absorption' by the South on the German model, but the South, with its current economic difficulties and political uncertainties, does not want to take on the responsibilities of looking after - or paying for - North Korea yet either.

For many Japanese, the real worry is not the shorter-term one of a maverick nuclear-armed North Korea (which may well be on the way out as a potential threat), but rather the longer-term impact of a reunified Korea, of whatever political hue, with significant armed forces, economic power and overtly anti-Japanese nationalistic tendencies (Foster-Carter 1992 pp. 80-81). This has been used by some Japanese to justify attempts to promote relations with the North - as a way of postponing the evil day of reunification. Yet, for most policy-makers in Japan, the real problem is not so much the end result, for they feel confident enough about Japan's economic strength to keep well ahead of even a reunified rival, but rather the process by which reunification is achieved. They see political risks involved in a violent and rushed reunification - either by Kim Il-sung embarking on a suicidal bid to reunify by force or by a dramatic 'implosion' in the North as food riots or demonstrations lead to virtual civil war and regime collapse. Japan would much prefer to see a gradual reduction of tensions and a measured economic and political rapprochement culminating in reunification, which would enable the costs of restructuring the North Korean economy to be spread over years.

The timing and manner of reunification depends now on the fate of Kim Il-sung's regime in the North, which is, of course, crucially bound up with the life and death of Kim himself. Can he withstand the economic problems and sustain his regime and the handover to his son? Will mounting internal difficulties lead to attempts - by the army or technocrats - to unseat him? Whether Kim Il-sung dies naturally or is removed forcibly, the successor regime will be forced by sheer economic necessity to overcome whatever ideological hang-ups it might have and be more amenable to contacts and cooperation with the South. Gradualism has been working in China, where it has proved possible to allow economic reform without political reform, but the old guard of the party there is now finding itself being pushed along directions that it does not want to go. The economic situation and the political isolation in the North is clearly worse than in China; opening up to the South - and to Japan - will make gradualism less viable. A successor regime to Kim Il-sung will not be able to sustain, as the Chinese have done, a reform movement dragged out over a decade or more. Changes will have to come faster.

The South is, therefore, in practice well on the way to achieving reunification by 'absorption'. Predictions for when this might happen vary: Aidan Foster-Carter suggests 'within the next five years - but it could be much sooner' (Foster-Carter 1992 p. 95), while Okonogi Masao suggests some time from 1996 onwards (Okonogi 1991 pp. 177-82). In June 1991, President Roh told his cabinet that reunification was possible by the mid-1990s or by 2000 at the latest (*The Times* 28 June 1991). Certainly, by the end of this decade Japanese policy-makers will have to learn how to deal with a reunified Korea.

A reunified Korea will obviously be a powerful economic force, although the initial disruption and adjustment needs will be similar to the transitional difficulties in Germany after 1990. However, the unified economy will have over 65 million people, a complementary mix of northern mineral resources and docile labour and southern technology and capital, and a combined GNP which would not be far off those of the geographically and demographically much larger India and China. But it would still be well behind Japan, in terms of domestic market, GNP and per capita GNP, and financial and technological prowess. The marked difference in the size of the skyscrapers in Hasegawa

Keitaro's unfortunate metaphor will be true.

A reunified Korea might want to flex its military muscles, especially against the Japanese; it would take some time for the two armies to be reduced down and the reunified country might find itself inheriting a nuclear weapon-producing capacity. But Korea has historically been 'the victim and not the perpetrator of aggression in North-east Asia' (Park 1992a p.129). The Americans, reduced though their direct involvement in the region might be, would certainly work hard to prevent any military tension between the unified Korea and Japan (and they are certain to maintain a military presence in the two countries well into the 1990s). It would not be in the interest either of the Russians or the Chinese, who wish to ensure stability in North-east Asia so as to carry on economic development. Gradual moves towards a sub-regional framework, something both looser and broader than a mere replica of the '2 + 4' structure employed on the eve of German reunification, can help to manage the traumas for neighbouring countries of the eventual Korean reunification.

Living with each other

The process of adjustment to new realities, both for people and for governments, can be painful. The relatively stable, if often unpleasant, world of the Cold War era has disappeared. Arguably, in the Asian context, it was never quite so immovable or so clear-cut as in Europe anyway. It has been replaced by the uncertainties deriving from the re-assertion of regional, ethnic, religious and national aims. The international economic order is in a state of flux too, as economic growth and technological development not only geographically redistribute power but also rebalance the relationship between governments and companies.

Japan, South Korea and North Korea are affected by these transitional processes, much as the North would like to pretend that it is not. At the same time, the inter-relationships between the three countries are in a state of transition. Japan and North Korea are moving towards normalising relations for the first time ever. North and South Korea are involved in a partial dialogue which might yet bring some degree of reconciliation on the divided peninsula. Japan and South Korea are working towards a more mature relationship. A reunified Korea is no longer a distant and impractical vision. Emotional legacies, ideological remnants, economic competition, and differing national security perspectives, however, will ensure that the leaders of these three countries will need to show responsibility and understanding in guiding their countries' complex relationships inside the triangle.

References

Ahn, Byung-Joon (1987) 'Korea: A Rising Middle Power in World Politics', *Korea & World Affairs*, Spring.

Ahn, Byung Sup (1989) 'Aesthetics in Korean Cinema', *Koreana*, 3(4).

Akao, Nobutoshi (ed) (1983) *Japan's Economic Security*, Aldershot: Gower.

Arai, Sawako (1990) 'Saharin no kankokujin wa naze kaeranakatta no ka', *Gendai Koria*, July.

Araki, Kiyoshi (1991) *Japan's Security Policy in the Regional and Global Context*, London: RIIA Discussion Paper.

Awanohara, Susumu (1989) 'Japan and East Asia: Towards a New Division of Labour', *The Pacific Review* 2(3).

Baerwald, Hans (1968) 'The Diet and the Japan-Korea Treaty', *Asian Survey*, December.

BBC (1986-1992) *Summary of World Broadcasts*, Daily Bulletin (cited throughout as BBC-SWB, issue no. and date).

Bloom, Martin (1992) 'Technological Change, in the Korean Electronics Industry', Paris: OECD Development Centre.

Bridges, Brian (1984a) 'Distant Neighbours: Japan and Korea in the Early 1980s', *Asian Profile*, February.

Bridges, Brian (1984b) 'South Korea: looking towards its friends', *The World Today*, October.

Bridges, Brian (1986) 'The Bamboo Islands: A Chronic Case of Neuralgia?' in *Proceedings of BAJS*, Vol. 11.

Bridges, Brian (1991) 'Japan: Waiting for Gorbachev', *The Pacific Review*, 4(1).

Bridges, Brian (1992) 'South Korea and the Gulf Crisis', *The Pacific Review*, 5(2).

Chapman, J.M.W., Drifte, R., and Gow, I.T.M. (1983) *Japan's Quest for Comprehensive Security: Defence, Diplomacy and Dependence*, London: Frances Pinter.

Cheong, Sung-hwa (1991) *The Politics of Anti-Japanese Sentiment: Japanese-South Korean Relations under the American Occupation, 1945-1952*, New York: Greenwood Press.

Choi, Sang-yong (1978) 'Post-war Nationalism in Korea: Three Problems' in Hahn Bae-ho and Yamamoto Tadashi (eds), *Korea and Japan: A New Dialogue Across the Channel*, Seoul: Korea University.

Chough, Il Chee (1987) 'Repatriation of Stateless Koreans from Sakhalin Island', *Korea & World Affairs*, Winter.

Chung, Chin-wee (1983) 'The Evolution of a Constitutional Structure in North Korea', in Scalapino, Robert and Kim, Jun-Yop (eds), *North Korea Today: Strategic and Domestic Issues*, Berkeley: University of California Press.

Chung, Joseph S. (1983) 'Economic Planning in North Korea' in Scalapino, Robert and Kim, Jun-Yop (eds), *North Korea Today: Strategic and Domestic Issues*, Berkeley: University of California Press.

Clough, Ralph (1987a) *Embattled Korea: The Rivalry for International Support*, Boulder: Westview Press.

Clough, Ralph (1987b) 'North Korea and the United States' in Park, Jae-kyu, Koh, Byung Chul and Kwak, Tae-hwan (eds), *The Foreign Relations of North Korea*, Seoul: Kyungnam University Press.

Colbert, Evelyn (1986) 'Japan and the Republic of Korea: Yesterday, Today, and Tomorrow', *Asian Survey*, 26 (3), March.

Conroy, Hilary (1960) *The Japanese Seizure of Korea, 1968-1910*, Philadelphia: University of Pennsylvania Press.

Cotton, James (1987) 'The Prospects for the North Korean Political Succession', *Korea & World Affairs*, XI (4).

Cotton, James (1990) 'APEC: Australia hosts another Pacific acronym', *The Pacific Review*, 3 (2).

Department of Defense (1990) *A Strategic Framework for the Asia Pacific Region*, Washington: USGPO.

Deuchler, Martina (1987) *Modern Korea in Historical Perspective*, Geneva: Graduate Institute of International Studies Occasional Paper.

De Vos, George and Wetherall, William (1983) *Japan's Minorities*, London: Minority Rights Group.

Dore, Ronald (1986) *Flexible Rigidities: Industrial Policy and Structural Adjustment in the Japanese Economy, 1970-80*, London: Athlone Press.

Drifte, Reinhard (1990) *Japan's Foreign Policy*, London: Routledge.

Drysdale, Peter (1988) *International Economic Pluralism*, Sydney: Allen & Unwin.

Foreign Broadcast Information Service (1988-92) *FBIS Daily Report* (cited throughout as FBIS, issue no. and date).

Foster-Carter, Aidan (1992) *Korea's Coming Reunification: Another East Asian Superpower?*, London: Economist Intelligence Unit.

Fujio, Masayuki (1986) '"Hogen daijin" oi ni hoeru', *Bungei Shunju*, October.

Fukugawa, Yukiko (1987) 'Korean Products: A threat to Japan?', *Economic Eye*, December.

Gordon, Bernard (1990) *New Directions for American Policy in Asia*, New York: Routledge.

Hahn, Bae-Ho (1980) 'Asian International Politics and the Future of Korea-Japan Relations' in *Korea-Japan Relations: Issues and Future Prospects*, Seoul: Korea University.

Harris, Stuart (1991) 'Varieties of Pacific Economic Cooperation', *The Pacific Review*, 4 (4).

Harrison, Selig (1977) *China, Oil and Asia*, New York: Columbia University Press.

Hasegawa, Keitaro (1986) *Sayonara ajia*, Tokyo: Nesco Books.

Hellman, Donald (1969) *Japanese Domestic Politics and Foreign Policy*, Berkeley: University of California Press.

Hirano, Kenichiro (1988) 'International Cultural Conflicts: Causes and Remedies', *Japan Review of International Affairs*, Fall/Winter.

Hoare, James and Pares, Susan (1988) *Korea: An Introduction*, London: Kegan Paul International.

Hyon, Kwon Su (1983) *Minzoku no shiten*, Tokyo: Dojidaisha.

Ichiki, Kazugi (1990) 'Zaikan hibausha shien e no teigen', *Gendai Koria*, August-September.

International Institute for Strategic Studies (1991) *The Military Balance, 1991-1992*, London: Brassey's.

International Institute for Strategic Studies (1992) *Strategic Survey, 1991-1992*, London: Brassey's.

International Monetary Fund (1992) *Direction of Trade Statistics, 1991*, Washington.

Ishii, Hajime (1991) *Chikazuite kita tooi kuni*, Tokyo: Nihon Seisansei Honbu.

JETRO (1988-91) *Kitachosen no keizai to boeki no tenbo*, Tokyo (annual volume for years 1988-91).

Johnson, Chalmers (1982) *MITI and the Japanese Miracle*, Stanford: Stanford University Press.

Jung Ku-hyun (1989) 'Direct Investment and Technology Transfer between Korea and the European Community' in Kim, Dalchhong, Gumpel, Werner, and Kindermann, Gottfried-Karl (eds), *New Dynamics in East-West Relations* Seoul: Yonsei University.

Jung Ku-hyun (1990) 'Internationalisation of Korean firms in the Global Context' in Kim, Dalchoong and Healey, Graham (eds), *Korea and the United Kingdom*, Seoul: Yonsei University.

Kakizawa, Koji (1992) 'Japan's Position on Suspected Nuclear Weapons Development by North Korea' *Korean Journal of Defense Analysis*,

Summer.

Kantaiheiyo Mondai Kenkyujo (1984 and 1987) *Kankoku kitachosen soran*, Vols I and II, Tokyo: Harashobo.

Kihl, Young Whan (1984) *Politics and Policies in a Divided Korea*, Boulder: Westview.

Kim, Dalchoong (1989) 'Two Koreas and Four Major Powers' in Kim, Dalchoong and Gumpel, Werner (eds), *New Directions in East-West Relations*, Seoul: Yonsei University.

Kim, Hakjoon (1978) *Unification Policies of South and North Korea*, Seoul: Seoul National University.

Kim, Hakjoon (1989) *Democratization under the Sixth Republic*, Seoul: Korea Overseas Information Service.

Kim, Hong N. (1983) 'Politics of Japan's Economic Aid to South Korea', *Asia Pacific Community*, Spring.

Kim, Hong Nack (1991) 'The Two Koreas' Entry into the United Nations and the Implications for Inter-Korean Relations', *Korea & World Affairs* 15 (3), Fall.

Koh, Byung Chul (1984) *The Foreign Policy Systems of North and South Korea*, Berkeley: University of California Press.

Koh, Byung Chul (1987) 'North Korea's Foreign Policymaking Process' in Park, Jae Kyu, Koh, Byung Chul and Kwak, Tae-Hwan, *The Foreign Relations of North Korea*, Seoul: Kyungnam University Press.

Komaki, Teruo (1991) (ed) *Kokusai jidai no kankoku keizai*, Tokyo: Ajia Keizai Kenkyujo.

Komiya, Ryutaro, Okuno, Masariho, and Suzumura, Kotaro (eds), (1988) *Industrial Policy of Japan*, Tokyo: Academic Press.

Kurata, Hideo (1989) 'Kankoku "hoppo gaiko" no hoga', *Kokusai Seiji*, October.

Kuroda, Katsuhiro (1986) '"Fujio hatsugen" to nikkan kankei', *Gendai Korea*, December.

Lee, Chae-jin and Sato, Hideo (1982) *U.S. Policy toward Japan and Korea*, New York: Praeger.

Lee, Changsoo and De Vos, George (1981) *Koreans in Japan: Ethnic Conflict and Accommodation*, Berkeley: University of California Press.

Lee, Chong-sik (1985) *Japan and Korea: The Political Dimension*, Stanford: Stanford University.

Lee, Hongkoo (1990) 'Call for Building National Community: As a Prerequisite to Reunification', *Korea & World Affairs*, Winter.

Lee, Jong Soo (1992) 'Changes of Policy Orientation and the Determinants: The Unification Policy of South Korea' in *Papers of the British Association for Korean Studies*, 3.

Lee, Jung-hoon (1992) 'Korean-Japanese Relations: The Past, the Present and the Future' in *Papers of the British Association for Korean Studies: Volume 3*, London: BAKS.

Lee, Tsao Yuan (1991) (ed) *Growth Triangle: The Johore-Singapore-Riau Experience*, Singapore: Institute of Southeast Asian Studies.

Lehmann, Ronald (1992) 'Arms Control, Negotiations and the Korean Peninsula', *Korean Journal of Defense Analysis* IV(1), Summer.

Lin, Bih-jaw (1991) (ed) *The Decline of Communism: Causes Processes and Prospects*, Tapei: Institute of International Relations.

Mack, Andrew (1991) 'North Korea and the Bomb', *Foreign Policy*, Summer.

Maswood, S. Javed (1990) *Japanese Defence: The Search for Political Power*, Singapore Institute of Southeast Asian Studies.

Maswood, S. Javed (1992) 'Japan and the Gulf War: Still Searching for a Role', *The Pacific Review* 5(2).

Matsumoto, Koji (1991) 'Mujun suru tainichi yokyu', *Gendai Koria*, October.

Mendl, Wolf (1990) 'Stuck in a Mould: The Relationship between Japan and the Soviet Union' in Newland, Kathleen (ed), *The International Relations of Japan*, London: Macmillan.

Ministry of International Trade and Industry, Industrial Structure Council (1992) *Report on Unfair Trade Policies by Major Trading Partners*.

Nakagawa, Nobuo (1981) *Nikkan kankei to Zentokan taisei*, Tokyo: Sanichi Shobo.

Nam, Joo-Hong (1986) *America's commitment to South Korea*, Cambridge: Cambridge University Press.

National Institute of Research Advancement (NIRA) (1986) *Nikkan keizai hatten hikakuron*, Tokyo.

Newby, Laura (1988) *Sino-Japanese Relations: China's Perspective*, London: Routledge.

Nijuisseiki, Iinkai (1991a) *Nikkan kankei no genjo to kadai*, Tokyo.

Nijuisseiki, Iinkai (1991b) *Saishu Hokokusho*, Tokyo.

Niksch, Larry (1992) 'Dealing with North Korea on the Nuclear Weapons Threshold', *Korean Journal of Defense Analysis*, IV(1), Summer.

Nish, Ian (1985) *The Origins of the Russo-Japanese War*, London: Longman.

Ogata, Sadako (1977) 'The Business Community and Japanese Foreign Policy: Normalisation of Relations with the People's Republic of China' in Scalapino, Robert (ed), *The Foreign Policy of Modern Japan*, Berkeley: University of California Press.

Okonogi, Masao (1989) 'The Political Dynamics of Japan-North Korea Relations', *Korea & World Affairs*, Summer.

Okonogi, Masao (1991) *Nihon to kitachosen: kore kara no gonen*, Tokyo: PHP.

Olsen, Edward (1985) *U.S.-Japan Strategic Reciprocity*, Stanford: Stanford University.

Onuma, Yasuaki (1986) *Tanitsu minzoku shakai no shinwa o koete*, Tokyo: Toshindo.

Park, Jin (1992a) 'Korea in the Post-Cold War Era' in Leslie Palmier (ed), *Detente in Asia?*, London: Macmillan.

Park, Jin (1992b) 'Japan-North Korea Rapprochement: Issues and Prospects' in *Japan Forum*, [forthcoming October].

Park, Moon Kyu (1987) 'Interest Representation in South Korea', *Asian Survey*, 27(8), August.

Peattie, Mark (1990) 'The Japanese colonial empire, 1895-1945' in Duus, Peter (ed), *The Cambridge History of Japan: Volume 6, The Twentieth Century*, Cambridge: Cambridge University Press.

Pyon, Jin Il (1991) 'Guests in their own home', *Look Japan*, February.

Radtke, Kurt (1990) *China's Relations with Japan, 1945-83: The Role of Liao Chengzhi*, Manchester: Manchester University Press.

Rhee, Sang-Woo (1992) 'North Korea in 1991', *Asian Survey*, January.

Roy, Denny (1988) 'North Korea's Relations with Japan', *Asian Survey*, December.

Sanford, Dan (1990) *South Korea and the Socialist Countries*, London: Macmillan.

Sato, Katsumi (1991) *Hakai suru kitachosen: nitcho kosho isogu bekarazu*, Tokyo: Nesco.

Sato, Kunio (1983) 'Nikkan bunka koryu ni tsuite no noto', *Kaigai jijo*, November.

Sato, Seizaburo (1974) 'Japan's World Order' in Scheiner, Irwin (ed), *Modern Japan: An Interpretive Anthology*, New York: Macmillan.

Satoh, Yukio (1982) *The Evolution of Japanese Security Policy*, London: International Institute for Strategic Studies, Adelphi Paper No. 178.

Scalapino, Robert (1977) (ed), *The Foreign Policy of Modern Japan*, Berkeley: University of California Press.

Scalapino, Robert and Kim, Jun-yop (1983) (eds), *North Korea Today: Strategic and Domestic Issues*, Berkeley: University of California Press.

Segal, Gerald (1990a) *Rethinking the Pacific*, Oxford: Clarendon Press.

Segal, Gerald (1990b) *The Soviet Union and the Pacific*, London: Unwin Hyman.

Segal, Gerald (1991) *Normalizing Soviet-Japanese Relations*, London: RIIA Special Paper.

Shibusawa, Masahide, Ahmad, Zakaria Haji and Bridges, Brian (1991) *Pacific Asia in the 1990s*, London: Routledge.

Shin, Jung Hyun (1987) 'North Korea's policy towards Japan: Perceptions, Goals, Trends' in Park, Jae Kyu, Koh, Byung Chul and Park, Tae-Hwan (eds), *The Foreign Relations of North Korea: New Perspectives*,

Seoul: Kyungnam University Press.

Simpson, John and Howlett, Darryl (1991) 'Nuclear non-proliferation: the way forward', *Survival*, Nov/Dec.

Song, Young Sun (1991) 'The Korean Nuclear Issue', *Korea & World Affairs*, Fall.

Sugimoto, Takashi (1992) *The Dawning of Development of the Tumen River Area*, Tokyo: International Institute for Global Peace.

Suh, Dae-Sook (1983) 'Kim Il-song: His Personality and Politics' in Scalapino, Robert and Kim, Jun-yop (eds), *North Korea Today: Strategic and Domestic Issues*, Berkeley: University of California Press.

Takagi, Kenichi (1990) *Saharin to nihon no sengo sekinin*, Tokyo: Gaifusha.

Tanaka, Hitoshi (1989) 'Nitcho kankei kaizen o susumeru gaimusho no ito', *Gendai Koria*, January.

Taniguchi, Koji (1990) (ed), *Taiwan-kankoku no taigai toshi no tenkai*, Tokyo: Institute of Developing Economies.

Tugendhat, Christopher and Wallace, William (1988) *Options for British Foreign Policy in the 1990s*, London: Routledge for RIIA.

Valencia, Mark (1991) 'Economic Cooperation in Northeast Asia: The Proposed Tumen River Scheme', *The Pacific Review*, 3(2).

Wagner, Edward (1951) *The Korean Minority in Japan, 1904-1950*, New York: Institute of Pacific Relations.

Weiner, Michael (1989) *The Origins of the Korean Community in Japan: 1910-1923*, Manchester: Manchester University Press.

Whiting, Allen (1989) *China eyes Japan*, Berkeley: University of California Press.

Wolferen, Karl van (1989) *The Enigma of Japanese Power*, London: Macmillan.

World Bank (1992) *World Development Report: 1992*, Oxford: Oxford University Press.

Yamaura, Koichi (1986) 'Japan-Korea Economic Relations', *Journal of Japanese Trade and Industry*, March/April.

Yayama, Taro (1983) 'The Newspapers Conduct a Mad Rhapsody over the Textbook Issue', *Journal of Japanese Studies*, 9(2), Spring.

Yun, Chung-ok (1992) 'Jungshindae - Korean Military "Comfort Women"' (memorandum submitted by Korean Council for Women Drafted for Sexual Service by Japan to United Nations Human Rights Commission).

Index

Academy of Social Sciences 41
Afro-Asian Study Group 30
Agency for National Security Policy 36
Agreement on Reconciliation and Non-aggression, see under North-South Korean relations
Air Defence Intercept Zone 55
Akihito, Emperor 139
    apology to Roh: 61, 63-5
Alien Registration Law 120-3
anti-dumping 33, 98
Arai, Shokei 126
Armacost, Michael 150
ASEAN (Association of South-east Asian Nations) 26-7, 52-3, 87-8, 96, 114
Asian Pacific Economic Cooperation (APEC) 114, 166
Asian-style CSCE, see under Conference for Security and Cooperation in Europe
Association of A-bomb Victims, see Atomic bomb victims
Asukata, Ichio 31
Atomic bomb victims 130-32

Baker, James 154
Blix, Hans 80
Burakumin 125
Bush, George 77, 79, 81, 161

Carter, Jimmy 13, 54, 76-7
Central People's Committee 39
Chaebol 37, 90, 99
Cheney, Dick 83
China
        and Japan: 26, 33, 82, 111, 119, 145-6, 156, 163;

and North Korea: 69, 72-5, 82-4, 110-11, 152, 160;
        and South Korea: 46, 59, 67, 82, 86, 165
Cho Young-pil 139
Choi Ho-joong 36, 57
Chongnyon 33, 40, 120-21, 123, 131
Chon In-chol 149, 155, 160
Chu Chin-kuk 40
Chun Doo-hwan 13-14, 16-17, 20, 29, 34-5, 54-6, 96, 103, 106
        visit to Japan: 16, 23, 38, 63
Chungang-chong 137
Cocom 111
Comecon 115
Comfort women 62, 132-6, 153, 157, 159-60, 164
Commonwealth of Independent States (CIS) 71-2, 130
Conference for Security and Cooperation in Europe (CSCE) 52, 168
Cross-recognition 85-6
Cultural exchanges 136-42
Cultural imperialism 136

Declaration on a Non-nuclear Korean Peninsula, see under North-South Korean relations
Democratic Confederal Republic of Koryo (DCRK) 47
Democratic Justice Party (DJP) 35-7
Democratic Liberal Party (DLP) 31, 36-7, 168
Democratic Party (DP) 57
Democratic Republican Party (DRP) 36
Democratic Socialist Party (DSP) 30, 32
Deng, Xiaoping 69, 86, 110, 167
DMZ (Demilitarised Zone) 49

DATE DUE